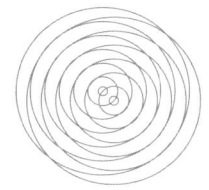

少年研究员：
Young Researchers:

探究中国非遗（1）—— 雕漆与评书篇
Exploring Intangible Cultural Heritage of China (1)—
Diaoqi and Pingshu

主编
沈忆文

外语教学与研究出版社
FOREIGN LANGUAGE TEACHING AND RESEARCH PRESS
北京 BEIJING

图书在版编目（CIP）数据

少年研究员：探究中国非遗．1，雕漆与评书篇：汉、英／沈忆文主编．－－北京：外语教学与研究出版社，2019.8
（UNIPLUS基础教育国际化特色办学系列丛书）
ISBN 978-7-5213-0963-8

Ⅰ.①少… Ⅱ.①沈… Ⅲ.①雕漆－研究－北京－汉、英②北方评书－研究－北京－汉、英 Ⅳ.①G122

中国版本图书馆CIP数据核字（2019）第138931号

出 版 人　徐建忠
项目策划　姚　虹
责任编辑　周渝毅
责任校对　徐　宁
封面设计　杰威国际　水长流文化
版式设计　范晔文
出版发行　外语教学与研究出版社
社　　址　北京市西三环北路19号（100089）
网　　址　http://www.fltrp.com
印　　刷　涿州市星河印刷有限公司
开　　本　650×980　1/16
印　　张　25
版　　次　2019年8月第1版 2019年8月第1次印刷
书　　号　ISBN 978-7-5213-0963-8
定　　价　56.00元

购书咨询：（010）88819926　电子邮箱：club@fltrp.com
外研书店：https://waiyants.tmall.com
凡印刷、装订质量问题，请联系我社印制部
联系电话：（010）61207896　电子邮箱：zhijian@fltrp.com
凡侵权、盗版书籍线索，请联系我社法律事务部
举报电话：（010）88817519　电子邮箱：banquan@fltrp.com
物料号：309630001

系列丛书专家委员会（按姓氏首字母排序）

卢慧文　上海协和双语学校总校长，上海市政协常委，上海市民办中小学协会副会长

陆云泉　北京一零一中学校长，中学特级教师，原北京市海淀区教育委员会主任

孙霄兵　北京外国语大学国际教育研究院院长，国家督学，教育部原政策法规司司长

吴颖民　原华南师范大学副校长、华南师范大学附属中学校长，广州中学校长

叶翠微　海亮教育集团总校长，原杭州第二中学校长

Mr. Barnaby Lenon　英国私立学校协会主席，原英国哈罗公学校长

Mr. Chris Whittle（魏克礼）　荟同学校主席、总裁，美国教育改革委员会理事

Advisory Board of the Book Series (In Alphabetical Order)

Mr. Barnaby LENON, Chairman of Independent Schools Council, UK; former Head Master of Harrow School.

Ms. Huiwen LU, Principal General, Shanghai United International School; member of Shanghai CPPCC Standing Committee; Vice President of Shanghai Association of Non-government Elementary and Middle Schools.

Mr. Yunquan LU, Principal of Beijing 101 Middle School; Master Teacher; former Director of Education Bureau of Haidian District, Beijing.

Prof. Xiaobing SUN, Dean of School of International Education Research, Beijing Foreign Studies University; National Education Inspector; former Director of Department of Policies and Regulations of Ministry of Education, China.

Mr. Chris WHITTLE, Chairman and CEO, Whittle School & Studios; member of Board at Center for Education Reform, US.

Mr. Yingmin WU, former Pro-vice-chancellor of South China Normal University and Principal of its Affiliated School; Principal of Guangzhou Middle School.

Mr. Cuiwei YE, Principal General, Hailiang Education; former Principal of Hangzhou No. 2 High School of Zhejiang Province.

本书编委会(按姓氏首字母排序)

曹　文　北京外国语大学国际教育集团首席学术官

范晓虹　北京外国语大学国际教育集团总经理

晋　军　北京外国语大学附属中学校长、书记

梁　彦　著名评书演员、文化研究学者

蔺　音　北京市西城区非物质文化遗产保护中心副主任

刘乙晨　北京外国语大学国际教育集团升学规划部总监

马　迪　北京外国语大学国际课程中心助理学术校长

马　宁　北京市工艺美术大师、东城区雕漆代表性传承人

沈忆文　北京外国语大学专用英语学院副教授、北京外国语大学国际教育集团教学顾问

王一虹　北京外国语大学国际教育集团学术委员会副主任

王　元　北京外国语大学国际教育集团"少年研究员"培养计划负责人

杨　飞　北京市西城区非物质文化遗产保护中心主任

Rehema Clarken　北京外国语大学国际课程中心学术校长、博士

Editorial Board of the Book (In Alphabetical Order)

Prof. Wen CAO, Chief Academic Officer of International Education Group, Beijing Foreign Studies University.

Dr. Rehema CLARKEN, Academic Principal, Beijing Foreign Studies University International Curriculum Centre.

Ms. Xiaohong FAN, CEO of International Education Group, Beijing Foreign Studies University.

Ms. Jun JIN, Principal and Party Secretary General of The Affiliated High School of Beijing Foreign Studies University.

Mr. Yan LIANG, Pingshu Performer; Scholar of Chinese Cultural Studies.

Mr. Yin LIN, Vice Director of Beijing Xicheng District Intangible Cultural Heritage Protection Centre.

Ms. Yichen LIU, Director of Counselling Department, International Education Group, Beijing Foreign Studies University.

Ms. Di MA, Assistant Academic Principal of Beijing Foreign Studies University International Curriculum Centre.

Mr. Ning MA, Master of Chinese Arts and Crafts in Beijing; Diaoqi Inheritor in Dongcheng District, Beijing.

Ms. Yiwen SHEN, Associate Professor of The School of English for Specific Purposes, Beijing Foreign Studies University; Academic Supervisor of International Education Group, Beijing Foreign Studies University.

Ms. Yihong WANG, Deputy Director of Academic Board, International

Education Group, Beijing Foreign Studies University.

Mr. Yuan WANG, Director of Young Researchers Programme, International Education Group, Beijing Foreign Studies University.

Mr. Fei YANG, Director of Beijing Xicheng District Intangible Cultural Heritage Protection Centre.

少年研究员参访儒匠传奇工坊

著名文化学者、评书演员梁彦与少年研究员

评书名家连丽如先生与少年研究员

雕漆技艺代表性传承人马宁

外教导师参与小组团建活动

外教导师和少年研究员一起研讨论文内容

外教导师讲授论文写作的过程和要求

导师李琛参加团建活动

少年研究员采访雕漆大师殷秀云

学生访谈

雕漆工坊访谈

雕漆访谈

儒匠传奇工坊体验

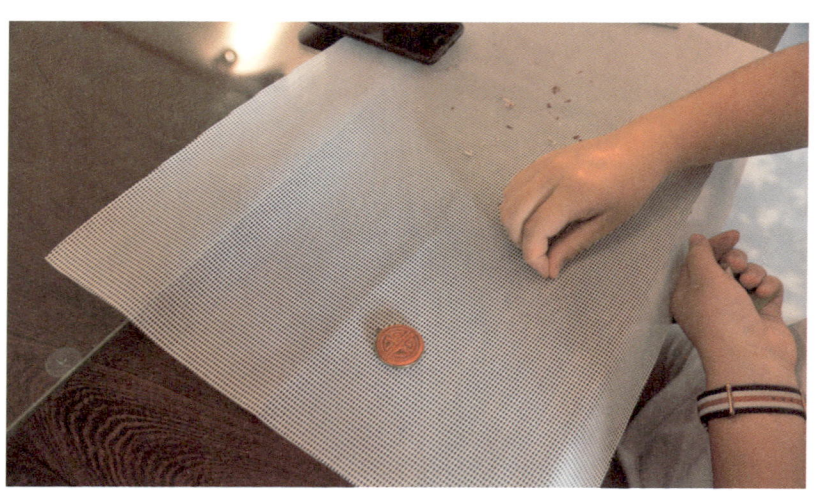

体验雕漆

马剑平、汤凡表演双语评书

学生访谈

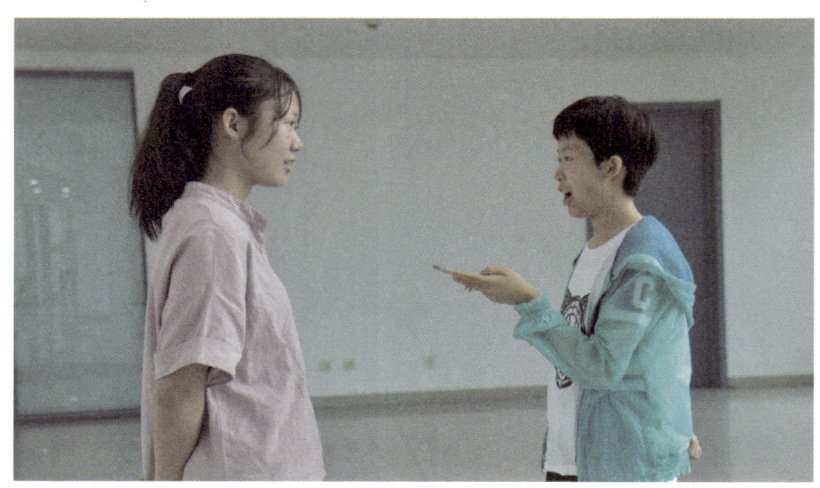

学生访谈

导师李琛和她辅导的"初心"和"敢死队"两组少年研究员

导师Sonje和她辅导的"少年时"和"甘嗣"两组少年研究员

导师郭倩和她辅导的"黑麻薯"和"Plan B"两组少年研究员

导师和他辅导的"MilkyWay"和"商一"两组少年研究员

"战斗民族"小组获得演讲比赛特等奖

"商一"小组获得演讲比赛一等奖

"Plan B"小组获得演讲比赛一等奖

"黑麻薯"小组获得演讲比赛二等奖

"少年时"小组获得演讲比赛二等奖

目录

开篇

传承中华文化，建立文化自信 …………………………………… 002

准确、规范把握有关"三个关注对象"的相关问题 —— 以北京市西城
区为例 …………………………………………………………… 010

传承中国非遗，弘扬优秀文化 …………………………………… 022

雕漆篇

雕　漆 ……………………………………………………………… 028

当代雕漆的艺术特色 ……………………………………………… 033

Artistic Features of Modern *Diaoqi* …………………………… 042

雕漆传承人的工作和生活现状 …………………………………… 052

The Life and Work Experience of *Diaoqi* Artists …………… 066

雕漆传承人的培养 ………………………………………………… 077

The Training Process of *Diaoqi* Inheritors ………………… 089

北京雕漆艺术发展障碍的研究 …………………………………… 101

Research on the Barriers to the Development of Beijing *Diaoqi* ……… 118

北京雕漆市场调查报告 …………………………………………… 134

Diaoqi Market Investigation Report ………………………… 149

北京高中生对于雕漆认知度的调查 ·· **165**
Beijing High School Students' Cognition of *Diaoqi* ························ **181**

评书篇

浅析北京评书的艺术特征 ·· **198**
二十一世纪北京评书的艺术特色与创新 ·· **208**
The Artistic Features and Innovations of Beijing *Pingshu* in the 21st
  Century ··· **220**
北京评书说书人的培养 ··· **232**
The Training of Beijing *Pingshu* Performers ································· **242**
书场说书和电视说书的区别 ·· **253**
The Differences between Performing in a *Pingshu* Theater and on TV ····· **270**
北京评书艺术发展障碍的研究 ·· **288**
A Study on the Obstacles to the Development of Beijing *Pingshu* ········ **309**
北京中学生对北京评书的认知度调查 ··· **330**
Beijing Middle School Students' Cognition of Beijing *Pingshu* ············ **349**

开篇

传承中华文化，建立文化自信

沈忆文[1]

一、调研报告的背景

"少年研究员"培养计划是北京外国语大学国际教育集团（以下简称"北外国际"）于2016年推出的针对青少年的学术研究项目，已经进行了三期。该项目中，学生以小组为单位，在北京外国语大学的教授及外籍专家的辅导下，完成包括明确研究问题、检索文献、设计问卷、收集数据、分析数据、撰写调研报告、宣读和发表报告等阶段的任务。在这个过程中，学生不仅提升了学习力、思考力和行动力，还培养了自律、坚韧的品格，完成了从"被动学习"到"主动学习"的过渡。同时，论文写作和英文演讲是大学学习必须具备的基础技能，"少年研究员"培养计划正是学习和掌握这两项技能的优选路径。

挖掘和继承中华文化，在青少年中建立文化自信，是新时代摆在我们面前刻不容缓的任务。2017年，习近平总书记在中国共产党第十九次全国代表大会上的报告中指出："深入挖掘中华优秀传统文化蕴含的思想观念、人文精神、道德规范，结合时代要求继承创新，让中华文化展现出永久魅力和时代风采。"基于此，2018年，北外国际"少年研究员"培养计划的第三期确定了以中国非物质文化遗产"北

---

1. 本文作者为"少年研究员"培养计划的策划者和学术负责人。

京雕漆"和"北京评书"两个项目为研究对象。首先，它们都具有浓郁的北京地方特色，北京的中学生对其有天然的亲切感。其次，它们都有很强的观赏性和实践性，中学生谈起来津津有味，做起来兴趣盎然。最重要的是，在当今社会，它们在传承和发展方面都遇到不小的障碍和阻力，这些阻力有些是来自这项技艺本身，有些是时代变化所致。中学生可以通过对它们进行深入的调查、访谈、对比和分析研究，发现技艺传承和时代变化这两方面因素之间的关系，从而发展出自己的历史观和文化观。我们欣喜地看到，在这个过程中，学生们开始喜爱非遗项目，理解中华文化，强化了对中华文化的认同感和自豪感。同时他们感受到了做中华文化的代言人、讲好中国故事的使命感。

通过检索中国知网等一系列学术网站，我们发现针对中国非遗项目的实证性研究非常少。相关论文主要集中研究雕漆和评书的艺术特色和历史发展等方面，而关于它们的生存现状、传承人培养、发展障碍、青年人对其的认知等，却鲜有研究。由此，参加第三期"少年研究员"培养计划的学生分为两个大组，分别负责北京雕漆和北京评书的研究。每个大组又分为若干小组，每个小组负责一个子课题。这样我们的研究就可以向读者全方位呈现北京雕漆和北京评书的现状。

研究论文以中英双语撰写，这样不仅能锻炼学生的语言能力，还帮助学生通过第二语言视角，反观中华文化，深入思考中华文化的现代意义，建立文化自信，成为传播中华文化的使者。

二、研究成员构成

研究活动共分为11个研究小组，每组3—4名成员。小组成员主要来自两所教育机构——北京外国语大学附属中学和北京外国语大学国际课程中心,包括高一和高二年级的共34名学生,年龄在15—17岁之间。每个小组配备具有丰富科研经验的北外教授和外教导师,负责小组的科研辅导和文字修改工作,以保证最终的论文成稿达到出版要求。

三、研究问题和研究方法

(一) 研究问题

对于北京雕漆和北京评书这两个非遗项目,我们设立了相似的子课题。

北京雕漆研究共有六个子课题,分别是:

1) 当代北京雕漆的艺术特色

2) 北京雕漆传承人的生活和工作现状

3) 北京雕漆传承人的培养

4) 北京雕漆的发展障碍

5) 北京雕漆的市场调查

6) 北京中学生对北京雕漆的认知度调查

北京评书研究共有五个子课题,分别是:

1) 北京评书的艺术特色与创新

2) 北京评书说书人的培养

3) 书场说书和电视说书的区别

4) 北京评书艺术的发展障碍

5) 北京中学生对北京评书的认知度调查

(二)研究方法

研究方法包括文献研究、数据收集和数据分析。

1. 文献研究

每个小组在参与项目初期，通过中国知网上的关键词检索，广泛收集并阅读了2010年至2018年上半年的相关文献，了解在自己的研究领域已有的研究方法和结果。在数据分析和论文撰写阶段，小组成员更有针对性地阅读相关文献的具体内容，并进行分析、总结和对比。

2. 数据收集

调研采取结构式访谈的方法，少年研究员以小组为单位，按照访谈单提问，不得随意添加或减少问题，也不得改变访谈或提问的措辞。

调研在数据收集方面主要包括以下四个方面的工作：

1）设计访谈问卷：每个小组根据调研问题，设计访谈问卷，对访谈开始、过程和结尾的话术进行统一。

2）小范围试访谈：每组少年研究员在听完雕漆和评书专家的讲座后，对专家进行试访谈，并根据试访谈过程中暴露出的问题，调整访谈问卷设计，完善访谈步骤，完成访谈单定稿。

3）实际访谈：少年研究员按照预先约定，到达访谈地点，对雕漆、评书艺术家及相关人员进行访谈。每次访谈结束后，访谈单随访谈录音一并上传，由北外国际工作人员保留。

4）访谈录音文字撰写：访谈结束后，所有录音通过语音转换软件转换为文字，并由少年研究员自己校对，提交给各组导师审核。

3. 数据分析

调研主要采取主题分析（thematic analysis）的方法，对数据进行分析和编码整理，提炼出共性。之所以采用这种分析方法，主要是考虑到它能够灵活适应各类理论视角，真正重视参与者的感受，最大程度地找到纷繁数据中的规律和意义（刘润清，2015）。另外，调研的问题尚没有充分的文献资料作为支撑，也没有数据分析模型可以参考，因此这种方法比较适合少年研究员。

调研的数据分析包括以下七个具体步骤：

1）第一步：熟悉数据。少年研究员以小组为单位阅读已有数据两至三遍，对数据产生总体认知。

2）第二步：标出关键词。少年研究员对本小组收集的所有数据进行关键词标记，即将数据中关键词的字体颜色改为红色。然后，各组员比较自己和同伴标红的部分，互相补充，形成最终的数据关键词标记结果。

3）第三步：初步编码。将常见的关键词记录下来，转换成统一用词，形成一份词语列表，作为初步编码。

4）第四步：形成编码体系。少年研究员将已有编码（三级编码）进行归类，形成二级编码，并为各类编码选择名称；之后，再将二级编码归类，形成主题。由此，则形成调研所使用的编码体系。

5）第五步：使用编码体系。小组各成员对每一条数据进行编码，即根据该数据中的关键词，从编码体系中选择适当编码，记录在该数据后方，形成一个条目。在这一过程中，小组各成员对编码体系进行相应调整，加入新出现的编码，修改已有编码名称，并删除没有使用的编码。最后，小组各成员比较自己和同伴的编码，互相补充修正，在完善、调整和补充之后重新审核各条目。

6）第六步：确定编码体系并核对每一条数据的编码。各条目审核完毕后，小组各成员对编码体系进行最后的调整，以确定每个条目都出现在编码体系中，且编码体系中没有多余的编码。

7）第七步：数据分析和总结。有些小组需要计算编码出现的频次，并以该频次除以总条目数，得出百分比，进行数据分析，发现规律。有些小组需要从编码中找到支持某个主题的数据并加以提炼，形成对主题的支持。

最后，论文的写作由小组的每个成员分头承担。雕漆组以英文论文开始，然后完成中文论文的写作；评书组以中文论文开始，然后完成英文论文的写作。小组各成员每完成论文的一部分，就提交给导师审阅；收到导师的修改意见后，成员修改论文。整篇论文的写作完成之后，导师审阅论文，提出修改意见，这样几次反复后才形成终稿。

四、培养计划的实施步骤

"少年研究员"培养计划的实施分为六个阶段，每个阶段都有明确的任务和具体完成时间。

阶段	时间	主题	任务
一	2018年3月	选拔期	学生通过面试考核，取得入选资格。
二	2018年3—6月	预备期	非物质文化遗产保护单位和非遗传承人进入校园作讲座宣传，帮助学生树立意识、培养兴趣。
三	2018年7月中旬	集训期	经过两周的集训，总体完成设计、文献研究、调研、分析等各阶段的学习，并基本完成调研报告所需的信息数据采集和相关准备工作。
四	2018年8—10月	写作期	用英文撰写调研报告，制作演讲PPT，准备演讲比赛。

续表

阶段	时间	主题	任务
五	2018年10月	竞赛期	参加2018年北外国际"少年研究员"培养计划英语演讲比赛。
六	2018年10—12月	出版期	修改调研报告，达到出版要求。

在第一阶段，培养计划导师组筛选学生的主要标准是学业成绩优秀，同时本人对参与此项目的意愿强烈，对项目要求的时间精力等方面的投入有清晰的认识。

在第二阶段，培养计划导师组邀请包括北京市西城区非物质文化遗产保护中心主任杨飞在内的三位专家，从非遗保护的各个层面向学生普及中华文化和非遗保护知识；同时，导师指导学生根据每次专家讲座的内容，开展小型的模拟调研。

在第三阶段，学生根据第二阶段所积累的知识和经验，开展实质性的调研工作。

在第四、第五阶段，学生参加2018年北外国际"少年研究员"英语演讲比赛，用英语展示他们的调研结果。

在第六阶段，中英双语论文结集出版，导师对少年研究员在项目中的表现给予评价。

五、总结

与量化研究相比，质性研究需要研究者具备更强的判断力、想象力和综合概括能力。本培养计划的调研报告多数出自第一次作研究的少年研究员之手，从数据的收集到分析都不免有偏颇和疏漏之处，尤其在田野调查中，由于采访对象少，少年研究员又缺乏访谈经验，收集的数据不够丰富，因此，调研报告不可避免地存在瑕疵。但我们希望这些研究成果能为后续的研究提供方向和基础。

更加难能可贵的是，少年研究员参与中华文化研究活动的意义超越了论文内容本身。他们带着强烈的求知欲，完全利用课余时间，挑战了他们从未涉足过的科研领域。在这个过程中他们得到了许多方面的收获，如时间管理能力，辩证思维能力，整理、分析、概括数据的能力等等。但最令人欣慰的是，他们对祖国灿烂的文化有了更深的认同感，对中华文明在世界文明中的地位产生了更强的信心，带着身份的认同和文化的自信，少年研究员们将成长为中国的脊梁和世界的领导者。

参考文献：

刘润清.外语教学中的科研方法[M].北京：外语教学与研究出版社，2015.

准确、规范把握有关"三个关注对象"的相关问题——以北京市西城区为例

杨 飞[1]

【摘要】 非物质文化遗产是中华传统文化的重要组成部分。中国民族民间文化保护工程从启动至今,已实施多年;但在实施过程中,以"三个关注对象"为观察点,非遗保护工作在名录体系构建、项目保护单位认定、代表性传承人社会认知、项目保护单位与代表性传承人辩证关系等方面存在理解误区,这限制了保护工作的开展,影响了工作成效。笔者作为基层非遗保护工作者,结合本职工作,尝试对相关问题进行梳理、思考,并力图寻求解决方案,为非遗保护工作的实施建言献策。

【关键词】 非物质文化遗产 工作 保护 探索

党的十八届五中全会提出"构建中华优秀传统文化传承体系,加强文化遗产保护,振兴传统工艺"的要求以来,非物质文化遗产作为传统文化的重要组成部分,其传承、保护、发展得到了社会各界的高度关注与积极参与。近几年,《关于实施中华优秀传统文化传承发展工程的意见》《中国传统工艺振兴计划》等重要文件的出台,更是将

---

1. 本文作者为北京市西城区非物质文化遗产保护中心主任。

非遗保护工作的重要性提升到前所未有的高度。

自2003年10月文化部在贵阳召开中国民族民间文化保护工程试点工作会议以来,非遗保护工作已开展了十几个年头,卓有成效。笔者作为基层非遗保护工作者,在工作开展过程中积累了一些思考,希望在此与专家、同人分享和探讨。

一、非遗保护工作的"三个关注对象"

什么是非物质文化遗产?2011年6月1日正式施行的《中华人民共和国非物质文化遗产法》(以下简称《非遗法》)有明确的界定:非物质文化遗产,是指各族人民世代相传并视为其文化遗产组成部分的各种传统文化表现形式,以及与传统文化表现形式相关的实物和场所。

在正确理解非物质文化遗产定义的基础上,笔者认为其保护工作应该关注非物质文化遗产保护名录(以下简称"名录")、项目保护单位及传承人这三个"对象"。笔者强调这"三个关注对象"的原因如下。

第一,名录。非物质文化遗产具有鲜明的地域特点和民族特色,有特定的场所和文化生态,其保护工作的原则为属地申报、属地管理;同时,本地区名录是各级文化主管部门开展非遗保护工作的重要依据。

第二,项目保护单位。作为非遗保护工作实施主体的重要组成部分,项目保护单位在非遗项目普查、整理、申报,保护工作计划和开展,保护资金申请、使用、管理,代表性传承人评审推荐等方面发挥重要作用,承担重要职责。

第三,传承人。此处所指的传承人与代表性传承人有所区别,在后文中有明确描述。非物质文化遗产区别于文物等物质范畴文化遗产，以非物质性、活态性为显著特征，以传承人为保护、传承、传播的主体。传承人的数量、技艺掌握程度及社会知晓率和影响力是非遗保护工作开展形式的依据及开展效果的判定标准。

二、名录的有关问题及解决方略

问题一：同一项目在各级名录中名称不一，缺乏规范性。在不同级名录中，存在相同项目（即传承脉络相同、技艺特点相同、代表性传承人相同、项目保护单位相同）名称不一的现象。

以西城区区级非遗项目"泥塑彩绘脸谱"为例，该项目通过区级评审，经区政府批准、公示后，正式入选。此后，该项目通过专家评审，由西城区推荐，进入北京市市级非遗项目评审。在评审过程中，经专家建议，项目名称变更为"彩塑京剧脸谱"。经市政府批准、公示后，该项目同样正式入选。

相同非遗项目在市、区两级名录中出现两个名称，这在宣传、传播过程中容易造成混淆，使人产生名录体系构建不规范的印象，不利于保护工作的开展。类似现象还存在于"京派内画鼻烟壶""北京内画鼻烟壶"等项目。

问题分析：名录由各级政府逐级批准、公示，存在时间的先后。项目级别晋升后，如发生名称变更，公示内容未涉及项目原名，前一级政府也未公示变更后的名称。

意见和建议：在各级政府有效沟通并达成共识的基础上，在确定某非遗项目进入上一级名录并发生名称变更时，各级政府对各级名录中的名称进行统一和公示。

问题二：各区名录构建工作中缺少横向沟通，缺乏科学性。在各区名录构建过程中，存在"此区不批彼区批""变个名称多区批"的现象。

以西城区为例，在连续两批非遗项目、代表性传承人评审的过程中，均有专家提出，存在项目、传承人在其他区评审未通过，转而在本区申报的问题，以及传承脉络、技艺特点、核心特质相同的项目在其他区已通过后变换名称在本区申报的问题。

此现象容易造成各区非遗评审工作相互否定的局面，使人产生名录体系构建掺杂人为因素，项目评审、代表性传承人认定工作不公平、不科学的印象，易对申报单位和个人造成不良影响。

问题分析：北京市各区非遗项目、代表性传承人评审工作由该区文化行政部门实施，而在此过程中，由于选择的专家不同，专家对项目的掌握情况、把握尺度不一，各区的评审工作无横向沟通，存在信息壁垒。

意见和建议：借助信息化手段完善非遗项目、代表性传承人评审信息库；在各区、各级评审过程中不断补充、完善并重点关注申报项目传承脉络、技艺特点、专家评审意见等内容，这些内容可作为各区、各级评审工作背景资料；不断加强评审工作的公开、透明程度，避免出现人为因素。

问题三：名录对项目技艺整体性的体现不足，缺乏严谨性、全面性。很多非遗项目需要不同工序、多个角色共同配合完成，但在名录体系构建、代表性传承人认定工作中，个别项目未体现出整体性、合作性。

以西城区非遗项目"单弦牌子曲"为例，演唱与伴奏是单弦演出的重要组成部分，缺一不可，且很多单弦演唱者是由"弦儿师"（伴奏者，即三弦演奏者）传授演唱技艺，业内称之为"夹磨儿"。可以说"弦儿师"对于该项目的传承、发展起到了至关重要的作用。现阶段，"弦儿师"的稀缺是"单弦牌子曲"项目传承、发展的重要瓶颈，但代表性传承人的认定工作仅关注了演唱者，未涉及"弦儿师"。此外，西城区从抢救、保护角度出发，将"三弦演奏"项目列入区级名录，但这割裂了"单弦牌子曲"项目的整体性。

问题分析：名录体系构建过程中存在未从非遗项目整体出发全盘考虑技艺传承、发展过程以及未充分尊重艺术创作、展示规律的现象。

意见和建议：从尊重艺术创作、展示规律及项目传承整体性的角度出发，完善名录；名录划分不宜过于烦琐，但项目的重要组成部分不可缺失，可将其列入扩展名录，或者在代表性传承人认定工作中关注全工序或认同多角色。

三、项目保护单位的有关问题及解决方略

问题：项目保护单位与代表性传承人"关联度"过高，单位法人代表只是代表性传承人的另一身份。

问题分析：非遗项目保护单位需要具备的基本条件及需要履行的职责，在《国家级非物质文化遗产保护与管理暂行办法》（文化部令第39号）、《国家级非物质文化遗产项目代表性传承人认定与管理暂行办法》（文化部令第45号）等文件中有明确表述。可以说保护单位是非

遗保护工作机构的重要组成部分，承担了重要职责，如以组织形式推荐代表性传承人、申报非遗保护专项资金、接受社会监督（包括对非遗保护工作开展情况、专项资金使用情况的监督）等。

项目保护单位与代表性传承人具有"关联度"有其可取之处，如保护工作响应及时、保护政策落实便利、保护资金使用便捷等，但"关联度"过高则存在风险，如代表性传承人申报推荐工作存在排他性，专项保护资金使用存在安全风险且无法促进、带动非遗项目所代表的整体行业发展等。从开展非遗保护工作长远考虑，代表性传承人与项目保护单位"关联度"过高，弊大于利。

以西城区为例，以代表性传承人或其后代、亲属作为保护单位法人代表的项目约占项目总数的10%（此数据无法准确统计，因为很多项目出于有利于通过项目评审的目的，借用申报条件成熟的单位作为其项目保护单位，但申报通过后经常变更项目保护单位）。这些过度"关联"的保护单位在西城区非遗保护工作统计中，经常无法提供非遗保护专项资金使用证明、绩效数据等相关保护工作的材料。

意见和建议：

1. 代表性传承人与项目保护单位不宜过度"关联"，在保护单位认定中应考虑其是否具备对名录项目所代表行业的保护能力，是否具有行业代表性。

2. 在明确项目保护单位"准入"条件基础上，根据成立时间、经营状况、保护工作开展情况、专项保护资金使用情况等内容对保护单位进行年度审核。对于那些为申报项目而刚刚成立的项目保护单位，以项目代表性传承人或其后代、亲属为法人代表的项目保护单位，或新申报项目以重要传承人代表[2]为法人代表的项目保护单位，应慎重对待，重点关注，对保护工作开展不利的项目保护单位应依规"准出"。

3. 加大项目保护资金申请、使用、绩效情况的公开力度，接受社会、代表性传承人、文化主管部门及相关部门的监督。

四、传承人的有关问题及解决方略

问题一：对代表性传承人定义的理解存在偏差，对代表性传承人与传承人之间关系的认知不到位，"以偏概全"，称谓众多，乱象丛生。

问题分析：《国家级非物质文化遗产项目代表性传承人认定与管理暂行办法》（文化部令第45号）中明确指出，代表性传承人是指经国务院文化行政部门认定的，承担国家级非物质文化遗产名录项目传承保护责任，具有公认的代表性、权威性与影响力的传承人。从上述表述中我们可以看出，代表性传承人从传承人中产生，代表性传承人与传承人是"子集与母集""点与面"之间的关系。

由于社会认知不到位，宣传、报道常过分放大代表性传承人的代表性，忽视其他传承人对非遗传承的贡献，这造成非遗项目只有代表性传承人一家而别无分号的错误认知；此外，很多文化行政部门及非遗保护机构机械地认为"扶植代表性传承人就是保护非遗项目"，将代表性传承人认定与否作为给予资金、优惠政策的判定标准。这样的双重误区打击了除代表性传承人之外的其他传承人的积极性，经常导

---

2. 由于非遗项目活态传承的特点，新申报项目为证明其影响力及活态性，须明确该项目的重要传承人代表，重要传承人代表多数为项目通过后的代表性传承人。

致代表性传承人受到"孤立"以及除代表性传承人之外的其他传承人得不到认同和关注，限制了非遗传承与发展。

同时，随着国家的重视和社会的关注，很多人受既得利益的驱使，打出"国家级项目传承人"或"国家级项目传人"旗号，混淆视听，严重影响了非遗保护工作的正常开展。

意见和建议：由文化主管部门牵头，加大《非遗法》普及、宣传力度，使社会各界正确理解代表性传承人的定义、权利与义务；尊重、关注、认可传承人对非遗保护工作的贡献；正确认识传承梯队建设对于非遗保护工作的重要性；在非遗保护工作中不要"过度关注"代表性传承人，做到非遗保护工作"点面结合"，真正实现传统文化振兴。

问题二："强势"项目保护单位不愿推荐、申报代表性传承人，"弱势"项目保护单位过度依赖代表性传承人。

问题分析：经营成规模，发展成体系，有独立知识产权或品牌、字号的"强势"保护单位，在保护工作开展之初希望被列入非遗名录，但并不愿推荐、申报代表性传承人。主要原因在于，对于有国企背景的单位，一旦代表性传承人退休，原则上除代表性传承人失去传承能力或年龄过大等原因之外，企业自身无法再申报代表性传承人，与此同时也失去了对代表性传承人的直接领导力；此外，一旦代表性传承人脱离单位，自立门户，会对企业自身的品牌、知识产权等造成不可控影响。相反，一些发展处于起步阶段、经营不善的"弱势"保护单位，急需利用代表性传承人的个人影响，扩大单位的社会认知度，以谋求发展，从而对代表性传承人"言听计从、百依百顺"，这同样不利于非遗保护工作的开展。

意见和建议：

1. 根据2008年6月14日起施行的《国家级非物质文化遗产项目代表性传承人认定与管理暂行办法》（文化部令第45号），非遗项目保护单位向所在地县级以上文化行政部门提出申请及征得被推荐人同意后，由保护单位向对应级别文化行政部门推荐代表性传承人；各级代表性传承人评审工作均照此执行。应由文化行政部门在传承人中进一步宣传，明确项目保护单位在代表性传承人认定工作中具有"推荐"职能，而非"垄断"职能。

2. 由文化主管部门牵头，充分发挥代表性传承人的能动性，组织其对项目保护单位保护工作计划的制订和落实、公益传承活动开展、专项保护资金使用等进行指导，并对项目保护单位的技艺保留情况和所生产产品的工艺、流程、质量进行监督；同时，加强《非遗法》普及力度，制定、完善相关细则，使代表性传承人明确，配合项目保护单位开展公益性非遗保护、传承、传播工作是其应尽义务，最终确立代表性传承人与项目保护单位之间的良性互动关系，形成相互监督、相互促进的良好局面。

五、由准确、规范把握"三个关注对象"相关问题引发的思考

以上是笔者以"三个关注对象"为出发点，结合西城区非遗保护工作现状，列举的一些问题及理解误区；同时，笔者有如下思考。

（一）非遗保护工作分为三个层面，应聚焦基础，实现可持续发展

非遗保护工作根据开展进程、形式、关注点的不同可分为三个层

面，即保护层面、传承层面、传播层面。

1. 保护层面：处于开展之初，是基础层面；以非遗项目的普查、整理、申报为主要形式；关注名录体系构建，如非遗项目的评审、代表性传承人的认定等。

2. 传承层面：在保护的基础上，以恢复、创造非遗项目传承的必要条件为主要形式；关注技艺的原汁原味保留及传承人队伍的扩大，如开展抢救性记录、鼓励传承人授徒等。

3. 传播层面：在保护、传承的基础上，非遗项目得到长足的发展与壮大；以宣传非遗和扩大其社会影响力为主要形式；关注非遗的历史、文学、艺术、科学、审美价值的传播与输出，如开展各类宣传、展示、交流活动等。

此外，这三个层面既相互渗透又彼此促进，保护层面是传承层面的基础，传承层面是传播层面的前提；同时，在传播过程中，通过文化交流、文明互鉴，又促进更高阶段的保护层面工作的开展，三个层面的工作呈波浪式前进、螺旋式上升态势。上文中讨论的种种现象与问题更多出现在保护层面，只有准确、规范地把握和解决上述问题，夯实非遗保护工作的基础，才能确保其正确的发展方向，实现非遗保护工作的可持续发展。

(二) 非遗保护工作的终极目标是实现中华民族传统文化的复兴

非遗保护工作由于阶段不同、层面不同，因此核心内容不同，但不应出现"脱离文化生态，片面讨论非遗项目保护""只关注传承不关注发展"等"以偏概全""舍本逐末"的理解误区。

以西城区国家级项目"北京评书"为例，笔者认为非遗保护工作并不应该仅仅关注北京评书表演艺术的传承，而应通过非遗项目的保护实现北京书馆文化的恢复与振兴。书馆文化中既有说书人的表演，又有观众的观演礼仪，还有演员与观众的互动关系。书馆服务人员熟知每位"书座儿"喝茶的口味、偏好，这种人文关怀是书馆文化；说书者开场之前不说书，先与台下观众互动，通过经验判定如何"使活""把点开活"，这种表演心理学是书馆文化；说书结束后，说书者门口送客，与观众互动，交流演出心得，这种观演关系是书馆文化。脱离书馆文化这个文化生态讨论"北京评书"项目的传承与发展，既不现实，也不全面。伴随着时代的变迁，很多新兴娱乐媒介和方式对传统文化的传承、传播影响深远。如何适应新时代的发展，弘扬中华民族传统文化，振兴中华传统手工艺，是非遗保护工作的时代命题与永恒实践。"抱残守缺"，只保留不发展，既不可行，也不可取。

参考文献：

北京市财政局 北京市文化局关于印发《北京市非物质文化遗产保护专项资金管理办法》的通知[EB/OL]. 北京市政府信息公开专栏 北京市文化局. http://www.beijing.gov.cn/zfxxgk/110021/gfxwj22/2016-12/13/content_769358.shtml.

本刊通讯员. 第三批国家级非物质文化遗产项目代表性传承人名单公布[J]. 中国中医药信息杂志, 2009, 16(7): 5.

国家级非物质文化遗产保护与管理暂行办法(文化部令第39号)[EB/OL]. 中华人民共和国中央人民政府. http://www.gov.cn/gongbao/content/2007/content_751777.htm.

国家级非物质文化遗产名录[EB/OL]. http://www.china.com.cn/culture/zhuanti/whycml/node_7021179.htm.

国家级非物质文化遗产项目代表性传承人认定与管理暂行办法(文化部令第45号)[EB/

OL]. 中华人民共和国中央人民政府. http://www.gov.cn/gongbao/content/2008/content_1157918.htm.

全国人民代表大会常务委员会关于批准《保护非物质文化遗产公约》的决定[J]. 中华人民共和国全国人民代表大会常务委员会公报, 2006, (2): 138—145.

中华人民共和国非物质文化遗产法[J]. 司法业务文选, 2011, (9): 30—37.

传承中国非遗，弘扬优秀文化
——记2018年北外国际"少年研究员"学术调研活动

任知行[1]

2018年3月28日，北外国际少年研究员遴选结束，本年度的少年研究员来自北京外国语大学国际课程中心、北京外国语大学附属中学、北京一零一中学等，共34名成员。4月12日，北外沈忆文教授主持了本年度"少年研究员"项目的启动仪式，标志着北外国际第三届"少年研究员"项目的正式开始。

在启动仪式后到集训前的三个月时间里，我们这些少年研究员带着问题，分别做了开营前的准备工作。我们不仅阅读了相关的文献资料，了解北京雕漆和北京评书，还听取了北京市西城区非物质文化遗产保护中心杨飞主任有关非遗保护知识的讲座、中华书局的梁彦老师带来的北京评书讲座，以及北京非物质文化遗产传承人刘晓迪老师带来的剪纸艺术讲座。

7月16日晨，小雨，尚在假期的我们按计划重返校园汇合，集体前往位于北京市大兴区的外研社国际会议中心，开始了为期13天的暑期集训。

在此期间，沈忆文教授给我们作了"少年研究员"项目的介绍，并分几次讲解质性数据分析的理论和方法；张虹老师从为什么要作科研及社会科学如何作科研两个方面为我们阐述了科研的意义；李琛老

---

1. 本文作者为北京外国语大学国际课程中心十一年级学生。

师讲解了访谈问题的设计；Sonja老师作了学术论文写作的讲解。

  集训期间穿插了搭建乐高、结绳记事、卡片排序、无敌骰子等游戏，旨在通过每个人的亲自动手参与，激发右脑思维，打开想象力，发现事物规律，学习信息统计与编排，为之后的调研工作打下基础。各种需要在小组内分工与合作的游戏让我们了解到每个人在认知上确实存在差异，我们从而尝试建立正确的沟通思路与方法，认识团队的利弊，从冲突中厘清问题，形成共识，共创团队共赢的局面。

  在此基础上，每个小组按照各自兴趣认领研究课题，之后完成问卷设计，制作完成指定研究课题的时间进度表，并按照要求进行访谈录音；录音后及时转换成文字，将内容导入Excel表格内，并在整理出来的访谈中认真寻找问题的答案。

  为期13天的集训中，我们聆听了北京雕漆传承人马宁老师关于雕漆和雕漆文化的故事。当马宁老师在屏幕上给我们展示精美绝伦的雕漆作品时，我们的感动之情简直无法用语言来形容。篆刻大师张国维先生带来了关于非遗项目篆刻的历史沿革的讲座，我们有幸亲眼见识到篆刻大家的篆刻过程。北外国际的王元老师向我们介绍了中国文化，王海兴老师给我们讲解了《易经》。

  我们走访了京城百工坊、北京儒匠传奇家具有限公司、宣南书馆、东城书馆、什刹海、南锣鼓巷等文化场所。我们欣赏了连丽如先生和她的徒弟们的现场评书，亲手制作了泥塑，参观了榫卯家具、上蜡技艺、雕漆技艺等与非遗相关的文化项目。不同的传承人为我们讲解了他们行当的奥妙与祖先的智慧。榫卯传承人讲解了榫卯的不同结构及用途，如一边宽一边窄的燕尾槽、既节省空间又能保持桌子稳定性的霸王撑等等；上蜡匠人讲解了蜡的原材料及上蜡的目的；我们还亲眼见证了雕漆制作的用时之长久、技艺之精细。

　　每一位中国非遗文化项目传承人都在采访中给我留下了深刻印象，其中以雕漆方面的国家级工艺美术大师、雕漆传承人殷秀云老师，核雕及雕漆传承人马宁老师为最。殷秀云老师出生在二十世纪四十年代，曾就读于北京市工艺美术学校。在学习、工作的几十年间，她在人物创作中不仅能够巧妙利用象牙雕刻的刀法展现人物的衣带飘飘，还能将人物面部的喜怒哀乐刻画得呼之欲出。她创作的《洛神赋》屏风、《丝绸之路》大瓶、《剔红鼎盛中华大鼎》等作品多次获得北京市及全国大奖。老一辈非遗传承人精益求精，新一代非遗传承人突破创新。二十世纪八十年代出生的马宁老师就是这样一位让人敬重的后生。马宁老师讲到了他与雕漆的渊源：他们家是核雕世家，而且他也是核雕这一非遗项目的传承人，他是因为喜爱雕漆而自寻师承。马宁老师平时话语不多，但讲起雕漆就滔滔不绝，比如讲到"漆"字的构成：上面的"木"是指漆树，中间的"人"其实是用刀在树上刮出的样子，两刀下面就是漆的颜色（奶茶色），左边的水则表示汁液。马宁老师还讲到漆自然风干是黑色的，唯有矿彩能易其色。他告诉我们，雕漆在工艺美术中的地位很高，是除了剪纸之外唯一的工比料贵的手艺。但无论哪一门手艺的手艺人，如果不是冬练三九、夏练三伏、日积月累、多年坐得住冷板凳，都不可能脱颖而出，成为非遗传承人。作为北京雕漆技艺最年轻的代表性传承人，马宁老师最近常常思考的问题是如何传承好老祖宗留下的技艺，让非遗很好地融入当代生活。相同的手艺，不同的年代，一个个非遗项目，作为中华文化的载体，就是这样代代相传、薪火不止的吧！

　　非遗传承人虽然与我们素昧平生，但对我们这些少年研究员有问必答，且热心、用心地向我们传授他们为之骄傲的技艺，这种热忱是对于我们传承非遗抱有殷切期望的体现。他们呈现的超凡技艺让人叹为观止！他们对品质严苛要求、一丝不苟的态度，以及心无旁骛、一生一事、专心致志的精神，让我们为之震撼！他们对于中华手工艺的热爱之情、敬畏之心就是我们中华民族的文化传统得以传承的根和魂！

通过参加北外国际的"少年研究员"项目，我获得的不仅仅是智力和能力方面的提升；作为一个中国人，我感到了自豪和骄傲。我真切地希望中国的每一项久经锤炼的文化遗产都可以广为人知。让更多的中国人更深刻地了解自己祖先的聪明才智，让更多的外国人了解中华文化源远流长的光辉历程，让中华文明发扬光大，这就是我们这些少年研究员的使命和责任所在吧！

雕漆篇

雕 漆
——千年之集萃　万世之流风

马　宁[1]　权宏力[2]

华夏精工六千年，刀耕火种漆器传。

殷商彩漆髹[3]世物，周礼祀器祭先天。

战国漆器若青铜，秦汉漆镴俱风流。

宋元美漆惊百邦，明盛髹饰风蔚然。

清史剔红醉当世，开辟雕漆新天地。

若欲书香继世长，国韵家宝永相传！

欲说雕漆，先说漆器。中国古代漆器的工艺，早在新石器时代就已经出现。夏代的木胎漆器不仅用于日常生活，而且用于祭祀，并常用朱、黑二色来髹涂。殷商时代已有"石器雕琢，觞酌刻镂"的漆艺。

从七千年前河姆渡时期的朱漆木碗开始，漆器一直以奢侈品的面貌在中国的历史中存在。尧、舜以漆器为祭祀用器；汉代漆器是富贵的标志；唐代一种叫"库露真"的雕漆被中原政权赐给西北少数民族，为西北少数民族所珍视。唐朝以后，漆器常被列为高档贸易品或

---

1. 北京市工艺美术大师，北京雕漆技艺代表性传承人，师从国家级非物质文化遗产北京雕漆技艺代表性传承人、国家级工艺美术大师文乾刚。
2. 儒匠工坊雕漆负责人。
3. 髹，读音为xiū，意为"把漆涂在器物上"。

者国际外交时的赠礼。

雕漆是一种技艺，是漆器随着社会的发展和进步，结合时代文化的注入和社会精神诉求，从而产生的一种高端艺术形式；雕漆让漆器从实用器具升华到文化艺术品。它至少有一千四百年历史，横跨唐、宋、元、明、清五个朝代，具有崇高的社会地位和艺术价值。

雕漆起源于唐，在中国漆艺的众多门类中是出现得最晚的，但得益于帝王的厚爱，雕漆在中国漆艺中可谓独领风骚，在宋、明、清三朝，采用雕漆工艺的漆器都成为皇家御用的宫廷器物。

雕漆一千四百余年的发展历程是一个逐渐丰富和完善的过程。最早的雕漆似乎是剔犀，后来品类逐渐丰富，出现剔红、剔黄、剔绿、剔黑、剔彩、复色雕漆、金银胎剔红。王世襄先生把中国的漆艺分为十四大类，其中剔犀和剔红属于雕漆。他用剔红囊括剔黄、剔绿、剔黑、剔彩等品类，因为这些品类制作技艺大体类似，主要是漆层颜色不同。剔犀单列是因为剔犀的制作工艺与剔红类不同。传世实物中剔红最多。中国人喜欢红色，而剔红的这种红色一般是用朱砂或者银朱入漆，看上去鲜明稳重，可以长久不褪色；并且经历的时间越久，色泽会越润厚，所以各个时代都不同程度地重视发展剔红，使剔红成为雕漆的代表品类。一般情况下，说到雕漆就是指剔红，而剔红也代称所有剔犀以外的雕漆。

雕漆，顾名思义，就是在漆上进行雕刻创作的艺术形式，所以要想全面了解雕漆，就要明晰"漆"与"雕"各自的含义。漆为质，雕为工，大漆为良材美质，美手为巧夺天工，良美的材质与精湛的技艺完美结合，造就了雕漆"冠众艺"的历史评价。

中国传统的"漆"指的是漆树皮层中流溢出的一种液体，主要由漆酚、漆酶、树胶质和水分构成，与现代化工漆是完全不同的：

> 就像京剧是"国剧"一样，大漆经常被称为"国漆"。漆液刚从漆树流出时是乳白色的，氧化干燥后变成红棕色，稍厚几近黑色，所以有了"漆黑"一词。它的色彩基调中含有内省静穆的审美趣味，东南大学教授张燕说："大漆的气质是中国人温柔敦厚气质的折射，谦冲而温厚，含蓄而神秘，接近诗的意境和诗教传统。"[4]

雕漆虽然以"雕"为名，但是绝不是只有"雕"，雕漆这项极其复杂的宫廷工艺，从大体上主要分为设计、制胎、髹漆、雕刻、抛磨等五大工序；如果从小的工序划分，会达几十道之多。

雕漆的首要工序是设计，这也是雕漆最为重要的一个环节，之后的一切工序都要以此为基础。一个好的设计首先要有一个效果图，根据雕漆的主题、用途、造价、使用对象等进行制作。

第二道工序是制胎，制胎是雕漆作品发展的空间。大漆必须附着于胎体上，这样才能为接下来的工序打好基础。现在雕漆主要使用的胎体有木胎、金属胎、脱胎、瓷胎和皮胎，每种胎体的选择都要考虑器物的不同特质。

第三道工序就是髹漆，也就是雕漆中的"漆"，是雕漆所有工艺中耗时最长的。髹漆就是将纯天然的大漆髹涂在胎型上，一遍遍地重复此道程序，等达到一定厚度就可以在胎体上进行雕刻。素有"髹漆

---

4. 见http://www.lifeweek.com.cn/2008/0128/20676.shtml。

百日"的说法,来形容髹漆所耗时之长。但在实际操作中,很多雕漆作品需要的髹漆时间远远超过百日。因为产自漆树的大漆结膜的特点是表面结成膜,而不是整体固化,因此髹漆只能在胎体上一道一道地刷,每次还不能涂得太厚,1毫米厚的漆要刷17遍。每天只能涂一道漆,涂完一道漆后就需要将胎体放置在一间湿度大概为70%、温度为25℃的黑暗房间中让大漆结膜。雕漆需要涂多厚的漆是由所做物品的大小和制作工艺决定的,这些都没有明确的标准,全部依靠雕漆大师丰富的经验。

第四道工序就是"雕",即雕刻。如果说髹漆是雕漆工艺中最需要耐心的工序,那么雕刻就是雕漆工艺中最需要速度的环节,也是最难的一道工序。由于大漆会逐渐硬化,匠人必须在4个月之内完成雕刻。不管雕刻图案有多么复杂,时间都必须限定在4个月之内。雕漆作品的雕刻程序大都需要多位匠人共同完成。雕漆雕刻的难点是它不能像一般的雕刻制品那样由雕刻师慢慢地去塑造被雕刻的形象,雕漆讲求一刀到位,不能重刀。因此雕刻必须由经验丰富的匠人来完成,若一刀出错,一件雕漆作品就有可能报废了。

根据髹漆的色彩分类,有剔红、剔黑、剔彩、剔犀等不同名目。剔红是最主要的品种,大部分时候,雕漆就是指剔红。明代黄成的《髹饰录》上说:"剔红,即雕红漆也。髹层之厚薄,朱色之明暗,雕镂之精粗,亦甚有巧拙。唐制多印板刻平锦朱色,雕法古拙可赏……"因为这几句话,剔红被认为始于唐代,虽然到今天传世最早的剔红是宋剔。明代官坊果园厂的剔红承袭了元代嘉兴西塘"藏锋清楚、隐起圆滑"的风格。清代,因为乾隆皇帝的偏爱,宫廷监制了大量的雕漆作品。不过,到光绪年间为慈禧太后60岁寿辰筹办剔红的时候已经"无匠造办",雕漆技艺几乎失传了。

第五道工序就是打磨、抛光。这同样需要匠人的耐心与技艺,一般一件小的雕漆作品完工需要6—8个月,而大型屏风则需要2—3年。这些都是常规雕漆作品的制作时间,如果制作大型雕漆作品,所需的时间就更久了。

简单来说,雕漆是用天然漆料在素胎(有木胎、铜胎、皮胎等)上涂抹出一定厚度,再用刀在堆起的平面漆胎上雕刻山水、花卉、人物等浮雕纹样的技法。通过对漆与雕漆的厘清,可知雕漆技艺是建立在大漆这种独特的材质上的,材质与技艺相互成就:材质承托了技艺的思考,技艺对材质充满敬意。

雕漆历经千余年的发展沿袭至今,位列国家级非物质文化遗产名录,成为全人类的智慧结晶和文化传承。我们当代人有责任、有义务继承和发扬中国传统文化中的精髓。在充斥着浮躁与功利的当代社会,雕漆的底蕴和醇厚更能让喧嚣归于寂静,让浮躁甘于淡然。

雕漆的继承与发展离不开全社会的关注与支持,希望社会中的有识之士能够给予这一古老中国技艺的延续以更多的帮助,让雕漆在新的时代焕发更加璀璨的光芒。

当代雕漆的艺术特色[1]

杨靖尧　孟家毓　刘紫璇[2]

【摘要】 雕漆有着鲜明的艺术特色。当代雕漆既保留了传统，体现了传统文化的特色，也融入了现代的多元化和个性化元素。当代雕漆的题材更广泛且侧重个人艺术创作，在制作材料、工具等方面更具创新性并增加了现代科技。雕漆一直是创作者思想与情感的体现，蕴含着创作者的美好期望，同时也是中国传统文化的一种呈现。

【关键词】 雕漆　艺术特色　艺术创新

一、研究意义

雕漆作为中国非物质文化遗产之一，有着非常鲜明的中国特色，而不同时期的雕漆总能以不同的艺术特色来反映当时的审美和文化。随着时代的发展，雕漆匠人们不断创新，以使传统文化能够适应时代潮流的发展。当今新一代雕漆工匠不断深入挖掘雕漆的传统艺术特色，并在此基础上融入鲜明的时代感，促进雕漆的艺术创新和发展。我们作为中国青年，研究雕漆的艺术特色和创新发展，对于雕漆的艺术传承具有重要的社会意义，这也是我们的使命和责任。

---

1. 本调研报告科研指导教师为北京外国语大学国际教育集团共建项目部教师刘文婕。
2. 本调研报告的三位作者均为北京外国语大学国际课程中心十一年级学生。

二、文献综述

目前,学界对于当代雕漆艺术特色的研究有一些初步成果。例如,我国第一个非物质文化遗产保护专业博士毕业生宋本蓉在《雕漆技艺》一书中表示,"雕漆经历了技艺的精致追求、文化的深度取向、皇家的政治考虑,不同的参与者对其不同层面和向度上进行锤炼淳化。它既在漆艺技术史上有重要的地位,也以其精致富丽的面貌呈现出中国文化的丰富内涵,既是物质文化,又是非物质文化"(宋本蓉,2013)。中国工艺美术大师、非物质文化遗产雕漆技艺传承人殷秀云老师将雕漆和当代其他工艺品进行对比,认为雕漆具有如下鲜明的艺术特色:一是要在器物胎骨上反复上漆;二是纯手工制作,注重雕工和磨工;三是历史悠久,可以从唐代追溯到现代,是一项重要的国礼。在目前中国雕漆艺术出现断层的背景下,研究当代雕漆的艺术特色、促进人们对雕漆的认知显得尤为重要。

三、研究方法

本研究采用结构式访谈的方法来收集数据,研究小组成员在2018年7月分别对三位雕漆工匠——马宁、殷秀云、赵海伟——进行了实地采访,并对采访数据进行编码和分析。

（一）受访者基本信息

表1：受访者基本信息

受访者	背景介绍
马宁	京作核雕代表性传承人、北京雕漆技艺代表性传承人、北京市工艺美术大师，目前北京最年轻的东城区雕漆技艺传承人
殷秀云	中国工艺美术大师、非物质文化遗产雕漆技艺传承人
赵海伟	北京儒匠传奇家具有限公司雕漆工作室雕刻师

（二）采访问题

本研究采取结构式访谈形式，不随意增加或减少访谈问题，采访问题如下：

1）您认为哪个时期的雕漆作品最具有代表性？这个时期雕漆作品的特点以及同当代雕漆的差异是什么？

2）当代雕漆作品的主要题材是什么？和以前作品的题材有什么不同？

3）当代雕漆的制作手法与过去是否有所不同？

4）当代雕漆制作过程中是否使用了一些我们现在才有的材料及工具？这些材料的获取是否会受时代的影响产生变化？

5）在雕漆的创作过程中，您会赋予作品怎样的个人情感或特殊含义？

6）您认为雕漆这门艺术蕴含了中国文化的哪些精髓？

（三）数据分析

本研究对收集的采访数据进行编码，通过对比传统雕漆和当代雕漆在艺术特色、主要题材、制作技艺、个人情感和文化传承方面的差异，探究当代雕漆的艺术特色。我们得到以下结果。

表2：雕漆的艺术特色

研究主题	解读	编码
艺术特色	在创作中所运用的各种具体的表现方法	雕漆的艺术特色体现时代特征
主要题材	作品中所表现的主体内容和素材	雕漆题材广泛但个人侧重不同
制作技艺	制作中的材料、工具、技术或品质性手艺	雕漆技艺既保留传统又加入创新
个人情感	作品中所表达的个人情绪、思想和感受	雕漆蕴含创作者的情感表达
文化传承	所创作作品的物质精神和文化精神的传递和承接	雕漆体现中国文化

四、研究发现与讨论

(一) 雕漆的艺术特色体现时代特征

雕漆在不同时代有着不同的艺术特征，而这些特征可以反映出各朝代独特的文化特征。通过对比历代雕漆和当代雕漆的艺术特色，本研究发现当代雕漆更加多元化和个性化。

雕漆起源于唐代的四川和云南地区，而最早被发现的雕漆手工艺品出自宋朝。由于宋朝时期的绘画技艺精湛，宋朝雕漆作品上的图案样式极为精美。而从元代出土的雕漆文物中发现，元代工匠创造了许多雕漆制作技艺，这些技艺对雕漆工艺的逐渐成熟起到了重要作用。雕漆在明清时期发展迅猛，达到了繁荣时期。在采访中，马宁认为，"明朝的雕漆气势更强，而清代工艺复杂，体现皇家思想"。在明朝永乐时期，因永乐皇帝对雕漆具有浓厚兴趣，雕漆有史以来首次完全由皇室制造，"御用监"甚至建立了果园厂这一工坊来承担雕漆的制作工作。在强大的财政支持和稳定的生产环境下，雕漆的发展突飞猛进，雕漆甚至经常被皇帝作为国礼赠送外宾。到了清代，人们更为追求雕漆的观赏性与装饰性，所以雕漆工匠更注重雕漆的制作风格。乾隆皇帝的龙椅和屏风便是由雕漆制作而成的，赵海伟提道："乾隆时期的雕漆注重观赏类，（例如他的）这些龙椅还有屏风，虽只是一个观赏，但看着又特别精巧，做工特别细致。"中华人民共和国成立后，北京雕漆变得更为重要，主要用以兑换外汇（宋本蓉，2013）。雕漆巨大的审美价值使其产业得到了政府的支持与资助。而更是由于北京雕漆艺术家的不懈努力，雕漆多次荣获国内外奖项，向世界表明了它的重要地位。

　　相比历代雕漆的特色，当代雕漆的设计更加自由多样，正如马宁在采访中提道："如今的雕漆更多的是一种自由的艺术创作。"因为当代雕漆有了更多的个人色彩，所以在艺术特征方面比古代作品更加个性化。雕漆的创作变得更加自由，有三个重要原因。首先，随着社会福利的改善，雕漆工匠不需要靠雕漆技术来维持基本生活需求。其次，正如殷秀云所说："如今，在传承文化的基础上，雕漆作品反映了新时代的一些东西。人们的精神层次更高，他们便会有更多的想法。"最后，大量涌入中国的西方文化扩展了雕漆创新的空间。当一门艺术的创作变得更加自由，它就会变得更多样化，更有价值，因为它不仅包含了社会对它的需求，还包含了创作者自身的情感。

　　当代雕漆同样极具包容性，融入了其他艺术元素，例如雕漆与黄金或宝石结合，用于装饰；另外，当代雕漆并非特别繁复，而是简单大方,如赵海伟所说:"雕漆简单大方,就跟山水画需要留白似的,让人看着特别舒服;但同时又具有美感,作品更能体现雕漆语言。"

(二)雕漆题材广泛但个人侧重不同

当代雕漆的主题仍保留着传统题材,但雕漆大师各有侧重,其雕漆作品也各具特点。在采访中,马宁和赵海伟都介绍了当代雕漆大师的选题特点:文乾刚先生侧重于山水画,擅长大型的山水屏风制作;殷秀云老师擅长精细人物的雕漆制作;马宁老师侧重于佛造像题材,擅长雕塑人体结构,推出背光的虚实层次;李志刚大师擅长比较前卫的现代雕漆题材。由此可见,当代雕漆题材更体现个人的艺术创作,而不再局限于传统器物的雕漆制作。

(三)雕漆技艺既保留传统又加入创新

雕漆的整体制作过程没有太大的变化,因为雕漆的制作仍然保持着传统的技艺和工艺。马宁提道:"我们可以在设计的形态上有我们的时代特色,但是在技艺上我们更多的是保留它的原汁原味。"基本技艺从未改变,这也是雕漆传承的最基本特征。然而,雕漆工匠现在已经在生产过程中作出了一些改进来辅助雕漆生产。

1.当代雕漆内胎材料选择多样化

在过去,雕漆作品中使用的内胎材料只有少数几种,如铜、木、麻布等,这些材料都具有延展性和易塑性。但它们的获取比较困难,对材料的质量要求也比较高,例如"木胎的材料选优红松,因为这种木材变形最小"(宋本蓉,2013)。在当代雕漆生产中,内胎材料的选择则变得非常多样化,"最早的漆器肯定是木胎,但是随着金属工艺发展，有了金属胎，我们今天也可以有一些现代材质的胎体"（马宁）。

2.现代科技在一定程度上有助于雕漆制作

雕漆制作是一个非常复杂的过程。由于雕刻的复杂性、工艺的特殊性和艺术的独有性，从设计到成品，雕漆的生产必须由许多工匠合作，经过多道工序才能完成。一般来说，一个普通雕漆成品的生产至少需要半年时间，一件更精致的雕漆艺术品需要一年左右的时间，而一件对制作要求更高的雕漆作品则需要两年以上的时间。虽然当代工艺水平有所提高，生产时间有所缩短，但雕漆的制作仍不能在短时间内完成。

当代雕漆在制作过程中确实有了一些改进。马宁在采访中提道："印房以前是靠天吃饭，现在我们可以保持印房恒温恒湿，这个是科技给雕漆制作带来的便利。"另外，赵海伟提到，现代科技提高了雕漆制作的便捷程度，例如以前雕漆的图纸是由雕漆工匠手绘的，但现在设计师可以运用电脑制图，打印贴纸，再进行描绘。这样的方式使得雕漆制作不再散户化，减少了设计师的工作量，避免了雕漆样板走样。

(四)雕漆蕴含创作者的情感表达

雕漆不仅体现了创作者的思想立意，还反映出他们的情感寓意。殷秀云说道："在创作任何一件作品时，都在作品当中讲一个故事，而这个故事必须是打动你的。你认为它是有意义的，你才去表现它。所以说很多作品，特别是一些比较大的、比较重要的作品，都是会有很强的个人感情在里边。"对马宁来说，他认为创作作品的思想立意传达着对幸福生活的期盼："我的每一个作品当中都有我对美好生活的那种期盼，这也是我创作的主题。"实际上很多雕漆创作都基于对吉祥的愿景，也表达了人民对美好生活的期待。例如，雕漆的常见形象有荔枝、牡丹、龙、凤等。荔枝表达了人们想要拥有子嗣的愿望，牡丹象征着吉祥与财富，龙和凤代表权力。这些对美好生活的期望从古至今都在传递，这也是雕漆的一大传统。

同时，雕漆也融合了创作者对雕漆本身的激情、投入与热爱。赵海伟说道："我做每件作品都有一种激动感。我喜欢那种做雕漆的工作状态，它是需要把你想象中的那种感觉做出来，而且这个东西做出来特别有意思。"从赵海伟的话中也能看出雕漆工匠耗尽心血、不计成本，执着于每一处细节，这也是一种吃苦耐劳、坚韧不拔、极具耐心的工匠精神。

(五)雕漆体现中国文化

当代雕漆不仅以其艺术性著称，更是中国文化的重要组成部分。从色彩到工艺，甚至到表现形式，雕漆都蕴含中国的传统题材和文化。首先，在色彩方面，雕漆的颜色是纯粹的红色，而红色正是中国文化的一种象征。其次，在工艺方面，"中国是最早利用漆、拥有漆文化的国家；而且中国运用的漆是趋于自然的，且环保无公害"(赵海伟)。最后，在表现形式方面，雕漆"处处充满了我们中国传统的题材和文化，所以雕漆的整个工艺史就是中国工艺美术史的重要组成部分，它是中国工艺美术的血脉所在"(马宁)。

五、结语

　　了解雕漆的艺术特色和创新，对推广和传承雕漆具有重要意义。雕漆的艺术特色反映了不同时期的文化特色，而在时代变更中，当代雕漆的艺术特色既保留了传统，又融入了多元化、个性化的特征。当代雕漆在题材方面更侧重于个人艺术创作，题材更加广泛；在技艺上继承了雕漆传统中精华的部分，但内胎材料选择更具创新性，并在制作过程中加入了现代科技，促进了雕漆的创新发展和便捷制作。另外，当代雕漆依然是一种思想和情感的表达方式，蕴含着雕漆创作者的美好期望。当代雕漆作为中国非物质文化遗产之一，还体现出丰富的中国传统题材和文化。因此，当代雕漆结合传统和创新，不断适应时代的发展潮流，从而促进雕漆受众的逐步增加，这有助于雕漆的不断推广和传承。

参考文献：

宋本蓉. 雕漆技艺[M]. 北京：文化艺术出版社，2013.

Artistic Features of Modern *Diaoqi*[1]

Yang Jingyao Meng Jiayu Liu Zixuan[2]

Abstract: *Diaoqi* (carved lacquer) has distinctive artistic features. Modern *Diaoqi* not only retains its tradition and embodies characteristics of traditional culture, but also includes contemporary diversification and individuality. Contemporary *Diaoqi* has a wider range of subjects and an increased focus on individual artistic creation, and is more innovative in production and technologically advanced with its materials and tools. In addition, *Diaoqi* is always the creator's thoughtful and emotional expression, which contains the creator's beautiful expectations, while it is also a representation of Chinese traditional culture.

Keywords: *Diaoqi*, artistic feature, artistic innovation

1. Research Significance

As one element of Chinese intangible cultural heritage, *Diaoqi* has distinctive Chinese characteristics, and *Diaoqi* of different periods always reflects the corresponding historical backgrounds with different artistic features. With the continuing development of the times, *Diaoqi* craftsmen are constantly innovating to adapt the traditional culture to the trend of the new era. Understanding the artistic features, and incorporating the distinctive characteristics of the times, for the innovation and development of *Diaoqi*, are not only the sacred mission of the new generation of *Diaoqi* artists, but also teenagers' responsibility as Chinese citizens. At the same time,

---

1. The academic advisors of this paper are Liu Wenjie, from the Counselling Division of BFSU International Education Group; and Dana Melchior, a teacher from EPlus of BFSU International Group, Beijing Foreign Studies University.
2. The authors of this paper are the 11th grade students of the International Curriculum Centre (ICC) of Beijing Foreign Studies University.

studying the artistic characteristics and creative development of *Diaoqi* also has important social significance for the artistic inheritance of *Diaoqi* itself.

2. Literature Review

At present, we have found some preliminary results of studies on the characteristics of contemporary *Diaoqi*. For example, Song Benrong, a PhD on Chinese intangible cultural heritage protection, said in her book, that *Diaoqi* has exquisite craftsmanship, deep cultural connotations, political considerations of the royal family, and the improvements in different aspects and dimensions by different participants. "It has an important position in the history of lacquer art, and it also represents the rich connotation of Chinese culture with its exquisite appearance. *Diaoqi* is both intangible culture and tangible culture." (Song, 2013)

Yin Xiuyun, a master of Chinese arts and crafts, an inheritor of the intangible cultural heritage of *Diaoqi*, has compared *Diaoqi* with other contemporary crafts, and believes that *Diaoqi* has the following distinct artistic features: layers over layers of natural lacquer are painted on the substrate; completely handmade through engraving and polishing; its long history can be traced back to the Tang dynasty, and now *Diaoqi* is an important national gift. Against a background of a shortage of inheritors of Chinese *Diaoqi* art, it is especially important to study the artistic characteristics of contemporary *Diaoqi* and raise people's awareness of it.

3. Research Method

In this study, structured interviews were applied to collect data. In July 2018, the research team conducted on-the-spot interviews with three *Diaoqi* artists, Ma Ning, Yin Xiuyun and Zhao Haiwei, and the interview data were coded and analyzed afterwards.

3.1 Basic information of the participants

Table 1: Biographical information of the participants

Participant	Information
Ma Ning	Representative inheritor of Beijing *Hediao* (fruit pit carving) Representative inheritor of Beijing *Diaoqi* Master of Beijing Arts and Crafts
Yin Xiuyun	Master of Chinese Arts and Crafts Representative inheritor of intangible cultural heritage of *Diaoqi*
Zhao Haiwei	*Diaoqi* artist of Beijing Legend Furniture Co., Ltd

3.2 Interview questions

This study took the form of structured interviews with prepared interview questions. The interview questions are as follows:

1) During which period of time do you think the *Diaoqi* works are the most representative of the craft? What are the characteristics of *Diaoqi* works of this period and the differences between them and contemporary *Diaoqi* works?

2) What are the main themes of contemporary *Diaoqi* works? How are they different from the subject matter of traditional works?

3) Does the production of contemporary *Diaoqi* differ from the past?

4) In the process of making contemporary *Diaoqi*, have you used some materials and tools that are only available in modern times? Do the process of carving, the materials and tools change with time?

5) In the process of making *Diaoqi*, what kind of personal feelings or special meanings do you give the work?

6) What do you think is the essence of Chinese culture embodied in the art of *Diaoqi*?

3.3 Data analysis

This paper encodes the collected data and explores the artistic characteristics of contemporary *Diaoqi* by comparing the differences between traditional *Diaoqi* and contemporary *Diaoqi* in terms of artistic features, main themes, craftsmanship, personal emotions, and cultural heritage. We have the following research findings.

Table 2: Artistic features of *Diaoqi*

Theme	Explanation	Code
Artistic features	Various concrete expressions used in the creation	The artistic features of *Diaoqi* paintings reflect the characteristics of the times
Main themes	Main content and material expressed in the work	*Diaoqi*'s themes are wide but the individual focus is different
Craftsmanship	Materials, tools, techniques, and quality of production	Craftsmanship retains tradition and innovation
Personal emotions	Personal emotions, thoughts and feelings expressed in the works	*Diaoqi* contains the emotional expression of the creator
Cultural heritage	Material spirit and cultural spirit of the works	*Diaoqi* expresses traditional Chinese culture

4. Research Findings and Discussions

4.1 The artistic features of *Diaoqi* reflect the characteristics of the times

Diaoqi has different artistic characteristics in different eras, and these characteristics can reflect the unique cultural features of each era. Comparing the *Diaoqi* in the past and in contemporary times, this paper finds that contemporary *Diaoqi* is more diversified and personalized.

Diaoqi originated in regions of Sichuan and Yunnan in the Tang dynasty. However, the earliest discovered handicrafts were from the Song dynasty. Due to the exquisite painting skills of the Song dynasty, the patterns on the *Diaoqi* works were extremely beautiful. From the unearthed *Diaoqi* works of the Yuan dynasty, we can see that the craftsmen invented a lot of *Diaoqi* production techniques, symbolizing the maturity of the *Diaoqi* process. *Diaoqi* developed rapidly during the Ming and Qing dynasties and experienced a prosperous period of its craftsmanship. In the interview, Ma Ning said, "The Ming dynasty's *Diaoqi* pattern is more powerful, and the Qing dynasty's craftsmanship is complex, reflecting royal thought." During the Yongle period of the Ming dynasty, because of the Emperor Yongle's fondness for *Diaoqi*, it was the first time in history that a workshop named "Orchard Factory" was established to undertake the production of *Diaoqi* exclusively for the royal family. With the strong financial support and peaceful environment, *Diaoqi* developed by leaps and bounds, and was even given by the emperor as a national gift to his foreign guests. In the Qing dynasty, people pursued the functionality of *Diaoqi*, alongside with its artistic and decorative nature. At that time, the *Diaoqi* craftsmen paid more attention to the quality of lacquer making. For example, the dragon chairs and screens of the Emperor Qianlong were made of *Diaoqi*. As Zhao Haiwei mentioned, "*Diaoqi* of the Qianlong period of the Qing dynasty focused on the ornamental style, like these dragon chairs and screens. Although they are ornamental, they are especially delicate and the craftsmanship is particularly meticulous."

After the founding of the People's Republic of China, Beijing *Diaoqi* became more important, and leaders used it as a national gift or export for foreign currency. Due to the economic role of *Diaoqi*, the industry received government support and subsidies. Moreover, due to the unremitting efforts of Beijing *Diaoqi* artists, *Diaoqi* has won many awards domestically and abroad, and thus it has shown the important position of *Diaoqi* to the world.

Compared with the characteristics of *Diaoqi* of the past, the design of contemporary *Diaoqi* is freer and more diverse, as Ma Ning mentioned in the interview, "Now *Diaoqi* is more like a free art creation." Because contemporary *Diaoqi* adds more personal thoughts, it is more diversified than the ancient works in terms of artistic features. There are three important reasons for the free creation within the contemporary *Diaoqi* making process. Firstly, with the improvement of social welfare, *Diaoqi* artists do not need to rely on the market to maintain a living. Secondly, as Yin Xiuyun mentioned, "Now, inherited on the basis of culture, *Diaoqi* works also reflect new features of the new era. People are highly inspired and they have more ideas." Lastly, cultural communication with the West has expanded the space for *Diaoqi* innovation. When the creation of art becomes freer, the artworks become more diverse and more valuable, because they not only meet the needs of the society, but also contain the emotions of the creators themselves.

Contemporary *Diaoqi* is very inclusive, incorporating other artistic elements, reflecting the innovation, such as *Diaoqi* being combined with gold or precious gems for decoration. In addition, contemporary *Diaoqi* advocates simplicity and gracefulness, not complexity and intricacy. For example, Zhao Haiwei said, "*Diaoqi* is simple and delicate, just like Chinese painting where much space is left for imagination. It makes people comfortable, but at the same time it is beautiful. That is the language of *Diaoqi*."

4.2 *Diaoqi* has a wide range of themes but the individual focus is different

The theme of contemporary *Diaoqi* retains traditional elements, such as flowers, mountains, and water. But modern *Diaoqi* masters have their own focuses, and their works bear their personal characteristics. In the interviews, both Ma Ning and Zhao Haiwei have introduced the characteristics of the contemporary *Diaoqi* masters: Mr. Wen Qiangang, who focuses on landscape painting, particularly large-scale landscape painting; Yin Xiuyun, who is good at carving fine facial expressions of human figures; Ma Ning, who specializes in Buddha statues, focusing on carving patterns of human bodies; Li Zhigang, who is good at the avant-garde, a modern theme of *Diaoqi*. It can be seen that the themes of contemporary *Diaoqi* embody individual artistic creation, and are no longer limited to the *Diaoqi* making of traditional artifacts.

4.3 *Diaoqi* techniques retain tradition and add innovation

The overall production process of *Diaoqi* has not changed much because the production of *Diaoqi* still maintains the traditional techniques and craftsmanship. Ma Ning said, "We can have our time's characteristics in terms of design, but we are more reserved in the art and craft of carving." The basic skills have never changed, which is also the most basic feature of *Diaoqi* inheritance. However, *Diaoqi* artists have now made some improvements in the production process to assist in the production of *Diaoqi*.

4.3.1 Diversification of contemporary *Diaoqi* materials

In the past, there were only a few materials used as the base of *Diaoqi*, such as copper, wood, and burlap. These materials are malleable but difficult to obtain, and there are high quality requirements for them. For example, the wood needs to be dry lest it should crack or deform. In the contemporary *Diaoqi* production, the choice of interior materials has become diverse. "The earliest *Diaoqi* has definitely a wooden base; but with the development of metal technology, we now have metal bases, and we can also have some modern materials today." (Ma Ning)

4.3.2 Modern technology contributes to the production of *Diaoqi* to a certain extent

The process of making *Diaoqi* is very complicated. Due to the complexity of the engraving, the particularity of the craft, and the uniqueness of the art, from the design to the finished product, the production of *Diaoqi* must be cooperatively undertaken by many craftsmen, and can be completed only after many different processes. Generally speaking, the production of an ordinary *Diaoqi* product takes at least half a year, and a more elaborate artwork takes about one year. It takes more than two years to produce a grand *Diaoqi* work. Although contemporary technology has greatly shortened the production time of many commodities, *Diaoqi* products are not included in them.

Contemporary *Diaoqi* has made some minute improvements in the production process. In the interview, Ma Ning mentioned, "In the past, the drying of lacquer in the painting room depends on the weather and season.

Now, we can maintain constant temperature and humidity in the room. This is the convenience brought by technology." In addition, Zhao Haiwei expressed that modern technology improves the ease of designing *Diaoqi*. For example, the drawings of *Diaoqi* design were hand-painted by the artists in the old days, but now, computer graphics and sticker printing come to their assistance. In this way, *Diaoqi* production does not need to be divided into many phases, and the workload of the designer is reduced. Most importantly, the complete carving process can stick to the design strictly.

4.4 *Diaoqi* contains the emotional expression of the creator

Diaoqi reflects not only the creator's ideological intention, but also their emotional meaning. Yin Xiuyun said, "When you create any work, you tell a story through your work, and this story must be impressive. You think it makes sense, so you want to show it. So many works, particularly some larger and more important works have strong personal feelings inside." For Ma Ning, he believes that the idea of creating works contains the artists' expectation of a happy life. He said, "Every one of my works has my expectation of a good life. This is also the theme of my creation." In fact, many *Diaoqi* creations are based on the auspicious will, and thereby express people's hope for a good life. For example, the common designs of *Diaoqi* are patterns of lychee, peony, dragon, and phoenix. Lychees express the wish for more children, peonies symbolize auspiciousness and wealth, and dragon and phoenix represent power. These expectations for a better life have been passed down from ancient times to the present, and they belong to the great tradition.

At the same time, *Diaoqi* displays the enthusiasm and love of the creator. Zhao Haiwei said, "I have a sense of excitement in every piece of work. I enjoy my mental state of making *Diaoqi*. I need to externalize the feelings and inspirations that excite me through my work, and this is why *Diaoqi* is so intriguing." From Zhao Haiwei's words, it can be seen that *Diaoqi* artists have spared no efforts for every detail of the work. This is the spirit of craftsmanship, hard work, perseverance, and meticulousness.

4.5 *Diaoqi* reflects traditional Chinese culture

Contemporary *Diaoqi* is known not only for its artistic features, but also as an important part of Chinese culture. From color to craft, and even to expression, *Diaoqi* is full of Chinese traditional themes and culture. First of all, we can see this in the color of *Diaoqi*. The color of *Diaoqi* is the purest red, and red is a symbol of Chinese culture. Secondly, we can see this in the technique of *Diaoqi*. "China is the first country to use lacquer in the world and the lacquer used in China is all natural and environmentally friendly." (Zhao Haiwei) What's more, we can see this in the design of *Diaoqi*. "The design of *Diaoqi* is full of Chinese traditional themes and elements, so the history of *Diaoqi* is an important part of the history of Chinese arts and crafts. I think it is the embodiment of Chinese arts and crafts." (Ma Ning)

5. Conclusion

Understanding the artistic features and innovations of *Diaoqi* has great significance for the promotion and inheritance of *Diaoqi*. The artistic features of *Diaoqi* reflect the characteristics of different eras and the cultural characteristics of different periods. With the change of modern times, the artistic features of contemporary *Diaoqi* retain the tradition while incorporating the modern characteristics of diversification and individuality. In the themes of contemporary *Diaoqi*, the main focus is on individual art creation and the scope of the subject is more extensive. The contemporary *Diaoqi* technique inherits the essence of the tradition, but the selection of base materials is more innovative, and new technology is added in the manufacturing process in order to facilitate effective production. In addition, contemporary *Diaoqi* is more of a way expressing thoughts and emotions than ever, containing the beautiful expectations of the creator. As one exemplar of Chinese intangible cultural heritage, contemporary *Diaoqi* also reflects Chinese traditional culture. Therefore, contemporary *Diaoqi* combines tradition and innovation, constantly adapts to the development trend of the times, and thus promotes the gradual increase in the number of *Diaoqi* audience, which contributes to the continuous promotion and inheritance of the cultural heritage.

References:

Song, Benrong. Diaoqi Craft [M]. Beijing: Culture and Art Publishing House, 2013.

雕漆传承人的工作和生活现状

郝罡[1]　沈忆文

【摘要】 雕漆传承人热爱雕漆工作，并因为热爱而克服工作中的艰辛与困难，从而成为雕漆技艺的大师级传承人。在雕漆的学习和制作过程中，他们面临四个方面的困难：原材料和工具、工作时间、作品本身，以及投资方的压力。在工作中，大师们的雕漆技术和个人自信心都有很大提高，也获得了成就感和个人荣誉。同时，在经过多年的学习成为大师后，他们仍不忘传承雕漆这项传统技艺，并在不同领域进行了创新，持续为这项技艺的发展贡献力量。雕漆传承人在业界享有很高的地位，也享有各项专业荣誉，然而，雕漆传承人的整体社会地位还有待提高。雕漆大师们还肩负着传承这项文化技艺的社会责任。

【关键词】 雕漆传承人　非物质文化遗产　传承与创新　社会地位和社会责任

一、研究背景与研究目标

雕漆是中国传统漆艺的重要代表，始于大约一千五百年前，是大漆加工过程、雕刻技艺、工具材料及其制品的总称（宋本蓉，2013）。从历史上看，雕漆技艺有一个逐渐丰富和完善的过程。"禹用大漆做祭器，并加以才回纹饰，开启了以漆器作为祭器的风俗。"（宋本蓉，

---

1. 北京外国语大学国际教育集团升学规划部教师。

2013）三国、两晋、南北朝是中国传统漆艺极为重要的转折时期，而经过唐代对于色彩和技艺的改良，雕漆在宋代开始兴盛，于明清时期进入鼎盛阶段。雕漆艺术是基于人类对色彩的追求发展起来的（张飞龙，2008）。通过查找相关文献，我们可以看到雕漆在中国古代繁荣的发展史，也可以了解到雕漆艺人在古代的工作情况和社会地位。然而在当代，雕漆行业一度从人们的视野中消失，雕漆的社会认知度也低于其他工艺美术类产品（中经视野，2019）。随着中国非物质文化遗产保护工程的启动，雕漆技艺的保护已经被广泛关注。北京雕漆技艺在2006年被列入国家级非物质文化遗产名录，雕漆技艺开始重新进入人们的视线中（宋本蓉，2010）。但是，关于雕漆传承人工作和生活现状的介绍和文章却很少，公众很难深入了解雕漆大师的现实状况。

本研究采访了雕漆的两位传承人——殷秀云大师和马宁大师，从他们的日常工作安排和对雕漆行业的思考出发，通过分析、对比等方式，着重呈现出雕漆传承人的实际工作和生活现状。希望本研究可以填补当代雕漆大师研究方面的空白，以便让更多人了解雕漆大师，并努力提高他们的社会地位。本研究不仅是对雕漆技艺传承人现状的探究，更是对雕漆行业传承和发展的思考和认识。

二、研究方法与研究步骤

(一) 数据收集

为了深入了解本课题，我们采访了两位雕漆技艺传承人——殷秀云大师和马宁大师。通过对采访内容的整理和分析，我们对雕漆传承人的工作现状有了更多了解。

1. 采访对象

殷秀云

中国工艺美术大师、国家级非物质文化遗产北京雕漆技艺传承人。1967年毕业于北京工艺美术学校，从事雕漆设计和制作工作五十余年。殷秀云大师在人物的创作上，融入立体雕塑和象牙雕刻技法，把人物的体貌和个性表现得惟妙惟肖，开创了雕漆作品以人物为主题的艺术风格。

马宁

京作核雕代表性传承人、北京雕漆技艺代表性传承人、北京市工艺美术大师、北京职工艺术家、北京玩具协会会员；师从国家级非物质文化遗产北京雕漆技艺代表性传承人、国家级工艺美术大师文乾刚；目前北京最年轻的东城区雕漆技艺传承人、西城区京作核雕传承人。

2. 采访问题

1）在您刚开始步入这个行业的时候，您的榜样是谁？

2）请您简单介绍一下您的日常生活。

3）在您制作雕漆的过程中，有什么事情是让您难忘的？

4）在您成为雕漆大师之后，您的工作是否让您感到自豪？

5）您是否会让您的孩子继承您的工作，继续学习雕漆？

6）您认为从事雕漆这项工作的人群的社会地位怎么样？

(二) 数据分析

表1：数据分析结果

主题	编码
对雕漆的热爱	• 因为热爱而接触雕漆，树立行业中的榜样 • 因为热爱而克服工作中的困难 • 因为热爱最终成为传承人
困难与成就	• 困难 原材料难获取，工具需自己制作 雕漆作品制作周期长达几年 雕漆作品制作难度高 来自投资方的精神压力 • 成就 雕漆大师获得了个人荣誉 完成作品获得成就感 雕漆技术不断提高 更加有自信心
传承与创新	• 雕漆传承人需要传承这项传统技艺 • 雕漆大师的创新 在雕漆技艺上的创新 在雕漆题材和领域上的创新
社会地位和社会责任	• 社会地位 雕漆大师在传统艺术界有很高的地位 雕漆大师的社会地位不高 • 社会责任 雕漆大师有很强的使命感 雕漆大师在履行各自的社会责任

三、研究分析和讨论

(一) 热爱成就了雕漆传承人

通过对雕漆技艺传承人的访谈，我们感受最深的是大师们对于雕漆的热爱。因为热爱，他们走进了雕漆行业。马宁大师早期学习核雕，出于对雕漆的喜爱，他进入雕漆这个行业，现在已经到了一天不拿刀就会难受的地步。殷秀云大师则是从艺校毕业之后直接开始从事雕漆工作。在艺校，她学习的是象牙雕刻，但在学习和实践的过程中，她逐渐感受到自己对于雕漆的热情并持之以恒地坚持了下去。殷秀云大师说："我觉得自己是幸运的，因为每天干的事情都是自己很喜欢的，而且如果在生活中有什么烦恼的事，做雕漆时也能忘掉这些不好的事情。"

出于热爱，雕漆大师们克服了雕漆工作中的各种困难。完成一件雕漆作品是非常困难和艰辛的，面对复杂的工艺和紧张的工期，大师们从没有放弃或抱怨，反而以更加积极的态度对待工作，在解决困难的过程中提升自己；在工作的时候感觉不到苦，反而乐在其中。而这一切，都是源于对雕漆事业的热爱。正是心怀对雕漆的热爱，殷秀云大师和马宁大师为人们带来一件又一件精美的作品，得到了业内和社会的认可。同时，他们也在工作中体会到作为非遗传承人的自豪和骄傲。除此之外，殷秀云大师还提到制作雕漆使她更加自信，让自己的生活越来越好。

(二) 雕漆传承人面临的困难与取得的成就

雕漆技艺繁杂且精细，需要雕漆艺人专心致志、倾心付出。在雕漆的学习和制作过程中，他们面临无数的困难与艰辛，但也有很多收获和成绩。

1. 四个方面的困难

通过访谈，我们看到雕漆传承人工作中的困难来自四个方面：原材料和工具、工作时间、作品本身，以及投资方的压力。

首先是原材料和工具。制作雕漆作品时所需的原材料——漆，很难达到大师们的标准和要求，所以他们在制作非常重要的作品时，一般需要从采漆开始，亲自完成所有的工序，这其中就包括上山采集漆；而采集漆使用的工具以及后续制作雕漆作品的模型模具也都需要他们亲自制作。除了原材料需要亲自准备，每一位雕漆艺人还需要制作他们自己的雕刻工具。这些准备工作是艰苦而枯燥的。正如马宁大师所说："我们从材质到工具全都很难获取。我老师教我的第一课居然是生火打铁。作为一个北京孩子，我自己一辈子从没弄过火，但是从我拜师学艺之后，我马上要学生火打铁。"马宁大师还提到让他非常难忘但又备感艰辛的事情，包括"上山去采漆，去做这些泥塑模拟雕漆的训练"。

其次，雕漆作品的制作周期很长。尤其是刷漆这个过程，雕漆艺人只能等待几百层漆自然风干，如殷秀云大师所说，"（一件普通的作品）涂漆要涂半年多"。再加上复杂的雕刻，这些工序更需要雕漆艺人静下心来慢慢完成。雕漆作品的工艺难度极大，一刀错，这件作品就毁了，尤其是透雕和多层次的彩雕。所以雕漆艺人的手法必须恰到好处，这样便更加耗费时间和精力。马宁大师在采访中提道："我恐怕一年也不能完全完成一件作品。"由此可见雕漆作品的制作周期之长。

因为制作雕漆的时间很长，雕漆大师们每天的工作也十分辛苦。马宁大师说："我基本上没有休息日，就是说我每天正常起来，起床之前做梦都是在想图纸怎么办。"他还觉得，在成为大师后，"比以前更累了"。殷秀云大师的说法更加具有代表性："刷漆的工作一旦结束，你就必须在三四个月之内给它雕刻完成，否则它会容易变硬，你就雕不动了。"因此，为了在最佳时间内获得最好的作品，大师们必须抓紧时间，有时甚至到了废寝忘食的地步。殷秀云大师是这样描述她在制作一件作品时的每日安排的："早上起来，有时候甚至不吃饭，七八点钟就坐那儿开始雕了，中间草草解决了自己的两餐，之后可能一做就做到夜里12点。"由此可见，大师们在制作作品时，"真的是从早忙到晚，非常紧张"（殷秀云）。

第三个困难来自作品本身的难度。每一位雕漆大师都希望不断突破自我，创作出有意义的作品，而创作的过程也是不断克服困难的过程。在殷秀云大师创作雕漆作品《剔红鼎盛中华大鼎》时，她遇到了无数困难。这个大鼎的设计是把《开国大典》这幅著名的油画雕刻到大鼎的一个主要侧面上，难度非常大。雕刻人物是雕漆技艺中最难的，为了体现出所雕人物的表情和精神状态，雕漆艺人需要有极高的雕刻水平。况且在制作群像的时候，里面的人物都很小，雕刻的时候需要全心投入，不能有任何差错。这个大鼎整体约1.33米高，"尺寸最大的朱德的头像才2.2厘米，最小的人像才1厘米，所以在那么小的人像中要把整个精神状态、面貌都给雕出来，是非常难的"（殷秀云）。

第四个困难是来自投资方的压力。雕漆大师们经常需要完成很多重量级的作品，比如上文提到的《剔红鼎盛中华大鼎》，便是为中华人民共和国成立60周年献礼的作品，其艺术和文化价值都很高。在雕漆艺人制作一个作品之前,投资方已经作了大量的前期投入。因此,在面对繁复的技艺要求的同时,雕漆大师们还需要承受非常大的精神压力。殷秀云大师曾说,接受这样的任务压力很大,由于前期投入非常大,如果做不好的话会觉得"对不起投资方"。由于雕漆制作需要很长时间,雕漆大师会在整个过程中持续承受这种压力,直到作品成功完成的那一天。

2. 两个方面的成就

尽管雕漆给大师们带来很多问题和困难,他们仍因雕漆这门技艺而收获了很多成就。

首先,雕漆大师们获得了很多个人荣誉。他们凭借一件件技艺精湛的作品,在社会上得到了褒扬。比如,雕漆界泰斗级人物文乾刚大师凭借他的雕漆作品,包揽了从2002年到2005年中国工艺美术大师作品展的金奖(司丽,2007)。殷秀云大师在其从业的五十余年中,设计了上千件作品,并且获得了中国工艺美术百花奖、国际艺术精品博览会金奖等荣誉,是雕漆技艺的国家级代表性传承人。同时,根据访谈中马宁大师的叙述,我们了解到他在成为雕漆大师之后,作品也有了很高的知名度,"会在不同的场所展示和出售"。

其次,雕漆大师们每完成一件作品时都会获得成就感,而且他们的自信心都会有很大提高。每一件大师级作品的产生都是大师们勤勉敬业的结果,每一项高难度的雕漆工作都需要极长时间和极大精力的投入。如殷秀云大师创作的《剔红鼎盛中华大鼎》,她认为该作品的制作难度非常大,整个制作过程令人难以忘怀,这件作品是她雕漆生涯里最重要的作品之一,"是一个很重要的里程碑"。此外,她还把雕漆与金漆、牙雕等工艺相结合,创作出如《凤船》《郑和宝船》《牙形摆件》等不朽之作,其中多件作品被有关部门当成"国宝"收藏。雕漆工作需要大师们日复一日不断创作,在雕漆技艺得到提高的同时,大师们的心理素质和自信心也有很大提高。就像殷秀云大师所说:"通过锻炼觉得自己什么困难都可以克服,这对于自身也是一种很大的锻炼。"

(三)雕漆传承人的传承与创新

为了保护雕漆这一非物质文化遗产,在传承雕漆传统的同时,还需要对技艺和内容进行不断创新,以适应现代社会对于工艺美术作品的审美和使用需求。

1.雕漆传统技艺的传承

为了传承雕漆技艺,雕漆大师们首先需要经过十年到二十年的学习,并且在成为大师后还要从事雕漆制作、培养传承人、宣传雕漆艺术等工作,持续为这项技艺的发展贡献力量。

作为第一代雕漆传承人,殷秀云大师的首要工作是将这项技艺传承下去。自1968年被分配到北京工艺美术厂从事雕漆的设计和制作工作以来,殷秀云大师便开始了漫长的雕漆传承事业。她以历史上的雕漆大师为榜样,鉴赏他们的作品,并将达到大师水平作为自己雕漆事业的目标。她说:"元末明初的张成、杨茂都是我的榜样。"为了更好地锻炼雕漆技艺,殷秀云大师拜访各地名师,她正式拜的师父有孙茂同、贾福华。此外,殷秀云大师还跟朱文林、刘文瑞等多位大师学习雕漆技法。

在继承的同时,殷秀云大师还表示:"面对严重萎缩的雕漆市场,作为一名老雕漆人,是很心痛的,就想多做些好作品,把这门古老的技艺传承下去。"

2. 雕漆行业的创新发展

为了更好地适应现代社会对于雕漆的需求，雕漆大师们在不同领域进行了创新和发展。殷秀云大师在雕刻技法上进行了创新，即在人物的创作上，将象牙雕刻技法融入其中，赋予人物鲜活的体貌和个性，开创了雕漆作品以人物为主题的艺术风格。

马宁大师则在创新方面有更多建树。从进入这个行业开始，他便思考如何将传承下来的文化进行提炼，并且加入自己的东西。他说自己没有什么榜样，而是希望后人能把他当作榜样。他结合现代社会的审美，将雕漆这项非物质文化遗产融入现代人的生活；在进入新领域、给雕漆带来新题材的同时，实现了雕漆技艺在当代社会的创新和发展。比如，马宁大师结合佛教题材，将木雕、象牙雕刻的手法应用到佛像雕漆的工艺中，制作了雕漆屏风《维摩诘演教图》，整个雕刻内容涉及24个人物。此外，他将雕漆技艺应用到哈雷摩托的装饰上，赋予传统工艺新的活力。这是一次将雕漆和现代化设施相结合的大胆尝试，使雕漆得到了当代消费者和市场的认可，为传统文化与现代需求的结合提供了一个重要的创新思路。此后，马宁大师不断地发展和实践雕漆的装饰性，制作出包括以壶胎和雕漆共存的适用性茶壶为代表的一系列雕漆产品。

(四)雕漆传承人的社会地位和社会责任

作为雕漆的大师级人物，雕漆传承人在业内享有很高的地位，也享有各种专业荣誉。然而，从整个社会的角度看，雕漆传承人的社会地位尚有待提高。同时，作为雕漆这项传统文化的传承人，雕漆大师们又肩负着传承这项文化技艺的社会责任。

1. 社会地位

在采访雕漆大师殷秀云和马宁的过程中，我们可以感受到雕漆大师的社会地位在不同的范围内有所不同。首先，雕漆大师在雕漆艺术界有很高的地位，在国内的艺术领域也有很高的知名度和认可度。根据马宁大师所述，他认为每当别人介绍他是雕漆工艺美术大师和非遗传承人的时候，对方都会表现出极大的认可和尊重，他也觉得自己的社会地位很高。雕漆大师们的作品也在一些宣传平台和销售平台上受人追捧，一件大师级雕漆工艺品的价格在几万到几百万元之间[2]。

然而，雕漆大师在中国社会中的整体地位仍有待提高。首先，在调查中我们发现，社会人士对于雕漆大师的认知度较低。马宁大师提到，在生活中没有人知道他是谁，甚至没有人知道他的老师是谁。其次，社会对于传统技艺和工匠精神的认可度不高。马宁大师说："(工匠精神)应当得到社会的认可和尊重。那么在这一点上，我想目前社会上缺失的还很多。"在日常生活中，雕漆大师往往不被了解，只有在对方知道他们是非遗传承人的时候，他们才能得到尊重。由于雕漆行业曝光率不高，雕漆和雕漆大师都没有被公众普遍认识，因此他们的整体社会地位仍有待提高。

2. 社会责任

从调查中我们可以看出，不管是老一代雕漆大师殷秀云，还是新一代雕漆传承人马宁，他们对于雕漆事业都有很强的使命感和责任感。

作为雕漆大师，他们将保留和传承雕漆技艺作为自己的使命。在

---

2. 见 http://www.gmmatrix.com。

谈到雕漆技艺传承人的责任时，马宁大师表示，他对这项非遗项目的继承和创新有着强烈的使命感。如他所说："没准儿我在人间的使命就是把它更好地传递下去吧。"在现实生活中，身为国家级的雕漆大师和非遗传承人，他们身体力行，承担起很多传承工作。他们积极培养传承人，向社会宣传雕漆技艺，并鼓励下一代学习雕漆。马宁大师表示："如果可能的话，我两个儿子我都想让他们去学雕漆。"殷秀云大师现在已经七十多岁了，但是她仍然亲自带徒弟，因为她觉得自己的责任很大，希望徒弟可以传承雕漆这项技艺。马宁大师积极参加各种社会活动和讲座，向更多人宣讲雕漆这项中国非物质文化遗产，从而让大众更好地认识和了解雕漆，扩大雕漆的社会认知度和影响力。他注重对青少年的宣传，并且和中央美术学院、北京工业大学等高校合作，办讲座、重调查，将学校传授的知识和实践相结合，让年轻人多了解中国传统文化。马宁大师还利用现代社交媒体进行宣传，他在2016年创办了自己的微信公众号"雕漆马宁说漆"。他说："虽然这样更累了，但我还是乐在其中。"

正是因为有了像殷秀云大师和马宁大师这样的传承人的不懈努力，且随着国家的重视，中国的雕漆行业才逐步回暖。在十年之前，雕漆行业一直处于衰落期，工艺美术慢慢好起来才是近十年的事情（殷秀云）。

四、总结

随着北京雕漆技艺在2006年被列入国家级非物质文化遗产名录，这项技艺开始进入人们的视线。我们采用结构式访谈的调查方法，采访了雕漆行业的两位大师和传承人，并根据访谈内容，结合文献研究，对雕漆技艺传承人的现状进行了分析和总结。

我们了解到雕漆传承人对于雕漆行业的热爱和坚持，同时也看到在雕漆的学习和制作过程中，他们面临无数的困难与艰辛，也在坚持过后收获了很多成就和荣誉。他们不仅继承了雕漆制作的技艺，还在为雕漆的传承和创新发展奉献力量。他们肩负着传承这项文化技艺的社会责任，也在雕漆业界享有很高的地位，但是从整个社会的角度看，雕漆传承人的整体社会地位仍有待提高。

本研究的不足之处在于：首先，由于受访者只有殷秀云大师和马宁大师两位雕漆传承人，调查得到的数据较为有限，导致本研究的结论可能具有随机性，不具有广泛的代表性。其次，由于目前有关雕漆传承人现状的研究很少，本研究的理论基础较为欠缺。通过对受访者的深入采访，本研究凭借现实依据，力图展现雕漆传承人的工作和生活现状，以填补此类研究的空白。最后，由于时间和精力的限制，本次调研的数据多来自受访者对于特定问题的口述。如果可以增加问题数量或扩展调查广度，我们相信可以得到更多、更全面的数据，呈现出更加完善和立体的雕漆传承人工作和生活的现状全貌。

参考文献：

工美矩阵[EB/OL].https://www.gmmatrix.com.
司丽.雕漆大师文乾刚(艺苑名家).人民日报海外版，2007-06-08(第7版).
宋本蓉.雕漆技艺[M].北京：文化艺术出版社，2013.
宋本蓉.非物质文化遗产保护视野下的传统手工技艺——以北京雕漆为例[D].北京：中国艺术研究院，2010.

张飞龙. 中国髹漆工艺溯源[J]. 中国生漆，2008，27（1）：21—37.
中国雕漆行业市场前景分析预测报告[EB/OL]. 中经视野(2019). http://www.cevsn.com/research/report/1/325875.html.

The Life and Work Experience of *Diaoqi* Artists[1]

Song Chenghuan Shen Yimei Ren Zhixing[2]

Abstract: *Diaoqi* artists inherit not only the traditional skills of lacquer carving, but also the spirit of innovation and development in their specific fields. In the process of learning and making *Diaoqi*, they encounter difficulties in many aspects. However, during the process of carving and painting, *Diaoqi* artists improve their professional skills and personal confidence and receive a great sense of accomplishment and personal honors. Meanwhile, they also take the social responsibility for inheriting and carrying forward this traditional art. Regarding social status, *Diaoqi* inheritors are wildly praised in their specific fields and enjoy various professional honors; however, their social status in China still needs to be improved. *Diaoqi* masters have a great passion for their profession.

Keywords: *Diaoqi* inheritors, intangible cultural heritage, tradition and innovation, social responsibility and social status, passion for *Diaoqi*

1. Research Background and Objectives

Carved lacquer, or *Diaoqi*, is an integral part of the intangible cultural heritage of the People's Republic of China. The government of the People's Republic of China is encouraging the society to pay more attention to Chinese intangible cultural heritage, which has contributed to significant improvements in the environment and the techniques. Our research, therefore focuses on the life of the artists who have inherited and improved the

---

1. The academic advisors of this paper are Hao Gang, from the Counselling Division of BFSU International Education Group; and Sonje Du Toit, a teacher from EPlus of BFSU International Group, Beijing Foreign Studies University.
2. The authors of this paper are the 11th grade students of the International Curriculum Centre (ICC) of Beijing Foreign Studies University.

skills of their ancestors. However, current literature pays more attention to the inheritance of the craft, which is a part of the technique, while there is not much mention of the craftsmen, namely the carrier of skills. We are of the opinion that Chinese intangible cultural heritage should be a combination of technique and the spirit of the artists; therefore, our research aims to find the impact of the artists' life and work experience on the work of *Diaoqi* production and procedures.

Our research focus is the life and work experience of *Diaoqi* artists, which concentrate on the human element of the artists. By examining the daily routines of *Diaoqi* artists, we aim to gain a deeper understanding of modern *Diaoqi* inheritors in order to raise awareness of this intangible cultural heritage. We furthermore aim to raise awareness about the art of *Diaoqi* and the status of the artists in recognition of their status as inheritors of this intangible cultural heritage and national treasure.

2. Research Method and Steps

2.1 Data collection

For data collection, our group uses the method of structured interview. We interviewed Ma Ning and Yin Xiuyun respectively. Through analyzing the data, we have drawn some conclusions on the life and work experience of *Diaoqi* artists.

2.1.1 Participants

There are several reasons why the research group has chosen the two masters of *Diaoqi* as interviewees. First and foremost, the masters are the people who lead their industry and drive it further, that is to say, they serve as symbols of artists in their field. Moreover, they have extensive work experience of making *Diaoqi* art pieces, as well as life experience of how *Diaoqi* affects their lifestyle. Lastly, they have distinctive experiences and unique views of the technique which are also valuable. The introduction to the two masters is as follows.

Ma Ning

Ma Ning is an inheritor of both *Diaoqi* and *Hediao* (fruit pit carving), which are both classified as Chinese intangible cultural heritage. He was initially interested in *Hediao*, due to the influence of his grandfather, a *Hediao* artist. He practiced carving skills when he was making *Hediao* art pieces, but he was drawn to *Diaoqi* by a *Diaoqi* art piece in the picture of a stamp. This encounter drove him to leave the *Hediao* industry and visit *Diaoqi* masters and learn to make a *Diaoqi* work. He studied with his teacher Mr. Wen Qiangang to learn the craft. He learned the necessary techniques used to produce *Diaoqi* art pieces, as well as how to make his own instruments.

After completing his apprenticeship with Mr. Wen Qiangang, Ma Ning chose to focus on producing works such as Buddha statues and screens with scenery. He also created a *Diaoqi* work combined with Harley-Davidson motorcycle which raised the value of the motorcycle significantly. He has also put huge efforts into increasing social awareness of *Diaoqi*.

Yin Xiuyun

Yin Xiuyun is a master of Chinese arts and crafts and a national inheritor of the intangible cultural heritage of *Diaoqi*. She graduated from Beijing Arts and Crafts School in 1967, having studied ivory carving. She was assigned a job as a *Diaoqi* artisan since the ivory carving workforce was saturated at that time. She was therefore able to apply her ivory carving skills to improve her *Diaoqi* work and make innovations. She has been engaged in the design and manufacture of engraving lacquer for more than 50 years. Her products are highly regarded, especially in her carvings of human characters as the theme of her art style.

2.1.2 Interview questions

1) Who were your role models when you first started in this industry?

2) Please briefly describe your daily life.

3) In the process of making *Diaoqi*, what aspects are memorable for you?

4) After you became a master sculptor, do you feel proud of your work?

5) Will you let your child inherit your work and continue to learn *Diaoqi*?

6) What do you think of the social status of the people engaged in *Diaoqi* work?

The six questions were set in accordance with the topic of this research which is "The Life and Work Experience of *Diaoqi* Artists". The first question concentrates on both the life and work experience based on the assumption that the life experience of the artists will help them foster the method or the habit of thinking and doing their own work. Furthermore, a similar impact can be deduced by their choice of role models.

The second question is led by the first question in terms of establishing details about the impact of their life, work experience and role models on day-to-day life. The third and fourth questions mainly focus on the work experience of the *Diaoqi* artists, the things that make their work experience different from others'. Things that are memorable are different from individual to individual, such as the reason why they are proud or not proud of their job.

Lastly, the life experience is precipitated in the last two questions since it can be assumed that their life experience would impact the hopes they have for their children. That is the reason why we chose to use the six questions to be our structured interview questions.

2.2 Data analysis

Table 1: Research findings

Theme	Code
Innovation	· Be an example to others at any time to conceive new drawings · Ivory carving technology for the creation of portrait theme

continued

Theme	Code
Difficulty	• No rest • Scarcity of the materials and facilities • Long time to make a workpiece • Time limited • Hard to carve a facial symbol • Pressure • Long time to train a craftsman
Achievement	• Pride in the work • Exhibitions of masterpieces everywhere • The pressure turns into a driving force • Skill improvement • Boost of self-confidence
Social responsibility	• Inheritance (teaching apprenticeships, fatherhood) • Promotion (participation in social activities) • Responsibility (honor)
Social status	• Low recognition and respect; status should be promoted • Be respected (not for a position, if you work hard enough)
Ardent love	• Love • Do not feel difficult • Gladly accept the challenge • Enjoy it; do only one thing in a lifetime • Be proud of your work; love it • Be able to make a living
Future prospective	• Keep the positive opinion • It is improving

3. Findings

3.1 Tradition and innovation

Diaoqi has a long history and was once widely known by people. In the past, it was often used as decoration on people's meal boxes. When it was in vogue, in ancient times, the royals used it to decorate the palace and national treasures. Nowadays *Diaoqi* has been classified as an intangible cultural heritage, the main object of protection of national art heritage. Although *Diaoqi* work is considered exquisite, few people have a deep understanding of this craft. At present, the active *Diaoqi* artists in China are very few. They hope to dedicate their youth to inherit the great art of *Diaoqi*.

The inheritance of *Diaoqi* art can be traced back to the period of the Wei, Jin, and Southern & Northern dynasties. To this day, *Diaoqi* artists rely on the traditional masters to learn the skills required for mastering this art. In the process of learning, the master not only teaches apprentices the craft of *Diaoqi* and instructs them what their shortcomings are, but also teaches them how to live and even how to behave.

From our interview with the contemporary master Ma Ning, we have learned that when the artists first entered this industry, most of their goals were set by what they learned from their own master, and they have striven to achieve a degree of mastery with their own master as an example.

After *Diaoqi* artists have mastered certain relevant historical knowledge, they can set more role models, for example, some of other masters in this industry, or the *Diaoqi* masters in history. These role models urge them to learn *Diaoqi*, and encourage their efforts to inherit this craft.

During our interview, Yin Xiuyun stated the following:

> "When I first entered the industry, my role model was actually the best in the industry. I was particularly impressed by his skills. So I want to be able to learn his skills in the future and be as good as he was."

By setting a role model, *Diaoqi* artists gain motivation, which drives them to perfect their artistry and create *Diaoqi* works that mark them as masters. Their love for the art also motivates them to inspire the youth and ensure the inheritance of *Diaoqi* for future generations.

The longevity of *Diaoqi* as a traditional craft can be attributed to more than its long history and tradition; it is also due to the innovation of design concepts and techniques developed by the artists. In terms of design ideas and techniques of *Diaoqi*, Master Ma Ning has a particularly innovative approach to this art. He applies his *Diaoqi* techniques to nontraditional, modern objects, an example of which is his *Diaoqi*-embellished Harley-Davidson motorcycle. This innovative approach can be linked to his desire to avoid derivative work. In the interview, he explained this desire as follows: "I wanted to be a role model for others, so I didn't think about whether I wanted to be like my master or like any other celebrities."

Master Yin Xiuyun is also a great innovator in *Diaoqi*. She incorporates the carving techniques used in ivory carving into her *Diaoqi* art and also uses portraits as a subject, which is not common in traditional *Diaoqi*. In our interview with Yin Xiuyun, she referred to an example of her innovative work, a piece titled "The Founding Ceremony of the Nation", in which she carved portraits of Chinese leaders.

3.2 Difficulties and achievements

The *Diaoqi* craft requires a diverse skill set combined with fine and precise carving. Artists need to pay attention to each step of carving and carve carefully. In the learning and making process of *Diaoqi*, they face numerous difficulties and obstacles.

The raw material that is required when making the lacquer for *Diaoqi* is itself an obstacle as it is very difficult to extract. The tools for making *Diaoqi* present further difficulties as the molds must all be created by artists themselves. Another major challenge is the fact that it takes a long time to make a *Diaoqi* work. The process of layering lacquer is especially long, since many layers are necessary and the lacquer must dry naturally. Furthermore, the artist of a *Diaoqi* work must carve meticulously and slowly. One wrong cut destroys the work, so the technique of the artist must be just right, which is time-consuming for the artist. The extent of the difficulty caused by time is illustrated by Ma Ning in the interview; he stated that he "can't complete a piece of work in a year."

Time proves a further challenge in that it takes more than ten years to cultivate a *Diaoqi* artist. The production process is also extremely time-consuming, which puts a great deal of pressure on the artists. The pressure comes not only from the complexity of the production process, but also from the urging of the investors. Our interviewees have noted that there are almost no days off for the *Diaoqi* artists, and sometimes they even forget to eat and sleep. Despite these challenges, the *Diaoqi* masters we interviewed stated that their love for the art enables them to overcome these difficulties. Having their works exhibited and seeing appreciation of their craft allow the artists to turn the pressure into motivation to improve their skills.

The masters are also able to take pride in their achievements, which in turn gives them the confidence to express their creativity. When Master Yin Xiuyun was creating the *Diaoqi* work "The Founding Ceremony of the Nation", she encountered numerous difficulties, but she overcame all the difficulties and completed the surprisingly successful work, as is evident in this statement from the interview:

> "I think the harvest is particularly great. I can say that after this time, I feel as if I can overcome any difficulties. I think this work is an important milestone for my life and also an exercise for me."

For an artist, a successful work can be a milestone, an achievement that makes it worthwhile to overcome the obstacles.

3.3 Social responsibility and social status

A master of any field has the potential to be a role model for others, which can instill a sense of social responsibility. Since information on *Diaoqi* is not widely spread, people are not often exposed to this art. Some people do not even know what *Diaoqi* is. In order to raise awareness, *Diaoqi* masters do a lot of extra work. Ma Ning gives lectures to spread this culture and to introduce the charm of *Diaoqi* to people. Yin Xiuyun, who is in her seventies, still serves the public. She teaches *Diaoqi* at university, and also has her own apprentices.

Diaoqi artists devote most of their life to *Diaoqi* and express a sense of responsibility for the art. They are willing to sacrifice more for this craft to be better inherited and ensure the future inheritance of the Chinese intangible cultural heritage of *Diaoqi*.

Despite their efforts, *Diaoqi* masters are not well-known to the public. Few people inherit this skill, and much fewer people actually specialize in *Diaoqi*. As these masters are inheritors of a Chinese intangible cultural heritage, one could assume that these national masters would attain a degree of fame. However, their social status as masters of an intangible cultural heritage craft is still not like that of celebrities in TV shows or movies.

In the interview, Ma Ning referred to a discussion with a Japanese scholar, regarding the elements of craftsmanship, public recognition, and respect. Ma Ning claimed:

> "The composition of the craftsmanship has three elements. The Japanese artists get all three, while the Chinese artists only have two. The first is that every artist should only take one job in a lifetime. The second is to be proud of their work. The third point, which is the most crucial point, is that every artist needs to get recognition and respect from the public. Therefore, Chinese artists still have a long way to go."

Despite the lack of recognition, Ma Ning retains a sense of responsibility for *Diaoqi* and its future by working to promote social awareness of the craft; he remains passionate about his art.

3.4 Passion

The masters we interviewed have frequently mentioned their love and passion for their art as defining factors in their success as *Diaoqi* artisans. When they face difficulties such as making tools, having little spare time, or doing stressful projects, they rely on this passion to persevere. They believe that they can improve their skills by overcoming problems and they attribute this ability to overcome obstacles to their love of *Diaoqi*. Thus, they do not feel bothered or bored while they are working. They claim to enjoy their work. Because of their passion, they do their craft work patiently, not rushing their work, and accepting the necessary time constraints.

Yin Xiuyun stated, "I am really lucky, because all the things I do every day are things I love." She went on to mention that *Diaoqi* improved her living conditions despite her age, and she still served this industry, which was also because of her passion for *Diaoqi*. Ma Ning has claimed that he cannot live without making *Diaoqi* artworks. He will feel uncomfortable if he cannot pick up his knives and make *Diaoqi* artworks.

Artists' love and passion for *Diaoqi* have contributed to their success and they have become masters and leaders in the *Diaoqi* industry. Because of their love and passion for *Diaoqi*, they are proud of their careers. In their opinion, love is a crucial factor in job satisfaction.

3.5 Future prospects

The two *Diaoqi* masters we interviewed have great expectations for the future of *Diaoqi*. As technology improves, the *Diaoqi* industry has found ways to benefit. For example, the works of Ma Ning are sold online. Buyers do not need to drive far to the furniture hall; they can just view the works online and click to buy what they like. This method benefits both sellers and buyers and makes this intangible cultural heritage modernized.

Modernization is insufficient for the survival of the art; an intangible cultural heritage requires inheritors to survive and to have future prospects. When asked about passing on his knowledge to future generations, Ma Ning mentioned that he wanted his children to learn *Diaoqi* in the future. That is to say, he thinks *Diaoqi* has great potential, and his children can support themselves if they work in this field. In Yin Xiuyun's opinion, the revival of arts and crafts began around ten years ago. She is still working hard for the future of *Diaoqi*. With the efforts of these masters, more and more people are getting to know *Diaoqi*, to be attracted by *Diaoqi*, and to expect a good future for *Diaoqi*.

4. Conclusion

In summary, findings from the present studies are in accordance with the trends of related policies, and the life and work experience of the *Diaoqi* masters. Data of this study were collected via the method of field research. The research group interviewed two masters of *Diaoqi*, Yin Xiuyun and Ma Ning, via structured interviews in order to collect answers pointing to certain criteria.

Based on our findings we can conclude that the masters we interviewed hold the belief that they should keep the fundamental and reasonable tradition in order to hold the ground of the technique and make innovation for the sake of improving this feat. They also face several difficulties; however, the difficulties also bring achievements. In the interviews, the masters have stated that the difficulties and pressure they experienced have improved their skills and work overall.

With regard to the effort that the *Diaoqi* masters put in, which embodies the social responsibility of them, their social status is relatively high. However, they have stated that they are regarded as masters only when others are already aware of the fact, which shows that the degree of social recognition of *Diaoqi* artists is still not high enough.

Ma Ning in particular stated that he would be happy for his children if they can inherit the craft, which shows his belief that there will potentially be positive prospects for the *Diaoqi* industry.

This study has some limitations. Firstly, the time of the research project was insufficient. There was also insufficient bibliographical information, which presented further challenges. This has also impacted the questions which cover a wide range of life and work experience of *Diaoqi* artists, therefore the depth and range of this study are limited. It has prevented the research group from reaching a certain professional level.

Further research could be done related to comparison between modern artists' and ancient artists' work and life experience, to broaden the scope of our understanding of *Diaoqi* artists from a humanistic perspective.

雕漆传承人的培养[1]

贺 晴[2] 周弈杉[3] 龙 奕[4] 关 铁[5]

【摘要】 作为非物质文化遗产雕漆的传承人，他们将对雕漆共同的热爱作为从事这项事业和克服工作中困难的动力，这最终使他们在雕漆领域成为卓越的大师。作为大师，他们感到有责任将雕漆作为一种艺术形式传承下去；他们选择符合条件的学徒，从雕漆技艺和流程方面对传承人进行培养。当雕漆大师承担起培养徒弟及推广雕漆文化的使命时，政府和国家也在提供相应的支持，如国家已经开始大力开展非物质文化遗产保护项目，建立相关部门并针对不同的非遗传承人进行分类与分级。对于雕漆艺术，政府主要采取资金补助的形式进行支持，如提供补贴或研究资金。然而，目前的资金支持无法满足雕漆发展对工资、培训和购买材料费用的需求。在未来，我们期待政府对雕漆技艺的保护给予更多支持。

【关键词】 雕漆艺术 雕漆传承人 培养 热爱 政府支持

---

1. 本调研报告科研指导教师为北京外国语大学国际教育集团升学规划部教师郝罡。
2. 北京外国语大学国际课程中心十一年级学生。
3. 北京外国语大学国际课程中心十一年级学生。
4. 北京一零一中学国际部高二年级学生。
5. 北京外国语大学国际课程中心十一年级学生。

一、研究背景与研究目标

雕漆技艺已被认定为国家级非物质文化遗产之一，但随着现代化进程的飞速发展，传统技艺日渐式微，这对于传统手工技艺来说尤其明显。雕漆作为一种手工技艺，其所有制作步骤都需要人力完成，但大部分雕漆工艺大师已步入花甲之年，已然无法继续操持这门手艺。因此，培养雕漆传承人便成为基本课题。传承人是延续雕漆制作的根本，是雕漆艺术的未来，所以他们不仅需要有精湛的技艺，还需要具备一定的文化和艺术底蕴，以成为延续这一重要文化艺术形式的带头人。但由于选择从事传统手工艺行业的年轻人越来越少，这些独特、珍贵的手工技艺正面临无人继承的困境。雕漆作为传统工艺之一，也面临同样的窘境（张传寿，2013）。正因如此，本课题以与雕漆大师、学徒的面对面采访为基础，进行信息整理与分析，希望揭示雕漆传承人的培养过程与培养中的困难。

笔者将探讨雕漆传承与传承人培养中的三个主题：大师们最初进入雕漆行业的动机、潜在学徒与传承人的特质，以及政府对于雕漆技艺的补助和支持。笔者旨在对以上主题获得更深入的了解，并由此调研雕漆是如何代代相传的。

二、雕漆技艺的传承

雕漆技艺是"活体的技艺"，是"思想的本身"，技艺本身承载着雕漆的历史和演变痕迹。自公元五世纪以来，一直不乏精妙的雕漆器物传世。雕漆技艺也是代代相传、不断完善的。在元代以后，雕漆艺人才开始在雕漆器物上留名，自此，雕漆艺人才被人们熟知。到了清末，北京的"继古斋"兴起，雕漆工匠才开始有了明确的传承谱系。（宋本蓉，2013）

光绪二十七年，北京的雕漆艺人合作创办"继古斋"并开始招收徒弟。这个举动大大推动了雕漆发展的繁荣局面。"继古斋"和"德诚局"的创办者李茂隆、肖乐安、肖兴达、宋兴贵等成为北京雕漆第一代传承人。（宋本蓉，2013）

此后的雕漆行业在"继古斋"和"德诚局"的艺徒推动下迅速发展。1954年，北京市授予工艺美术行业27位领军人物"老艺人"的称号，其中雕漆行业获得这一荣誉的是吴瀛轩、孙彩文、董茂林、刘春林。这4位雕漆"老艺人"在行业中均有很大的影响力，他们是北京雕漆第二代传承人的代表。在这一时期，艺人之间的技艺交流是非常开放的，他们愿意分享自己的经验，展现出精湛的技艺与卓著的成就。（宋本蓉，2013）

进入二十世纪八十年代，杜炳臣、刘金波、朱廷仁等北京雕漆厂的技术工人作为北京雕漆第三代传承人的代表，被政府授予"工艺美术大师"的称号。他们从少年时代就开始学徒生涯，跟随老师傅学习，在技艺传承上延续"继古斋"的传统。在进入北京雕漆厂后，他们在雕漆设计和技艺上都有重大的突破和进展。第三代传承人对北京雕漆厂的产品制作起到引导性的作用，他们的作品成为北京雕漆厂雕漆制作的典范。（宋本蓉，2013）

自1958年北京工艺美术学校建立起，从前师徒相授的传艺模式被打破。但是，大多数从学校出来的工艺设计师不具备独特而不可替代的技能，他们中只有那些肯于动脑、深入研究的佼佼者才能成为行业的大师。九十年代之后,北京雕漆的代表人物为文乾刚、殷秀云、曾朝万、徐文生、满建民,他们被誉为雕漆技艺第四代传承人。这个时代的传承人面临着人们审美观念的发展、雕漆技艺的变革等多重困难和挑战。他们需要从一个新的角度看待雕漆的文化传统和技艺传统,并肩负着新时期雕漆技艺传承与发展的重任。(宋本蓉,2013)

三、研究方法与研究步骤

(一) 数据收集

为了深入研究本课题,我们采访了雕漆行业的两位传承人——殷秀云大师和马宁大师,以及北京市西城区非遗保护中心主任杨飞。通过对采访内容进行整理和分析,我们对雕漆和雕漆技艺的传承有了深入的了解。

1. 受访对象

表1:受访者基本信息

姓名	年龄	职业	工作时间	专业知识
殷秀云	72	国家级雕漆大师	55年	传统雕漆
马宁	38	北京市市级雕漆传承人	10年	雕漆与现代创新
杨飞	未知	北京市西城区非遗保护中心主任	未知	非物质文化遗产保护

2. 访谈问题

我们把研究问题分为三个主要部分:首先,学习和制作雕漆的个人经历;其次,传承人的挑选标准和特质;最后,政府提供的支持,这是在雕漆的保护和支持方面至关重要的一个部分。

采访问题：

1）您是从什么时候起跟随您的师父学习雕漆这门手艺的？是什么使您对雕漆产生兴趣？

2）作为一名雕漆传承人应该具有什么样的特质？成为一名合格的雕漆传承人需要经历哪几个阶段？

3）政府对于雕漆传承人有没有补助？

(二) 数据分析

表2：雕漆传承人的培养

主题	编码（相同点）	编码（不同点）
兴趣来源	他们都热爱雕漆	• 因为热爱而工作 • 因为工作而热爱
传承人品质	• 热爱和毅力 • 雕漆技艺	• 花费时间和金钱去做这件事 • 克服各种困难 • 从小开始学习 • 学习美术的专业知识 • 了解文化 • 技能技巧的学习 • 锻炼毅力和坚持练习
政府支持	有支持	支持并不充足

四、研究分析和讨论

(一) 热爱是成为雕漆传承人的必要因素

通过第一个问题的采访，我们发现由于所处的社会时期和拥有的早期经历不同，殷秀云大师和马宁大师学习做雕漆的原因是不同的。

尽管如此，他们对雕漆的热爱是他们从事这项事业的动力，最终使他们在雕漆领域成为卓越的大师和传承人。

1. 热爱指引他们进入雕漆行业

马宁大师开始做雕漆是出于个人爱好，后来才将它当作自己的职业。作为核雕的传承人，马宁大师在28岁时才第一次接触雕漆。当他看到文乾刚大师及其作品时便对雕漆一见钟情，因为他看到了文乾刚大师在每一个雕漆作品中投入的个人心血和热爱。"我感受到了这个艺术给我的冲击力，所以我决定去学习雕漆。"（马宁）可以说，是因为热爱，马宁大师才进入了雕漆行业，最终成为一名雕漆传承人。

殷秀云大师对雕漆的兴趣是逐渐产生的。她开始做雕漆是把它当成一份谋生的工作，之后对其产生了浓厚的兴趣，并把它变为自己一生的专长。据殷秀云大师说，她1967年从北京工艺美术学校毕业后开始学雕漆。当时她被分配到了雕漆制作车间工作，这使她很失望，因为她从1963年就开始在艺校学习象牙雕刻，并打算以此为毕生的职业。尽管雕漆和象牙雕刻有很多相似之处，殷秀云大师还是在很长时间内不能适应这个转变。但经过长时间的雕漆工作，尤其是在跟随老一辈的雕漆师傅学习之后，殷秀云大师渐渐喜爱上了雕漆并且愿意用一生去学习。她说："通过比较长的时间进入之后，我慢慢地发觉了它的这种特性和它的美。"

2. 热爱可以克服工作中的困难

在调查中我们发现，雕漆的学习和制作存在很大的困难，比如学艺时间长且艰苦、制作困难等等。只有真正热爱雕漆的人，才能够在长期的工作中去克服这些困难。马宁大师认为，雕漆需要全身心的投入，尽管会遇到很多困难："当你爱这个事业的时候，所有的困难在你面前都可以被解决。"同样，殷秀云大师提到，只有热爱雕漆的时候，才能勇于面对和接受制作中的各种挑战。而一部分人在面对困难和挑战的时候选择了知难而退。

3. 热爱是大师们坚持的动力

雕漆工作是困难的，作品制作的时间也很漫长，只有真正的热爱才能让一个人在这一领域钻研数十载。殷秀云大师讲到，雕漆的制作是十分艰苦的，三到五年是雕漆工艺师学习的基本周期："三年到五年之内，能够踏踏实实地坐下来，这时候不要想在经济上回报怎么样。"面对时间长和回报慢的困难，殷秀云大师认为，只有"真的喜欢它，真的爱它"才可以投入到这个行业中。她认为是因为对于雕漆的热爱，她才能在技术上取得一些成就，并且可以坚守一辈子。

另外，殷秀云大师喜欢尝试新的事物，她是第一位在雕漆中雕刻人物的艺术家。为了避免雕漆的没落并力争发展，殷秀云大师一直在招收学徒。马宁大师经过多年的不断付出，不仅自己成为北京市市级的雕漆传承人，他现在还有两名学徒。

总而言之，这两位雕漆大师能够坚持多年，一心一意地做雕漆，其中的根本原因是他们对雕漆的真正热爱。经过多年的刻苦锤炼，两位大师最终功成名就。不仅如此，他们一直致力于培养更多的雕漆艺术家，以促进雕漆艺术的长远发展。

(二) 雕漆传承人的培养

经过多年的努力，殷秀云和马宁已经成为雕漆领域的大师。他们的大师地位使他们有责任将雕漆作为一种艺术形式传承下去。因此，我们请他们分享了各自对雕漆行业下一代传承人的看法。这个问题的重点是雕漆技艺的传承人需要具备什么样的素质、什么样的基本技能,以及应该如何培养传承人。

1. 传承人的基本素质

殷秀云大师认为,从事这个职业最重要的是应该真正热爱雕漆艺术。她希望选择学习这门艺术的人能够为了雕漆而不顾其他:"如果一个人想成为一名杰出的工匠,他需要为艺术作出牺牲。"马宁大师也认为,成为传承人必须拥有的品质是爱。在他看来,只要爱雕漆就够了。他相信热爱和动机之间有一种关系,这可能影响艺术家生活的很多方面。

2. 传承人的培养

个人对于雕漆的情感和激情是成为传承人的必要条件。而对年轻人培养、培训的过程则是使其成为传承人的关键环节。

殷秀云大师进一步阐述了雕漆传承人的培养过程,并提出知识和毅力是传承人必要的品质。她认为学徒应该从小就开始学习,即"从娃娃抓起",因为这会让他们有更多时间来理解这种艺术。而从培养传承人的角度来看,最好从20岁左右开始培养,那时他们有更清楚的思维及逻辑。这样,艺术的生命就会更长。(杨卫华,2014)此外,殷秀云大师还建议学徒在中学或大学时更好地掌握艺术的基本知识,这些都可以作为学习雕漆的基础。同时,学徒也应该有一种鉴赏和欣赏美的能力,这种能力会让他们的作品脱颖而出。殷秀云大师说:"首先(学徒)要有一个美术的基本知识,对美的东西,你要有认识和感觉。那么在你雕刻当中,你会自觉地去爱雕刻,把你认为美的东西给表现出来。"因此,当学徒雕刻时,他们会自然地感受到雕漆的美并喜欢雕刻这个过程,从而展示他们认为美的雕塑形式。最后,在殷秀云大师看来，传承人"对雕漆、对这种文化要有了解"，并将其视为自己真正欣赏的东西。这样才能全方位地培养出合格的雕漆传承人。

马宁大师详细阐述了传承人所需的技能。首先，需要掌握制作工具的技能。"他们必须知道如何制作和使用工具，因为没有地方购买雕刻漆器所需的刀具。"（马宁）这就是他们自己制作工具的原因。马宁大师将制造工具的过程视为一个特殊的挑战。其次，传承人需要具备雕漆的基本功。雕漆的基本功训练包括刺、起、片、铲、剔，这几个工序的技法通常需要很多年的学习和练习。"真正要掌握这个技术是需要时间的堆垒的。"马宁说，"如果传承人决定学习雕漆，他们必须愿意花上一辈子的时间来奋斗。"

挑战无时无刻不存在于雕漆传承人的学习过程中，他们需要克服许多障碍。殷秀云大师和马宁大师在谈到这一问题时都提到了原材料漆。殷秀云大师解释，这种漆本身是一种酸，大多数人在接触到这种物质时都会产生过敏现象。马宁大师也提到，漆本身是一个难以克服的障碍，因为漆是无法直接雕刻的，只有通过长时间的刷漆过程，形成可以被雕刻的厚度之后，才能将漆转变成漆器。

根据我们的发现，雕漆传承人因为热爱而选择从事并传承雕漆，而且他们的培养是一个漫长且艰辛的过程，需要知识和毅力，更需要时间来打磨。所以当传承人学习雕漆时，当他们做雕漆产品时，都需要政府的补贴和支持来维持生活。另外，当雕漆大师们承担训练学徒及推广雕漆文化的使命时，同样也需要财政和政策上的支持，因为他们个人负担不起高昂的材料和时间成本，也没有能力把雕漆艺术传递给更多的人。因此，我们的下一个研究问题是政府对于雕漆传承人的支持。

(三)政府对于雕漆传承人的支持

对于传统手工艺正在面临传承人数量逐渐减少这一问题,我国政府近些年来已经开始大力开展关于非物质文化遗产的保护项目,建立相关部门并针对不同的非遗传承人进行分类与分级。

1. 政府目前的支持政策

通过采访北京市西城区非遗保护中心的杨飞主任,我们了解到,中国的非遗传承人通常被分成三类:国家级传承人、市级传承人和区级传承人。政府对于不同级别的传承人有不同标准的补助,而且不同级别传承人的收徒标准也会有所区别。近些年来,政府加强了对雕漆这一传统手工艺的保护措施,目前主要采取资金补助的形式。具体来说,非遗保护资金可以分为两种,一种是对于代表性传承人的补贴,另一种是为非遗项目推广和研究提供的资金。前者会每年或每月根据传承人的级别按时下发。

马宁大师是北京市市级雕漆传承人,他为我们提供了很多关于政府支持情况的介绍。我们从采访中了解到,政府会定期给他一笔带头津贴,但数额有限,每个学徒一个月可以拿到一百元。补贴不足以维持生活,学徒仍需通过努力工作来赚钱。殷秀云大师是国家级雕漆传承人,她也认为虽然政府有定期的资金补助,但数额只够一个学徒的工资,并不足以促进雕漆行业的发展。作为一名国家级传承人,她每年可获得两万元的津贴。

2. 对于政府支持的需求

政府补助是按照传承人的级别来分配的,马宁大师作为市级传承人得到的补助会比殷秀云大师的少。他们表示,目前的资金支持无法满足雕漆发展对工资、培训和购买材料费用的需求。

虽然如此，政府对于雕漆的支持力度正在逐渐加强，并且未来的支持会是多方面的。除了财政补贴，政府目前还通过精准扶贫项目帮助雕漆发展。据杨飞主任介绍，西城区非物质文化遗产保护中心按照传承人的数量对文化遗产进行分类，数量最少的被列为濒危文化遗产。对于濒危文化遗产项目，政府将搭建一个平台进行宣传推广，并招募志愿者。人们可以通过这个平台来了解非物质文化遗产项目，并选择去学习传统手工艺。

五、总结

随着现代化进程的飞速发展，很多的工艺美术类技艺都被科技取代。然而，作为中国非物质文化遗产的雕漆技艺却仍然保留着人工制作的传统工艺。为了进一步了解雕漆技艺的传承现状，本研究以雕漆传承人的培养为主题，采访了两位大师级雕漆传承人。通过访谈，我们了解到，热爱是成为雕漆传承人的必要因素。在热爱的基础之上，雕漆传承人的基本素质，如艺术基础知识，以及雕漆技艺学习，也是培养传承人的要素。此外，尽管目前政府给予的资金帮助尚且不足，但是政府对于雕漆的支持力度正在逐渐加强，支持政策也在不断完善。

本研究的不足之处在于，我们只采访到了两位雕漆大师，得到的支持性观点和数据较少。此外，很多信息都是受访者的主观意见，可能并不具有普遍性。受到时间和调查背景的限制，本文尚未能够获得更多的受访数据和理论性的文献支持。但是，在完成本调研的过程中，我们都感受到了雕漆大师对于雕漆的热爱，并且由衷地希望雕漆行业可以发展得越来越好,雕漆技艺可以通过培养传承人的方式而不断地传承下去。

参考文献:

宋本蓉.雕漆技艺[M].北京:文化艺术出版社,2013.

杨卫华.传统手工技艺传承教育的思考——以雕漆技艺为例[J].非物质文化遗产研究集刊,2014:26—33.

张传寿."非遗"视角下的传统手工艺人保护[J].非物质文化遗产研究集刊,2013:44—52.

The Training Process of *Diaoqi* Inheritors[1]

He Qing[2] Zhou Yishan[3] David Long[4] Guan Tie[5]

1. Research Background and Significance

This study investigates the training process of inheritors of the Chinese intangible cultural heritage, *Diaoqi*. We discuss three topics regarding the inheritance and inheritors of *Diaoqi*, namely the motivation of *Diaoqi* masters when they first entered the industry, the potential apprentices and characteristics of the inheritors, and finally government support of *Diaoqi* craftsmanship. We aim to gain a deeper understanding of these topics in order to determine how *Diaoqi* is passed on through generations.

1.1 Background

With the rapid progress of globalization and modernization, traditional arts are diminishing. Most masters are elderly, and some of them are no longer able to practice their skills. These unique and valuable manual skills are in danger of not being inherited by the next generation, because fewer young people choose to continue learning these traditional arts. According

---

1. The academic advisors of this paper are Hao Gang, from the Counselling Division of BFSU International Education Group; and Sonje Du Toit, a teacher from EPlus of BFSU International Group, Beijing Foreign Studies University.
2. The 11th grade student of the International Curriculum Centre (ICC) of Beijing Foreign Studies University.
3. The 11th grade student of the International Curriculum Centre (ICC) of Beijing Foreign Studies University.
4. The 11th grade student of the International Program of Beijing 101 High School.
5. The 11th grade student of the International Curriculum Centre (ICC) of Beijing Foreign Studies University.

to Zhang (2013), *Diaoqi*, as one of these traditional arts, faces the same situation. With recorded details through interviews and evaluations from both masters and inheritors, this study aims to investigate the inheritance of *Diaoqi* by exploring the training process.

1.2 Introduction of *Diaoqi*

Diaoqi, or carved lacquer, is an ancient traditional Chinese art form that has been passed down through generations for centuries. Cartwright (2017) described *Diaoqi* as follows:

> "Lacquer was a popular form of decoration and protective covering in ancient China. It was used to colour and beautify screens, furniture, bowls, cups, sculpture, musical instruments, and coffins, where it could be carved, incised, and inlaid to show off scenes from nature, mythology, and literature. Time-consuming to produce, Chinese lacquerware became highly sought after by those who could afford it and by neighbouring cultures."

Diaoqi combines the qualities of the lacquer and layering process as well as the carving skills of the masters, with each factor essential in the process of making *Diaoqi*.

1.3 Inheritance of *Diaoqi*

Inheritance and inheritors are essential to the survival of *Diaoqi* as an art form in Chinese culture. It is a manual skill and all procedures must be finished by hand, and apprentices must learn to replicate these procedures. Cultivating inheritors therefore becomes fundamental. Inheritors are the ones to carry on the inheritance of *Diaoqi*, so they have tasks involving both learning skills at their best, and choosing potential future inheritors as a continuous extension for this culturally significant work.

2. Literature Review

In order to understand the complexities of training *Diaoqi* craftsmen, it is necessary to grasp the complexities of the craft itself first. We will therefore provide a brief overview of the *Diaoqi* crafting process.

The technical process of *Diaoqi* is very complex. There are many aspects to the craft such as design, lacquer making, base making, ground making, varnishing, carving, polishing, and other major procedures. The complex nature of the craft makes *Diaoqi* a very time-consuming process, and causes difficulties for training apprentices.

In order to achieve the best effect, the lacquer used is chosen carefully with every step. Firstly, natural raw material is required, which must undergo physical purification in order to remove impurities. During the transportation process, certain amount of water and tung oil needs to be added so that the moisture can be balanced. Tung oil improves the quality of the lacquer, and it can modify the softness, elasticity and brightness of the material. Finally, pigment is required to color the lacquer.

Master Yin Xiuyun explained the difficulties of acquiring the raw material as follows:

> "The *Diaoqi* lacquer comes from lacquer trees growing in different environments, and the quality varies. The changes of temperature, humidity and other factors make the process of *Diaoqi*-making difficult to control. It is impossible to control the techniques without years of practice."

Processing the raw lacquer consumes a large amount of time before carving can even begin. Environmental factors must also be considered because they can lead to a decline in the quality of the raw lacquer. These issues may affect the training of craftsmen as the costs and time required can demotivate potential apprentices.

Beijing *Diaoqi* commonly uses some materials as its base, such as wood base, Bakelite base, metal base, and porcelain base. With different types of materials of the base, the making methods are different. The undercoat is not only the undercarriage of the sculptured lacquer, the physical embodiment of the design idea, but also the base of painting and engraving on the lacquer. So the process is very strict. This step can be seen as a small part during the whole process, but it still has several requirements that need to be noted.

The process of creating *Diaoqi* is very precise and complex, and potential apprentices must be trained for many years to master these procedures. This research aims to further explore the training process according to *Diaoqi* masters who have successfully completed their training and now train the future generation of craftsmen in their apprentices.

3. Research Methodology

3.1 Data collection

Research data were gathered by the authors through structured interviews.

3.1.1 Participants

We interviewed two masters/inheritors in the *Diaoqi* industry, Master Yin Xiuyun and Master Ma Ning. Through conversations with them, we have gained a better understanding of the current situation of training in this industry.

Table 1: Biographical information of the participants

Name	Age	Occupation	Years of work experience	Expertise
Yin Xiuyun	72	National representative inheritor of Beijing *Diaoqi*	55	Traditional *Diaoqi*
Ma Ning	38	Beijing local representative inheritor of Beijing *Diaoqi*	10	*Diaoqi* with contemporary creativity

continued

Name	Age	Occupation	Years of work experience	Expertise
Yang Fei	Unknown	Director of Beijing Xicheng District Intangible Cultural Heritage Protection Center	Unknown	Intangible cultural heritage protection

3.1.2 Research questions

We divided the whole study into three main parts. The first part is personal experience of learning and making *Diaoqi*. The second part mainly discusses the standards and characteristics of being an inheritor. Finally, we extend to the support of the government, which plays an important role in protecting and sustaining the *Diaoqi* industry.

The interview questions are as follows:

1) When did you start to learn *Diaoqi* from your master? Why did you become interested in *Diaoqi*?

2) What qualities should a qualified inheritor have and how many stages does it take to train a qualified inheritor?

3) Does the government have any support for *Diaoqi* inheritors?

3.2 Data analysis

Table 2: Data analysis results

Theme	Code (similarities)	Code (differences)
Personal interests	They both love *Diaoqi*	· Work because of love · Love because of work
Qualities of inheritors	· Love and persistence · Techniques of *Diaoqi*	· Spend time and money doing it · Overcome difficulties · Start training at an early age · Knowledge of the fine arts · Understand culture, skills and techniques · Willpower and more practices
Government support	There is support	The support is insufficient

4. Research Findings and Discussion

4.1 It is all because of love

The first aim is to determine what makes our interviewees learn the art of *Diaoqi*, and what inspires them to become masters themselves. The masters believe that it is their deep passion of the art that motivates them to pursue their careers and inspires them to become masters.

Through the first interview question, we find that even though Ms. Yin Xiuyun and Mr. Ma Ning underwent their early training for different reasons, it is their love for *Diaoqi* that keeps them engaged in this profession and drives them to excellence.

Ms. Yin began to do *Diaoqi* as a wage-making job, and later developed interest in it and made it her lifelong profession, whereas Mr. Ma started to do *Diaoqi* out of interest and later made it his career.

Love and affection for *Diaoqi* developed over time. According to Ms. Yin, she started to learn *Diaoqi* in 1968 when she graduated from the art school. She was assigned a job in a *Diaoqi* factory, which extremely disappointed her, because she had been doing and learning ivory carving since 1963, and planned to have it as her career. Even though *Diaoqi* and ivory carving share similar techniques, Ms. Yin had no interest in *Diaoqi*. However, she could not do anything about this arrangement but to obey. She was forced to give up her passion for ivory carving and accepted *Diaoqi* as her career. She explained her experience as follows:

> "I was very reluctant at first, and very passive. However, at that time jobs were allocated by the government… People used to stick to one work place for their entire life. When I realized it was impossible to change my situation, I settled for *Diaoqi* and learned to accept it."

After some time, she gradually discovered *Diaoqi*'s unique features and beauty. She developed genuine interest in *Diaoqi* and worked hard at perfecting her skills and creating art pieces. As a result, Ms. Yin later became a national-level *Diaoqi* master. Ms. Yin likes trying new things, and she was the first person to incorporate human figure as the subject in *Diaoqi* works. In order to keep *Diaoqi* alive and prosperous, Ms. Yin takes apprentices.

Mr. Wen Qiangang, a national-level *Diaoqi* master, now in his seventies, had the similar experience with Ms. Yin. After graduating from art school studying sculpture, he was put in the *Diaoqi* factory and worked there ever since. Over time, he developed a passion for this art form and grew into a *Diaoqi* master. (Song, 2013)

Master Wen Qiangang is an inspiration for our next interviewee, Mr. Ma, who, unlike his master and Ms. Yin, began to learn *Diaoqi* in 2009 when he was twenty-eight. He is from a family that has been doing *Hediao* (fruit pit carving) for generations, and is also an inheritor of *Hediao*, which is similar to *Diaoqi*. He had little interest in *Diaoqi* at first but things changed when he walked into the studio of Master Wen Qiangang:

> "I was in my teens when I first knew about *Diaoqi*. But the time when I was really interested in it was the exact moment when I first entered the studio of my mentor Mr. Wen Qiangang at the age of twenty-eight." (Ma Ning)

The reason why he did not start to do *Diaoqi* earlier was that the works he had seen in other workshops and stores did not impress him at all. After Mr. Ma saw the works of Master Wen Qiangang, he decided to learn *Diaoqi* from him. He was deeply moved by the magnificent works Master Wen Qiangang created, and also by the perseverance and craftsmanship that the master demonstrated. Then through his efforts and devotion for many years, Mr. Ma became the Beijing local-level inheritor of the *Diaoqi* art and now has two apprentices.

The *Diaoqi* masters, in spite of different reasons for entering the field, could not persevere without the true love for this art.

4.2 Qualities of an apprentice, training process, and challenges

After training, practicing, and honing their skills, Ms. Yin and Mr. Ma have become masters in this field. Their status also means responsibility for the future and inheritance of *Diaoqi*. We therefore asked them to share their opinions on potential apprentices and the training process, including the qualities that apprentices needed, the stages of training process, and basic skills required to become an inheritor.

According to Ms. Yin, one should really love the art, and that is the most important part in her opinion. She hopes that a person who chooses to learn this art will be able to do it for life. She stated that if one wanted to be an outstanding craftsman, one needed to make sacrifices for the art.

Mr. Ma also emphasized that the main quality one must own was love. If a person is committed and loves his career, all difficulties can be solved. He believes that there is a relationship between love and incentives, and that may influence many aspects of an artist's life.

Personal feelings and passion are not the only qualities required to become an inheritor. The training process itself is a key part. Ms. Yin explained this process, listing knowledge and persistence as further necessary qualities. She advised that apprentices should start at an early age, as this would give them more time to learn and understand this kind of art. She pointed out, "From the perspective of an inheritor, it is better to start from around 20 years old when one has a quick mind and clever fingers to learn, so that the art life would be longer." (Yang, 2014)

Furthermore, Ms. Yin recommended that it would be better for students to gain basic knowledge of fine arts when they were in secondary school or college. These things are a basis for learning *Diaoqi*. Students should also have a sense of beauty, because such sensibility promotes them to excel in their craft. As a result, when they carve, they will automatically sense the beauty and demonstrate what they think is beautiful in the carving. In her opinion, inheritors need to know *Diaoqi* and its culture very well, and consider it as something they truly admire.

Mr. Ma expanded on the required skills of potential inheritors by pointing out that they have to know how to make and use tools, because there is no place to buy necessary types of knives required for carving. He identified the process of making tools as a particular challenge and added that inheritors must be willing to dedicate a lifetime if they decided to learn *Diaoqi*.

It is essential to note that, both Ms. Yin and Mr. Ma mentioned the obstacles when they talked about *Diaoqi*. Ms. Yin explained that the lacquer itself was a kind of acid and it might make some people sick if they were allergic to it. Mr. Ma also mentioned the complex procedures in converting the lacquer into *Diaoqi* that could be carved was another challenge.

According to our findings, *Diaoqi* inheritors commit themselves to the art for their entire lives because of love. This is why they study *Diaoqi* and create *Diaoqi* art works. They believe that government subsidies benefit and support their work, and further support is necessary for training apprentices to promote *Diaoqi*.

4.3 Government support of the inheritors of *Diaoqi*

With all kinds of crafts facing the problem of losing heritage gradually, the Chinese government has begun to vigorously develop a protection project of "Intangible Cultural Heritage" in recent years, for which relevant departments have made detailed classification and grading of various inheritors of intangible cultural heritage.

According to Yang Fei, director of Beijing Xicheng District Intangible Cultural Heritage Protection Center, Chinese intangible cultural heritage inheritors are generally graded as national level, provincial level, and district level. The government has different ranks of financial subsidies for inheritors at different levels, and there are also differences in admission standards of apprentices for masters at different levels.

Currently, the government provides support for *Diaoqi* training, but the financial aid is limited. Specifically, the protection funds of intangible cultural heritage can be divided into two types: an inheritance subsidy for inheritors and an intangible cultural heritage project funding for some protection work. The former is issued to each inheritor every month or every year, and the amount of the subsidy depends on the status of the inheritor. A regional inheritor like Mr. Ma receives fewer subsidies than a national inheritor like Ms. Yin. However, the current financial support is insufficient to provide adequate salaries, fund training, and purchase materials for *Diaoqi* work.

As a *Diaoqi* inheritor of Beijing municipal level, Mr. Ma receives government grant on a regular basis, but the amount is so limited that it is not enough to sustain life. Each of his apprentices can only receive ¥100 a month. They need to work hard to earn money.

Ms. Yin is a national inheritor. She also thinks that the government's regular financial subsidies are limited, enough for an apprentice's salary, but not enough to promote the development of the industry. She receives an allowance of ¥20,000 a year.

The government's support for *Diaoqi* is gradually strengthening and will become better in the future. In addition to financial subsidies, the government sometimes helps the development of *Diaoqi* through "Targeted Poverty Alleviation" program. According to Yang Fei, Beijing Xicheng District Intangible Cultural Heritage Protection Center has set up a platform to promote and publicize those endangered intangible cultural heritages so as to recruit volunteers. People can learn about the intangible cultural heritage projects through the platform and choose to study the craft of *Diaoqi*.

5. Conclusion

This paper consists of three research questions. The first one is related to the time and reasons that *Diaoqi* masters started to make *Diaoqi*. The second one focuses on the prerequisites and standards of becoming a *Diaoqi* inheritor. The last one analyzes the role that government plays in supporting the *Diaoqi* industry.

In summary, the research findings are as follows. Firstly, the reasons for *Diaoqi* masters of different generations to enter a career in this field vary. Compared to modern times, back in the 1960s, government allocation was a major factor that influenced people's careers, which meant people were assigned jobs by the government, despite the fact that some individuals might not like their jobs, such as Ms. Yin. Nowadays, people have more freedom to choose their occupations based on their interest, such as Mr. Ma. Nevertheless, Ms. Yin and Mr. Ma both had an artistic or a crafts training background, and developed a keen interest and passion for *Diaoqi*. After years of training, practice, and hard work, they thrived and have become masters. Moreover, they all care about the survival and prosperity of *Diaoqi*, and devote themselves to cultivating more artists in *Diaoqi*.

Secondly, Ms. Yin and Mr. Ma both mentioned love as an essential element for a qualified apprentice, and after that, they stated several additional requirements that an apprentice should possess, such as professional art skills and a young age to start from. From their perspectives, obstacles and difficulties are unavoidable. No matter what kind of person he or she is, one should be able to persist in *Diaoqi* for life. An apprentice is able to become a mature craftsman of *Diaoqi* only if he or she persists and overcomes these obstacles.

Finally, government support is a vital aspect which has improved and continues to strengthen over time. From the findings of our interviews, masters like Ms. Yin and Mr. Ma already have financial support. However, most ordinary craftsmen working in this industry cannot get enough income, and even for the masters, the support is limited. As the importance of the development and sustainment of traditional culture is increasing, it is hoped that the government financial support will increase.

Throughout the project, we faced several problems when collecting data and analyzing results. First of all, as we only had two main interviewees, the supportive evidence and data were insufficient for us to form a concrete hypothesis. Secondly, because of the characteristics of the topic, most information is subjective and presented as personal opinions. Additionally, with limited time and research background, we were unable to obtain more supporting interview data or an extended practical literature review.

In conclusion, throughout our investigation of this topic, we have gained a deeper understanding of how the training process and inheritance of *Diaoqi* are passed down through generations. Based on different time periods and backgrounds, people have different reasons to enter the *Diaoqi* industry. The defined characteristic of an inheritor is the love of the art. As government support for traditional arts and crafts improves, *Diaoqi* craftsmen will be able to get more financial support, which will allow them to continue the craft and ensure the inheritance and continued survival of *Diaoqi*.

It is our hope that *Diaoqi* will continue to develop and prosper, as the masters and craftsmen in this industry really have a passion for *Diaoqi*. We also hope that *Diaoqi* will be inherited by future generations as a continuous extension of this cultural work. As young researchers, we may not become the inheritors, but we will endeavor to provide support by raising the public awareness of this art form in the future.

References:

Cartwright, Mark. Chinese Lacquerware [EB/OL]. Ancient History Encyclopedia (2017-06-30) [2018-09-16]. https://www.ancient.eu/article/1090/chinese-lacquerware/.

Song, Benrong. Diaoqi Craft [M]. Beijing: Culture and Art Publishing House, 2013.

Yang, Weihua. The Thinking of Education on Inheriting Traditional Handicraft – The Carved Lacquer Craft as an Example [J]. Journal of Intangible Cultural Heritage Research, 2014: 26-33.

Zhang, Chuanshou. Protection of Traditional Craftsmen from the Perspective of Intangible Cultural Heritage [J]. Journal of Intangible Cultural Heritage Study, 2013: 44-52.

北京雕漆艺术发展障碍的研究[1]

张舒娴　黄祎琳　何廷傲[2]

【摘要】 北京雕漆是一项古老的地方传统手工技艺。虽然已经传承了一千四百余年，但它在当代的发展却遇到了很多困难。通过对雕漆艺人的采访，并分析访谈数据，笔者发现手艺传承的不易和艰苦的条件导致雕漆行业人才的缺失，而雕漆自身的一些特性也限制了其发展的广度与速度；加之国内外不景气的市场和伪品的出现，雕漆的市场销量一直处于低迷状态。

【关键词】 北京雕漆　手工技艺　困难　人才缺失　特性　市场　适应　宣传度

一、研究意义

北京雕漆是一项古老的地方传统手工技艺。随着时代的变迁，它的知名度和受欢迎程度变得越来越低。笔者在街头对15个路人进行随机采访时，发现没有一个人知道雕漆是什么。为了保护和宣传这项传统工艺，我们有义务研究是哪些因素限制了其发展。只有这样，传统文化才有可能得到改进并继续发扬光大。基于这一思路，笔者对一部分目前仍在从事北京雕漆工作的工匠进行了采访，希望可以通过采访调查发现目前限制雕漆发展的因素，帮助雕漆在保留原有特色的基

---

1. 本调研报告科研指导教师为北京外国语大学国际教育集团共建项目部教师郭旻硕。
2. 本调研报告的三位作者均为北京外国语大学国际课程中心十一年级学生。

础上取得进一步发展。

二、文献综述

笔者在中国知网、维普网检索"北京雕漆"时发现，相关文献主要集中在北京雕漆的历史、发展现状及传承前景方面，也有学者曾对雕漆发展遇到的困难进行研究。丛玲玲（2008）指出，在二十世纪八十年代末出现的注漆，即一种一次性灌模成型的化工合成树脂产品，因其外表与北京雕漆极为相似，引起了市场的混乱。注漆因其低廉的价格占领了北京雕漆市场的大半壁江山，而传统雕漆工艺惨遭践踏，名声扫地。丛玲玲发出呼吁："我们有没有能力守住祖先留下的珍贵的工艺文化遗产？"笔者经过检索，虽然找到了上述资料，但是并没有发现以"北京雕漆艺术发展障碍"为主题进行的深入研究，因此笔者认为本研究是很有必要的。

三、研究方法

（一）受访者介绍

本研究通过结构式访谈收集数据。笔者于2018年7月17—19日分别采访了马宁、赵海伟、黄杰3位师傅，于8月3日在南锣鼓巷街头随机采访了15名路人，并于8月4日在百工坊采访了殷秀云大师。

表1：受访者基本信息

姓名	性别	年龄	职业
殷秀云	女	72	国家工艺美术大师，北京雕漆国家级传承人
马宁	男	中年	北京工艺美术大师，北京雕漆北京市市级传承人
赵海伟	男	中年	雕漆工匠
黄杰	男	中年	雕漆爱好者、收藏者
路人1	男		
路人2	男		
路人3	男		
路人4	男		
路人5	男		
路人6	男		
路人7	男		
路人8	男		
路人9	女		
路人10	女		
路人11	女		
路人12	女		
路人13	女		
路人14	女		
路人15	女		

（二）数据收集

本研究采用结构式访谈形式，访谈问题为五个：

1）您认为雕漆发展至今，是否遇到过一些瓶颈？

2）您认为当前原材料的获取对于雕漆的制作有何影响？

3）您认为当前雕漆的制作时间对于雕漆的发展和推广有何影响？

4）您认为当今社会的主流消费观念会如何影响雕漆市场？

5）您认为为了适应当今客户需求和市场的变化，雕漆作出了改变吗？

（三）数据编码

笔者通过仔细研究数据，对数据进行编码，得到以下研究结果。

表2：阻碍雕漆发展的主要因素

阻碍雕漆发展的主要因素	编码
人才缺失	• 学习雕漆的过程漫长、艰难、乏味 • 学习成果不可预测 • 薪资低
雕漆本身因素	• 价格高 • 生产过程长 • 原材料难以获取
市场不景气	• 不成熟的国内市场 • 萎缩的国际市场 • 假冒产品的入侵 • 不理想的市场推广

四、发现与讨论

作为一项传承了一千四百余年的传统技艺,雕漆曾一度处于鼎盛时期,然而雕漆在当代的发展却遇到了很多困难。通过对雕漆手艺人的采访,我们发现如今阻碍雕漆发展的有三个主要因素:人才缺失、雕漆本身因素,以及市场不景气。

(一) 人才缺失

如今,对于雕漆行业来说,发展新一代传承人是至关重要的事情。即使是一些著名的工厂也面临着后继无人的困境,小作坊的情况就更加糟糕了。如果没有传承人,雕漆的生存空间将会越来越小。二十世纪七八十年代,北京雕漆厂共有600多名工人,而现在靠雕漆生活的手艺人可能还不到20个。人才缺失对于雕漆行业的发展是一个不可忽视的挑战。殷秀云大师曾在一次采访中表示:

"现在全北京的雕漆从业者已不足百人,人数最多的凌云雕漆厂也不过二三十人,最年轻的技工也已经四十多岁,青年徒工几乎没有。这样下去,再过10年,该怎么办?"(丛玲玲,2008)

通过研究我们发现,雕漆行业人才缺失的主要原因包括以下三个方面。

1. 学习雕漆的过程漫长、艰难、乏味

学习雕漆的过程是漫长的。现在,越来越多的人追求快节奏的生活,只有很少人有耐心花很长时间学习一门手艺,或是从小就开始学习这项技术。"雕漆行业中，难度最大的就是设计策划和雕刻两道工序，大师的精彩设计，要靠高水平的雕刻技师来表现。一个高水平的雕刻技师，需要十多年的磨炼。"[3] 国家级雕漆艺术传承人文乾刚大师分享了他的学习过程：

> "从我进入雕漆厂到'文革'前的将近五年时间里，基本上是在学习，通过学习和实践熟悉雕漆各个工序的技艺，尤其是在雕刻方面，雕刻将近做了三年，全面掌握了雕漆技艺。"（宋本蓉，2010）

这一长期的学习过程，使得雕漆学徒不论在身份还是收获方面，都处于一个非常尴尬的境地。宋本蓉指出：

> "没有3—5年在师傅的悉心指导下学习，很难全面掌握雕漆技艺，如果3—5年的时间是学习，学费从哪里来？学生又如何养活自己？如果3—5年的时间是工作，一个对雕漆技艺完全不了解的年轻学生，进入这个行业，并能很快找到自己不可替代的位置，几乎是不可能的。雕漆制作还需要一定量的实践探索，如果不能全面掌握雕漆技艺，没有实践经验，很难在这个行业立足。"（宋本蓉，2013）

同时，学习的过程也很艰难，不是每个人都能学好它。学徒通常

---

3. 见 https://www.douban.com/note/362123430/。

需要有一定的绘画基础；学习的过程也是极其辛苦的，很多学徒都半途而废。文乾刚分享了自己的经历：

> "我用了一年的时间，就基本掌握了上手的技艺，因为对于我来说，只是工具的掌握，我本身就已经具备了很好的造型能力。因为做上手实际上就是做浮雕，所以学过美术的和没学过美术的就是不一样，掌握了刀具的特点之后，没学过美术或者造型能力不过关的，他还得掌握技巧才知道上面的浮雕应该怎么做。"（宋本蓉，2010）

宋本蓉（2010）也提道："1997年北京市雕漆厂曾经委托工美技校培养工人40人，但是由于厂子效益不好，很大一部分人不能忍受，他们选择了另谋职业。一部分有美术基础的，他们去做家装或者其他设计，其他的人转行去做销售、保安。年轻人吃不了苦，不愿意做这一行，这是很现实的问题，也能够理解。"

更重要的是，学习过程是乏味的。学徒重复做同样简单的工作，直到他们能够熟练地掌握这项技能。这个过程真正测试了他们对雕漆这门技艺的耐心和热情。殷秀云大师表示："我们厂里唯一的一位制漆师傅已经六十多岁了，从上个世纪七十年代末干到现在也没有人愿意跟他学，觉得又脏又累。很难想象，到他做不动的时候，制漆的这个环节怎么办。"

2. 学习成果不可预测

不仅雕漆学习的过程是漫长、艰难、乏味的，结果也是不可预测的。要学好雕漆的制作，不仅需要吃苦的决心，更需要一定的理解力和天赋。对于雕漆技艺来说，口传身授是最重要的传承方式，因为雕漆技艺难度大，有很多细节和感悟是无法诉诸文字的。没有几年师父的指导，不去在技艺运作过程中学习和体悟，很难了解雕漆的文化内涵和技艺传统。正如宋本蓉所说：

"一个优秀的手工艺术家所需要的专注、耐心、坚持的精神，在很大程度上依赖人与人的情感交流和行为感染，这种精神是在一个行业里达到精湛技艺的保证，也是有效使用其精湛技艺的精神基础，这些无法以文字记录，也无法以程序指引，他们只能口传身授地自然传承，并在实践中领悟。"（宋本蓉，2010）

"一般人通过学习可以掌握技能，掌握了精湛的技能可以成为优秀的雕刻技师，在漆面上雕刻出精美的形象。只有少部分人，可以从艺术面貌来考虑雕漆，在与技艺和材质的相互论证中，创造出有力的作品和新的样式或者找到新的雕漆语言，这是一般人不能轻易达到的。"（宋本蓉，2013）

3. 薪资低

除了艰难的学习过程和不可预知的结果，低工资也是雕漆人才缺乏的重要原因之一。宋本蓉记录了29位北京雕漆工人在2009年的工资，有8人每年只赚8000元。据《北京日报》报道，北京职工2009年的平均年薪为48444元。但雕漆工人当时最常见的年薪是10000—30000元，比平均年薪低得多。即使是殷秀云大师，她当时的年薪是15000元，更不用说新学徒了。没有足够的薪水，工匠们就无法生存，无法专心制作雕漆。雕漆大师文乾刚说：

"因为这个行业不能靠一个人来完成的，最少需要一个小团队，尽管这个团队中每个人的分量不一样，但是没有不行。既然是团队，就得给每个参与者带来一定的经济上的收入，能够赖以生存，并且生存得不错，他就愿意干了。"（宋本蓉，2010）

更重要的是，政府的补贴远远不够。政府希望工匠能带出更多的学徒，但在工艺品行业实行的是计件制，这导致工匠们带学徒成了一个纯粹的义务。因为工作紧张，他们没有时间和金钱来教导徒弟。采访中马宁大师表示："政府每月给我每个学徒100元，这只够他们的一顿饭钱。"

大部分传承人都将这笔补贴用作徒弟们的生活费，但这并不是对艺术的真正补贴。不理想的工资很难吸引年轻人去学习雕漆。许多工匠希望政府对雕漆行业给予更多的支持。殷秀云大师说："希望政府能合理、充分地发挥导向作用，并对传统雕漆产业进行大力扶持。"（丛玲玲，2008）

综上所述，漫长、艰难、乏味的学习过程，不可预测的学习成果，以及低薪资导致雕漆行业人才的缺失。年轻一代的传承人决定了雕漆的未来，但新生代人才的缺乏无疑给雕漆行业未来的发展带来了严峻考验。

(二)雕漆本身因素

1.价格高

通过研究，笔者发现雕漆本身的局限性是制约其发展的另一个因素。北京雕漆是一项古老的地方传统工艺，始于唐代，兴于宋、元，盛于明、清。传统上，它几乎只用于皇室：它是明朝永乐皇帝的外交赠礼，也深得清朝乾隆皇帝的喜爱。其细致的生产过程需要数百道工序、十几个人一起工作来完成，并且动辄耗费数年。雕漆的制作工艺极其精细、复杂，故而雕漆产品价格很高。因此，对于普通人来说，它是不亲民、不易接近的，这就是雕漆人气较低的原因。根据对赵海伟先生的采访我们也得知，雕漆是一种服务于皇家的手工艺品，普通人很难了解或学习它。

作为中国的非物质文化遗产，雕漆并不像其他一些工艺品那样流行。其历史背景造成的高价格、低人气极大地制约了它的发展。因此，普通收藏家也很难接触到这个领域。雕漆的这些特点为收藏家设定了一个很高的门槛。

2.生产过程长

由于雕漆有许多极其复杂、精致的细节，其生产过程较为长久。"漆的整个生产过程需要得到财富和时间的支持。一件作品，十几个人，做了三年。"（宋本蓉，2010）。赵海伟在采访中表示：

"工匠很难在短时间内完成雕漆的制造。设计、填料制作、涂料、油漆、雕刻和抛光工艺是雕漆生产的基本制作工艺。所有的生产程序都应该分步进行。即使是一小部分工作，从开始到结束，也可能持续六到七个月。我认为没有什么环节是可以缩短的，因为这是一个细致的、一步一步的工作。"

经过查阅资料，笔者得知，制作雕漆需要很多步骤。首先，工匠要花很多时间来制作漆和髹漆。例如，一件5—10毫米厚的产品，需要髹涂160多道漆，每天髹涂1—2道，持续3个月左右，所以雕漆的漆工称其为"髹漆百日""百髹成胎"。大部分像髹漆这样的过程都反反复复进行。完成雕刻步骤后，生产者应在自然环境中干燥半成品4—6年。每一步都专注而认真，工匠无法改变它的生产要素。（宋本蓉，2010）很明显，雕漆的生产过程是艰苦且复杂的，每一件作品都需要长时间的积累，这也是雕漆产量极低的原因。

然而，漫长的生产过程也有一些优点。首先，长久的制作过程可以体现雕漆的传统和古典文化。宋本蓉提到雕漆是一种极其传统的手工艺。其次，制作时间长可以保证雕漆的质量。艺术家们对雕漆制作有着近乎执拗的态度，他们不会通过缩短生产时间来加快生产。赵海伟说："我的观点是，需要两天完成，我就花两天时间完成，也许我花三天时间完成。但我不想把它变成一天就完成的产品。"

然而，由于制作过程漫长，雕漆的产量很低，消费者对雕漆的需求也就下降了。大多数消费者都渴望在短时间内获得产品，不会花太多时间等待雕漆生产。这就是为什么有些人试图找到替代品以取代雕漆，最大限度地满足消费者的需求。由此，注漆作为仿冒品大行其道，也是因为它有其赖以生存的市场基础。

总而言之，低产量和较长的制作时间导致人们对雕漆的需求低于其他工艺品，因而雕漆的消费群体更小了。

3. 原材料难以获取

人们普遍认为，雕漆的原料难以满足需求，因为不容易获得。一棵10年以上树龄的漆树，漆液的平均日产量仅为75—125克。一个漆农一天能采收750—1000克漆液，故有"百里千刀一斤漆"的说法。(宋本蓉，2013)雕漆的原材料是难以获取的，这被猜想为使雕漆发展缓慢的第三个因素。令笔者惊讶的是，马宁先生并不这么认为，他说："原材料可以保证，因为我们有自己的种植基地。"他的团队目前由湖北省竹溪县的工业基地提供原料，工业基地可以为雕漆提供足够的资源。此外，随着雕漆文化的复苏和发展，原材料仍然存在发展空间。换句话说，随着传统文化的发展，原料的数量可以得到提升。如果雕漆的人气增加，原料的数量将随之增长。

虽然原材料目前可能不会阻碍雕漆的发展，但如果对这一点不加以重视，原材料就会变得更加难以获得。到那时候，原材料也许会成为雕漆发展的障碍之一。

(三) 市场不景气

1. 不成熟的国内市场

在明朝和清朝，雕漆曾经作为国礼和时玩风靡整个皇家贵族阶层。可是后来由于战争不断、经济衰退，晚清的皇族及贵族对雕漆器物的需求锐减。同时，大多数皇族供养的雕漆工匠也都为生计奔波。在二十世纪初期，有工匠意识到雕漆器物盈利丰厚，于是与他人合作，创办了雕漆商会，专门制造仿清代风格的雕漆器进行售卖。由于修补并仿造传统的雕漆器物报酬丰厚，又陆续有雕漆作坊开业。

由肖兴达、肖乐安、吴瀛轩等人制作的《剔红群仙祝寿图五尺屏风》曾在美国旧金山举办的巴拿马万国博览会上获得金奖(宋本蓉，2010)，这代表了当时北京雕漆自清朝末期后的再一次辉煌。

"从洋务运动开始，工业化的影响不只是外来的、侵略性的，中国开始从社会、技术、文化等各个角度反思并批判自己的文化传统，传统文化成为落后的根源，被怀疑、否定、背离。一些主张工业救国的学者主张全力实现工业化，他们认为，只要中国实现了工业化，有关政治、道德、社会教育等问题就会迎刃而解。……雕漆虽然因其不可替代性还以自己的方式生存着，但是它已经陷入一种窘境，因为雕漆所依附的文化传统已经开始被质疑和背离。"(宋本蓉，2010)

这段文字说明，雕漆在经历了辉煌之后，遭到了国人的"抛弃"，从原来的国礼变得名声逐降，甚至除了制作雕漆的人之外，没有人知道它是何物。中华人民共和国成立后，当景泰蓝、紫砂壶等大受欢迎之时，雕漆在国内市场上仍然不为人知。可以看出，传统雕漆艺术家对于雕漆在国内市场的影响力无可奈何。

2. 萎缩的国际市场

雕漆在国内市场不受欢迎，在国际市场的表现更加糟糕。二十世纪初，雕漆作坊生产的雕漆产品主要面向外国游客。此外，还有一些作坊提供老雕漆产品的修复服务。部分雕漆产品也作为文物出售。雕漆出口的利润相对丰厚，所以雕漆产业得到了一定的发展。

但是自"七七事变"后至1949年，北京雕漆行业进入萧条时期。"太平洋战争爆发是在1941年，战乱使雕漆的外销逐渐难以维持，雕

漆的生产经营逐渐崩溃。由此可知，北京雕漆一定量的外销制作，前后持续大概有二三十年的时间。"（宋本蓉，2010）

中华人民共和国成立后，国家急需大量的外汇，北京雕漆再一次受到重视，雕漆产品开始向国外销售。到1966年，雕漆市场受到人们思想的影响开始再次萎缩。

二十世纪八九十年代，北京雕漆厂停止了雕漆产品的出口，导致雕漆退出国际市场，影响了其在国外的推广和销售。殷秀云大师表示："贸易不景气，技术支持被撤回。他们(指北京雕漆厂)只能在瓶子和盒子里生产一些小东西，而不能承担生产高档精细产品的责任。"

由此可知，雕漆产品数量的逐渐下降对其国际市场的影响是显而易见。如果能够在国内乃至国际市场进行大力推广，雕漆可能会迎来另外一番景象。

3.假冒产品的入侵

目前，雕漆面临着一个非常严峻的知识产权问题。马宁大师说："我们现在真正的问题在于对知识产权的保护和假雕漆对于真品的冲击。但关键是普通人无法区分真伪，这使得许多人对雕漆持怀疑态度，不会触碰这门艺术。"

许多假冒产品在市场上以雕漆的名义进行销售，且大多数消费者倾向于购买更便宜的商品，又无法区分真正的雕漆和假冒产品。因此，这些假冒产品正在逐渐侵入原本属于雕漆的市场。殷秀云大师期望政府更加重视对雕漆知识产权的保护，以确保雕漆市场不会继续受到压制。

4.不理想的市场推广

我们曾在街头采访过15个路人，询问他们是否知道和了解雕漆，答案都是否定的。由此可见，雕漆在市场上的推广程度较低。由于雕漆价格昂贵、制作时间长，大部分仅作装饰之用，所以群众的接受度不高。赵海伟说："雕漆的受欢迎程度很小，我们才更有必要推广和使用雕漆技艺。"

现如今，没有一个组织对不同年龄的雕漆爱好者进行专业培训，这导致理解和热爱传统手工艺的准专业雕漆人的数量逐渐减少，也意味着介入雕漆的团体越来越少。准专业人才和群体会在自己的经济能力范围之内购买收藏雕漆产品，他们对于雕漆的喜爱会传承和保护雕漆。正是因为喜爱雕漆的个人和群体数量减少，仅存的雕漆爱好者不能完全发挥他们的作用，致使雕漆日渐远离大众生活，也使人们理解和欣赏中国传统文化之美的能力下降。所以雕漆的市场推广并不是非常完善。

五、结论

在整个调查研究过程中，我们发现制约雕漆发展的因素主要有三个方面：人才缺失、雕漆本身因素和市场不景气。漫长烦琐的学习过程、不可预知的学习结果、低工资导致雕漆行业人才匮乏。产品本身的高价、漫长的制作过程影响了雕漆的发展；然而与人们普遍认为的不同，原材料并没有严重限制其发展。最后，不成熟的国内市场、萎缩的国际市场、假冒产品的入侵以及不理想的市场推广导致雕漆市场整体的不景气。

除了上述困难，部分受访者也提到了雕漆行业一些亟须改善的方面。马宁大师说："大部分雕漆工匠都是墨守成规的，他们不敢创新，使得当代雕漆作品没有加入现代元素，发展缓慢。想象力不足限制了工匠的行为。"他认为雕漆的发展取决于产品性质的改变，在保持高质量并符合大众审美的前提下，未来最有可能的趋势是加强雕漆的功能性，这样雕漆将被越来越多的人接受和喜爱。"因为每一个时期的雕漆作品都有其时代特点，我觉得今天的雕漆更应该兼具美感和实用性，这样才能让它得到长远的发展。"（马宁）黄杰则在提出雕漆产品实用性的基础上，也提出价格的调整：

"首先，它应该有一定的实用性，并且价格可以被大多数人接受。例如茶壶、小杯子或其他小玩意儿，它们的价格不是那么高，大多数人可以负担得起。对他们来说，把它介绍给朋友和亲戚是很方便的。"

总之，雕漆应该顺应时代潮流，更加实用。虽然雕漆的发展遇到很多问题，但如果能作出一些改变，未来的前景是可以期待的。作为一项历史悠久的非物质文化遗产，雕漆有其独特的魅力和生存之道。为了适应当代的发展与未来的传承要求，雕漆行业需要兼顾实用性与美观性，在保持高质量的同时尽量使价格更加亲民，同时辅以更好的宣传。这样，雕漆这块中国文化的瑰宝一定能有更美好的发展前景。

参考文献：

北京雕漆走在失传边缘[EB/OL].(2014-06-24).https://www.douban.com/note/362123430/.
丛玲玲."北京雕漆"之痛：并非只因"注漆"[J].美术观察，2008，(8)：92—96.

宋本蓉.雕漆技艺[M].北京：文化艺术出版社，2013．

宋本蓉.非物质文化遗产保护视野下的传统手工技艺——以北京雕漆为例[D].北京：中国艺术研究院，2010．

涂露芳.北京2009年职工平均工资48444元[N].北京日报，2010-07-17．

Research on the Barriers to the Development of Beijing *Diaoqi*[1]

Zhang Shuxian (Clara) Huang Yilin (Lyn) He Ting'ao (Mike)[2]

Abstract: Beijing *Diaoqi* is a Chinese ancient traditional handicraft. As a heritage for more than one thousand and four hundred years, *Diaoqi* was once in a very splendid period. However, it has met a lot of difficulties in the contemporary development. By interviewing *Diaoqi* craftsmen and analyzing the interview data, we find that the difficult and arduous conditions of the inheritance of the craft have led to the lack of talents. Some of the characteristics of *Diaoqi* itself limit the breadth and speed of its development. In addition, because of the domestic and foreign stagnant markets and the emergence of counterfeit products, *Diaoqi*'s market sales have been in the doldrums. In order to better adapt to the contemporary development and future inheritance, the *Diaoqi* industry needs to give consideration to both practicality and aesthetics. While maintaining high quality, *Diaoqi* should make its price as close to the public as possible, so as to get better publicity.

Keywords: Beijing *Diaoqi*, handicraft, difficulties, lack of talents, characteristics, market, adapt, publicity

1. Research Significance

Beijing *Diaoqi* is a Chinese ancient traditional handicraft. As time changes, its popularity is getting lower and lower. Through random street interviews of 15 passersby, it was found that none of them knew anything about *Diaoqi*. We believe that for traditional culture, it is necessary to un-

---

1. The academic advisors of this paper are Eli Smith and Guo Minshuo, teachers of BFSU International Education Group, Beijing Foreign Studies University.
2. The authors of this paper are the 11th grade students of the International Curriculum Centre (ICC) of Beijing Foreign Studies University.

derstand what barriers restrict its development. Only in this way can this traditional culture be improved and continue to flourish. Based on this idea, we interviewed some of the craftsmen who are still working on Beijing *Diaoqi*. We hope to find the barriers that restrict the development of Beijing *Diaoqi*, and help it develop further while retaining the original features.

2. Literature Review

When we searched "Beijing *Diaoqi*" as keywords on cnki.net and cqvip.com, we found that the related literature mainly focused on the history, development status and prospects of Beijing *Diaoqi*. Some scholars have studied the difficulties in its development. Cong (2008) pointed out that in the late 1980s, *Zhuqi*, a chemical synthetic resin product formed by one-time injection molding, caused chaos in the market because its appearance was very similar to Beijing *Diaoqi*. *Zhuqi*, because of its low price, has occupied more than half of the market in Beijing. Cong appealed, "Can we preserve the precious cultural heritage of craftsmanship left by our ancestors?" However, there is no literature that has conducted in-depth research on the barriers to the development of Beijing *Diaoqi*. Therefore, the authors think this research is significant.

3. Research Method

3.1 Data collection

For data collection, our group used the method of structured interview. We interviewed Ma Ning, Zhao Haiwei and Huang Jie respectively from July 17 to 19, 2018. Fifteen random interviewees were interviewed at South Luogu Lane on August 3, 2018. And we interviewed Master Yin Xiuyun at Baigongfang on August 4, 2018.

3.1.1 Participants

Table 1: Biographical information of the participants

Name	Gender	Age	Career
Yin Xiuyun	Female	72	National representative inheritor of Beijing *Diaoqi*
Ma Ning	Male	Middle-aged	Representative inheritor of Beijing *Hediao* (fruit pit carving) Beijing local representative inheritor of Beijing *Diaoqi*
Zhao Haiwei	Male	Middle-aged	One of the craftsmen of the *Diaoqi* production studio
Huang Jie	Male	Middle-aged	*Diaoqi* collector
Passerby 1	Male		
Passerby 2	Male		
Passerby 3	Male		
Passerby 4	Male		
Passerby 5	Male		
Passerby 6	Male		
Passerby 7	Male		
Passerby 8	Male		
Passerby 9	Female		
Passerby 10	Female		
Passerby 11	Female		
Passerby 12	Female		
Passerby 13	Female		
Passerby 14	Female		
Passerby 15	Female		

3.1.2 Interview questions

We used the structured interview to ask the participants a series of questions which was prepared in advance. The interview questions are as follows:

1) What are the factors which restrict the development of *Diaoqi* nowadays?

2) Do you think the scarce raw material is a difficulty to the promotion of *Diaoqi*?

3) Do you think long making process is a difficulty to the promotion of *Diaoqi*?

4) How do you think the mainstream consumption concept influence the *Diaoqi* market?

5) What changes do you think *Diaoqi* has made to meet the changes in the present customer demand and market?

3.2 Data analysis

The data are analyzed and coded.

Table 2: Data analysis result

Theme	Code
Lack of talents	· The learning process is long, hard, and tedious · The learning outcome is unpredictable · The salary is unstable and relatively low
Limitation of *Diaoqi* itself	· High price · Long production process · Raw material
Unpopular market	· The immature domestic market · The shrinking international market · The invasion of fake products · The weak market promotion

4. Research Findings and Discussion

The difficulties of three aspects are discussed: the lack of talents, the limitation of *Diaoqi* itself, and the unpopular market.

4.1 Difficulties in terms of lack of talents

Presently, it is crucial that *Diaoqi* industry should develop a younger generation of inheritors. Even the famous factories face the challenge of having no apprentices. The situation is even worse in those small workshops. Without inheritors, the room for *Diaoqi*'s survival is smaller and smaller. In the 1970s and 1980s, there were more than 600 workers in Beijing Diaoqi Factory. Nowadays, there are probably no more than 20 craftsmen who still make a living by *Diaoqi*. Through the interviews with Master Yin Xiuyun, we find that lack of talents is an assignable challenge for the *Diaoqi* industry.

> "These years, Beijing *Diaoqi* practitioners is less than 100 people. The largest factory, Lingyun Diaoqi Factory has only 20 or 30 people. The youngest artist is more than 40 years old, and there is no younger generation. So in 10 years, what should I do?" (Cong, 2008)

4.1.1 The learning process is long, hard, and tedious

The learning process is long. As more and more people pursue fast-paced life, only a very few people have the patience to spend long time learning a craft. Apprentices of *Diaoqi* need to learn the craft from an early age. "In the *Diaoqi* industry, the two most difficult learning procedures are designing and carving. A master's wonderful design depends on high-level craftsmen to display. A high-level *Diaoqi* craftsman needs more than 10 years of training."[3] National *Diaoqi* inheritor Wen Qiangang shared his learning process:

> "In nearly five years before the 'Cultural Revolution', I was doing nothing but learning hard. Through learning and practicing, I got familiar with the techniques of various procedures, particularly carving. Carving took most of my time. I practiced for nearly three years and mastered the carving techniques comprehensively." (Song, 2010)

---

3. https://www.douban.com/note/362123430/.

This long learning process makes *Diaoqi* apprentices' situation very awkward in terms of both identity and rewards. Song (2013) pointed out:

> "Without 3-5 years of learning under the instruction of masters, it is difficult to fully grasp the skills. If 3-5 years are for learning, who will pay for the tuition? How can students support themselves? If 3-5 years are for working, it's almost impossible for a young student with no knowledge of the art to make any contributions and quickly find his position."

Meanwhile, the learning process is hard. Not everyone can learn it well. Usually apprentices need to have some foundation or talents on drawing. The learning process is toilsome; many apprentices give up halfway through the training process because they do not want to bear the hardship. Wen Qiangang shared his own experience:

> "It took me one year to master simple skills. Because for me, it was just to learn how to use tools. I had already known how to carve relief. So it was relatively easy for me. People who have learned drawing or carving before are totally different compared with those who haven't. After mastering the use of the cutter, those who haven't learned the art of carving relief still need to master this skill." (Song, 2010)

Song (2010) also mentioned:

> "In 1997, Beijing Diaoqi Factory trained 40 workers. However, most of them could not bear it, and they chose to seek other careers. Some workers who had studied art design before worked on home decoration or other design. Others switched to sales and securities. It is easy to understand why young people are unwilling to do it."

What's more, the learning process is tedious. Apprentices do the same simple work again and again until they can master the skill craftily. The process really tests their patience and passion to this craft. Yin Xiuyun said, "Our factory only has one craftsman, who is more than 60 years old and has been working till now since the late 1970s. He does not have any apprentice, and no one is willing to follow him because the job is dirty and tiresome. It is hard to imagine that, when he cannot work anymore, how will *Diaoqi* be like in the future?"

4.1.2 The learning outcome is unpredictable

Not only is the learning process long, hard, and tedious, but the outcome is unpredictable. To learn the making of *Diaoqi* well requires not only the determination to endure hardship, but also a certain understanding and talent.

> "For *Diaoqi*, learning from practice is the most important way of inheritance. Its craft is difficult. There are a lot of technical details and perceptions that cannot be resorted to words. It is difficult to understand the cultural connotation and technical tradition of *Diaoqi* without learning and realizing the craftsmanship under the guidance of the master. The concentration, patience and perseverance are basic requirements for a good craftsman, but the maintenance of these spirits depends, to a great extent, on the emotional communication and behavior interaction between people. These spirits are the assurance of consummate skill in an industry and the spiritual basis for the effective use of this skill. They cannot be written down or guided by procedures. They can only be passed on orally and in practice." (Song, 2010)

4.1.3 The salary is unstable and relatively low

In addition to the tough learning process and the unpredictable outcome, the low salary is also a significant reason for the lack of talents.

According to a table which recorded the salaries of 29 *Diaoqi* craftsmen in Beijing of the year 2009, there were 8 craftsmen who only made ￥8,000 per year (Song, 2010). According to *Beijing Daily*, the average annual salary of the year 2009 of workers in Beijing was ￥48,444. (Tu, 2010) But the most common annual salary for *Diaoqi* craftsmen in 2009 was ￥10,000 - ￥30,000, which was much lower than the average annual salary. Even Master Yin Xiuyun only made ￥15,000 per year at that time, not to mention the green apprentices. Without sufficient salary, a craftsman cannot survive and be dedicated to the making of *Diaoqi*. *Diaoqi* Master Wen Qiangang said:

> "The work of *Diaoqi* can't be done by one person. At least it needs a small team. As a team, we have to bring income to each participant. If they can live on it, and live well, then they are willing to do it." (Song, 2010)

What's more, government's subsidies are far from sufficient. The government wants craftsmen to take more apprentices, but it implements the piece rate in the arts and crafts industry. Training apprentices becomes a pure obligation, which is also hard to do because of the strain of work. Artisans have no time and money to teach and train apprentices. Ma Ning pointed out that every apprentice gets ￥100 per month from the government and this is only enough for their food.

Most inheritors use the subsidies as their apprentices' daily allowance, rather than developing the workshop. Also, the unsatisfactory salary cannot attract many young people to learn the craft. Many craftsmen expect government to give more support to this industry. As Master Yin Xiuyun said, "I hope that the government can give full play to its guiding role and give strong support to the traditional *Diaoqi* industry." (Cong, 2008)

To sum up, the long, hard and tedious learning process, unpredictable learning results and low salaries lead to the lack of talents in the *Diaoqi* industry. Inheritance of the younger generation which determines the future of *Diaoqi* is crucial, but the lack of the new generation of talents is undoubtedly a severe test of future development of *Diaoqi*.

4.2 Difficulties in terms of limitation of *Diaoqi* itself

4.2.1 High price

Through the research, the authors find that the limitation of *Diaoqi* itself is one of the biggest challenges. Beijing *Diaoqi* is a traditional craft, beginning in the Tang dynasty, and becoming popular in the Song, Yuan, Ming and Qing dynasties. Traditionally, it was almost only used in royal families. It was used as diplomatic gifts by the Emperor Yongle of the Ming dynasty, and was described favorably in the poems of the Emperor Qianlong of the Qing dynasty. Its meticulous production process, with hundreds of procedures and more than a dozen workers, takes years to complete. Its exquisite workmanship leads to the exorbitant price. Therefore, it has never been approachable for ordinary people. According to the interview with Mr. Zhao Haiwei, the high price seems to set a natural barrier for the collectors of *Diaoqi*.

As part of the national intangible cultural heritage of China, *Diaoqi* is not as popular as some other crafts. Due to its historical background, the high price and low popularity greatly restrict the development of *Diaoqi* at the present. Therefore, it is difficult for collectors to enter this field.

4.2.2 Long production process

The long production process is due to its complicated and elegant details. "The entire production process is supported by wealth and time. One piece of work, occupying the time of a dozen people, has been made for three years." (Song, 2010)

> "It's hard for craftsmen to complete the manufacturing of *Diaoqi* in a short time. Design, padding making, paint making, painting, carving and polishing are the basic procedures of *Diaoqi* production.

The whole production process should be taken step by step. Even making a very small piece of work, from start to finish, may last six to seven months. I think there is nothing to spare because this is meticulous, step-by-step work." (Zhao Haiwei)

To begin with, the craftsmen spend a lot of time producing the paint and then the layering of paint. More than 160 layers of paint need to be painted for a product with a thickness of 5 - 10 mm. The paint needs to be painted 1 - 2 times per day, and the painting procedure takes about 3 months. Most of the procedures, just like painting, should be repeated again and again. After finishing the carving step, the craftsman should dry the semi-finished product in natural environment for 4 - 6 years. Each step should be made dedicatedly and seriously. A craftsman can't change the production process at all. (Song, 2010) It is clear to see the whole production process is strenuous and highly intricate. That is the reason why the output of *Diaoqi* is extremely low. Producing a piece of *Diaoqi* work needs long-time accumulation.

However, there are also some advantages of the prolonged production time. Firstly, the long production process can demonstrate the tradition and the classical culture of *Diaoqi*. In Song's book which has made a detailed introduction of *Diaoqi* production, Song mentioned that *Diaoqi* was an extremely traditional art craft. (Song, 2013) Secondly, long manufacturing time can guarantee the quality of *Diaoqi*. The artists have a dedicated and devoted attitude on the production. They won't reduce the time to speed up the production. "My point is, if it takes two days to finish, I will spend two days to complete, or maybe I will spend three days on it. I don't want to turn it into one day's work for more money." (Zhao Haiwei)

But the long production time has limited *Diaoqi*'s output and one of its drawbacks is the decreasing of consumers' demand. Most consumers expect to get something in a short time. They do not have the patience to wait for *Diaoqi* production. However, other kinds of art are fast, with abundant supply, so some people switch their demand and find other crafts which can replace *Diaoqi*. Consequently, the demand for *Diaoqi* decreases.

As a result, low output and long making time will cause the demand for *Diaoqi* to become lower than that of other crafts. People change their interests, and the consumption of *Diaoqi* is less.

4.2.3 Raw material

It is commonly accepted that the raw material of *Diaoqi*, the paint, is in short supply and this is regarded as the third reason for the slow development of *Diaoqi*. On average, a lacquer tree of 10 years old only produces 75 - 125 grams of sap daily. A sap gatherer can only collect 750 - 1000 grams of sap daily. (Song, 2013) To our surprise, Mr. Ma Ning felt that the lack of raw material is not a problem at all. To begin with, he said, "Raw material can be guaranteed, because we have our own planting base." This base is located in an industrial park in Zhuxi, a county in Hubei province. Mr. Ma thinks the base can provide sufficient material for *Diaoqi*. Furthermore, with the recovery and development of *Diaoqi* culture, there still exists some room for the expansion of raw material. In other words, the production of raw material can be boosted with the development of demand. According to Mr. Ma, if the popularity of *Diaoqi* increases, the market of raw material supply will accordingly grow larger instead of becoming withered.

Although the raw material may not hamper the development of *Diaoqi*, if the government does not take any actions to preserve it, somehow the raw material will become more difficult to acquire. At that time, the raw material may become one of the obstacles in the development of *Diaoqi*.

4.3 Difficulties in terms of unpopular market

4.3.1 The immature domestic market

During the Ming and Qing dynasties, *Diaoqi* was once used as national gifts and regarded as a symbol of royal aristocracy. However, due to constant wars and economic recession at the end of the Qing dynasty, the demand of *Diaoqi* in royal and noble families dropped sharply. At the same time, most of the *Diaoqi* craftsmen supported by the royalties went bankrupt. However, in the early 20th century, some craftsmen realized that *Diaoqi* was profitable, so they cooperated with other people and founded *Diaoqi* workshops, which specialized in making and selling *Diaoqi* of the Qing dynasty style. Due to the rich profit, many *Diaoqi* workshops successively opened.

According to Song (2010), the *Diaoqi* screen made by Xiao Xingda, Xiao Le'an, Wu Yingxuan and others won gold medal at the 1915 Panama World Expo in San Francisco, USA. It represented the glory of Beijing *Diaoqi* since the end of the Qing dynasty.

> "From the beginning of the Westernization Movement, the impact of industrialization was not only external and aggressive. China also began to reflect and criticize its cultural tradition from various angles, i.e. social, technological, and cultural. Traditional culture was regarded as the root of backwardness, and was suspected, denied, and abandoned. Some scholars who advocated self-salvation through industrial revolution believed that as long as China achieved industrialization, issues related to politics, morality and social education would be solved... Although *Diaoqi* survives because it cannot be replaced, it has fallen into an awkward situation. It's because the traditional culture that *Diaoqi* attaches itself with has been questioned and betrayed." (Song, 2010)

This passage shows that while *Diaoqi* was once in glory, it has been "abandoned" by Chinese people. From national gifts of the royal families to common daily utensils, the reputation of *Diaoqi* gradually declined and now few people know what it is. Nowadays, different from other handicrafts, such as the cloisonné and the purple clay pot, which are popular, *Diaoqi* is still unknown in the domestic market. Traditional *Diaoqi* craftsmen can do nothing to influence the market.

4.3.2 The shrinking international market

The domestic market of *Diaoqi* is not popular, and the international market is even worse. At the beginning of the 20th century, the main consumer groups of *Diaoqi* products were foreign tourists. In addition, there were some businesses of repairing old *Diaoqi* products. Some products of *Diaoqi* were also sold as cultural relics. The profit of *Diaoqi* for export was relatively rich, and the *Diaoqi* industry was developed.

"The outbreak of the Pacific War in 1941 made the export of *Diaoqi* extremely difficult, and the production and operation of *Diaoqi* business gradually collapsed. It can be seen that Beijing *Diaoqi* was booming at the early years of the 20th century, and it lasted for about two or three decades." (Song, 2010)

However, after the founding of the People's Republic of China, the government needed a large amount of foreign currency urgently, and Beijing *Diaoqi* was once again stimulated to sell products abroad. In 1966, *Diaoqi* was affected by people's thoughts and the market began to shrink again.

In the 1980s and 1990s, Beijing Diaoqi Factory stopped the export of *Diaoqi*, causing the retreat of *Diaoqi* on the international market, and affecting its promotion to foreign countries. Master Yin Xiuyun said, "The trade was sluggish and the technical support was withdrawn. They (Beijing Diaoqi Factory) could only produce some small things such as bottles and boxes, and could not undertake the production of high-grade fine products."

The impact of the gradual decline on its international market is evident. If *Diaoqi* can be protected and promoted in both domestic and international markets, it can regain its popularity.

4.3.3 The invasion of fake products

Nowadays, *Diaoqi* is facing a very pressing issue of intellectual property. Ma Ning said, "The real problem we have now is the protection of intellectual property rights against the impact of fake products on the real thing.

But the ordinary people have no way to distinguish the genuine products from the fake ones, which makes many people skeptical about *Diaoqi*. They refuse to explore the art."

Many fake products are sold in the market under the name of *Diaoqi*. Most consumers tend to buy cheaper goods, and they can't distinguish real *Diaoqi* products from fake ones. Therefore, these fake products are gradually encroaching on the market. Master Yin Xiuyun expects the government to pay more attention to the protection of the intellectual property of *Diaoqi*, in order to ensure that the market of *Diaoqi* will not continue to be suppressed.

4.3.4 The weak market promotion

Through random street interviews of 15 passersby, it was found that none of them knew anything about *Diaoqi*. The promotion of *Diaoqi* is insufficient and ineffective. *Diaoqi* was a royal craft since ancient times, so most people did not use it. Modern *Diaoqi* products are expensive, and most are decorative rather than practical, so the recognition of *Diaoqi* from ordinary people is not high enough. Zhao Haiwei said, "Even though the market of *Diaoqi* is small, it is still necessary to promote *Diaoqi* and preserve the cultural heritage."

What's more, no organization or individual offers professional training for *Diaoqi* lovers, which results in the fact that there are few chances of accessing *Diaoqi*, and of discovering real *Diaoqi* talents who understand and love traditional handicrafts, thus people's understanding and appreciation of Chinese traditional culture are flagging. The lack of quasi-professional talents of *Diaoqi* also means that there are fewer and fewer collectors and purchasers of *Diaoqi* products, and fewer and fewer people are willing to protect *Diaoqi*, because it is too far away from their lives.

5. Conclusion

This research finds that there are mainly three difficulties for the development of *Diaoqi*: lack of talents, limitation of *Diaoqi* itself, and unpopular market. The long, hard and tedious learning process, unpredictable learning outcome and low salary lead to the lack of talents in the *Diaoqi* industry. In addition, high price of the product itself and long making process are the inherent limitation of *Diaoqi* itself. Contrary to common belief, raw material may not be a restriction to its development. Last but not least, the immature domestic market, shrinking international market, invasion of fake products and weak market promotion result in the unsatisfying market of *Diaoqi*.

Apart from the difficulties, some participants also mentioned the potential improvement of the *Diaoqi* industry. Ma Ning said, "Most of the *Diaoqi* craftsmen are fettered by old conventions. They dare not innovate, which makes them fail to add modern elements to contemporary *Diaoqi* crafts. Poor imagination limits *Diaoqi* craftsmen's creativity." It is inevitable that *Diaoqi* is to make some changes to adapt to the trend of contemporary aesthetics. We also find some answers about the changes that *Diaoqi* will probably make in the future. The most likely trend is to be more functional. It should keep the high quality and conform to the public aesthetics. In this way, it will be accepted and loved by more and more people. "*Diaoqi* of every dynasty has its own characteristics. I think that today's *Diaoqi* should combine both beauty and practicality." (Ma Ning)

> "First of all, it should have certain practicability, and should be affordable to most people. For example, the prices of a teapot or a small cup are not so high, and most people can enjoy and afford it. It's convenient to introduce them to friends and relatives." (Huang Jie)

In contemporary society, compared with other prevalent traditional art crafts, *Diaoqi* is still unknown to most people. However, it also means that *Diaoqi* has a lot of room to grow. As an intangible and historic art form, *Diaoqi* can not only represent the Chinese traditional culture, but also increase the popularity of China.

In short, *Diaoqi* should adapt to the contemporary trend and be more functional. At the same time, while maintaining its high quality, *Diaoqi* should keep the price more affordable to ordinary people. Coupled with proper and effective promotion, the prospects of *Diaoqi* are to be expected.

References:

Beijing Diaoqi on the Verge of Extinction [EB/OL]. (2014-06-24). https://www.douban.com/note/362123430/.

Cong, Lingling. Pain of "Beijing Diaoqi" : Not Just Because of "Zhuqi" [J]. Art Observation, 2008, (08): 92-96.

Song, Benrong. Diaoqi Craft [M]. Beijing: Culture and Art Publishing House, 2013.

—. Traditional Handicraft Skills from the Perspective of Intangible Cultural Heritage Protection – Beijing Diaoqi as an Example [D]. Beijing: Chinese National Academy of Arts, 2010.

Tu, Lufang. Beijing Workers' Average Salary at ￥48,444 in 2009 [N]. Beijing Daily, 2010-07-17.

北京雕漆市场调查报告[1]

高艺径　张艺馨　王泽华[2]

【摘要】　通过对雕漆大师和雕漆销售人员的采访，我们得出的结论是：在未来，排除已有的障碍，雕漆市场会保持稳定的态势；雕漆的消费者有两种特质，分别是有经济实力和有丰富知识去理解雕漆；雕漆的销售渠道分为线上和线下两种，地区不同，其销量也有所不同。

【关键词】　北京雕漆　市场发展趋势　成本　消费群体　销售量　销售渠道　注漆影响　淡季与旺季

一、研究背景与研究目标

北京雕漆是一项古老的地方传统手工技艺，以雕刻见长，在漆胎上涂几十层漆，再以刀进行雕刻制作成漆器。虽然雕漆原材料的价格非常低廉，无法和市场上常见的工艺品如玉器、瓷器等的高价格原材料相媲美，但雕漆注重雕刻的手法和技艺，因此人工成本较高，耗费时间长。此外，由于宣传较少等原因，雕漆在市场上的知名度并不高。本研究希望通过对目前雕漆市场的调查研究，总结分析市场现状，从理性的角度对雕漆未来的市场走向作出有效的判断。

---

1. 本调研报告科研指导教师为北京外国语大学国际教育集团共建项目部教师郭旻硕。
2. 本调研报告的三位作者均为北京外国语大学国际课程中心十一年级学生。

二、文献综述

笔者以"北京雕漆""雕漆市场现状"等为关键词在中国知网等学术网站进行搜索,仅发现大量关于漆艺与漆艺传承保护的研究,并未发现市场方面的研究。笔者通过浏览关于漆艺的论文、采访雕漆匠人、走访门店和制作工作室等,进一步了解雕漆制作成本、销售渠道、销售量、客户群体、淡季和旺季等影响市场的因素,从而得出结论:虽然北京雕漆市场较小,但在未来将保持稳定。

三、研究方法与研究步骤

本文通过上网查找论文、采访雕漆匠人(访谈法)、走访雕漆工作室(田野调查)等方法获得研究数据。

(一) 受访者基本信息

表1:受访者信息

姓名	职业	工龄
马宁	京作核雕代表性传承人、北京雕漆技艺代表性传承人、北京市工艺美术大师,目前北京最年轻的东城区雕漆技艺传承人,西城区京作核雕传承人	10年
权国立	北京儒匠传奇家具有限公司雕漆工作室负责人之一	
张女士	百工坊殷秀云雕漆工作室售卖员	
赵师傅	北京儒匠传奇家具有限公司雕漆工作室雕刻师	

(二) 数据收集

本研究采用结构式访谈的形式向雕漆匠人和销售人员询问了下列问题：

1）您是否了解目前雕漆艺术品在市场上的售价？

2）您觉得是什么决定了雕漆的价格？

3）您认为雕漆的主要消费群体如今有哪些？

4）您所知雕漆艺术品如今的销量如何？

5）在中国特定节假日期间，雕漆销量相对于平时是否有所改变？

6）雕漆艺术成品的销售渠道有哪些？

7）就您所知，注漆对雕漆有什么样的市场影响？

(三) 数据编码

笔者通过仔细研究数据，对数据进行编码，得到以下研究结果。

表2：数据研究结果

主题	一级编码	二级编码
雕漆在未来市场将保持稳定	成本稳定	1. 雕刻作品价格稳定 2. 雕刻工匠人工成本稳定 3. 雕刻纹样难度稳定 4. 原材料价格稳定
	消费群体稳定	1. 经济能力高 2. 知识水平高
	供应没有增长	1. 生产耗时，无法大量供应 2. 劳动力缺乏 3. 消费者没有增加
	销售渠道没有变化	1. 线上：量小，低端 2. 线下：主要渠道，高端

续表

主题	一级编码	二级编码
雕漆在未来市场将保持稳定	替代品	只影响低端市场，不是竞争对手
	淡旺季	旺季：低端产品促销，影响不大

四、发现与讨论

(一) 雕漆的成本

1. 雕漆作品本身的价格波动较小

"相对于整个中国历史文化收藏品来讲，我认为雕漆目前还处于一个价格低谷，整个价格并没有太大的起伏。"(马宁)虽然雕漆作为一种曾经的贵族工艺——燕京八绝[3]之一——流传至今，但它并没有像景泰蓝、花丝镶嵌等那样为众人所知，其市场也不像其他工艺品的市场那般火热。大多数人都不能理解为什么雕漆的原材料那么廉价(相比于其他工艺，如玉雕、牙雕等)而它的售价却那么昂贵。其实，这是因为他们不知道雕漆的价格是由什么因素决定的。

"像目前最贵的雕漆艺术品，差不多可以在千万级以上。目前我知道最贵的可能就是文乾刚老师的一幅屏风，可能标价会到1.3亿。基本上一些顶级大师的作品的评估价是每平方米300万

---

3. 燕京八绝，即景泰蓝、玉雕、牙雕、雕漆、金漆镶嵌、花丝镶嵌、宫毯、京绣八大工艺门类。它们充分汲取了各地民间工艺的精华，在清代均开创了中华传统工艺新的高峰，并逐渐形成了"京作"特色的宫廷艺术。

到500万。像中等的大师，如马宁老师这样的，作品是每平方米50万到80万。所以雕漆的价格空间幅度是非常大的。"（权国立）

虽然价格区间很大，但由于工匠的资历和水平不同，雕漆的价格在未来将不会有太大波动。从雕漆项目其他研究小组的成果中可以得知，培养一位雕漆大师非常困难，而且需要相当长的一段时间（见本书论文《雕漆传承人的培养》）。"当代的雕漆艺术品也和我们现在很多的现代艺术品是一样的，它分大师级、补充级，然后还要分体量。"（权国立）

2. 劳动力成本将不会有太大改变

由于一个好的工匠需要长期培养，而漫长的工作时间和乏味的工作内容使得在雕漆市场上找不到新的工匠，所以劳动力成本将不会有太大改变。

> "一个高水平的雕刻技师，需要十多年的磨炼。文乾刚说，假设100个人学雕刻，两三年后，会有50人被淘汰去从事相对容易的制胎、打磨等工种，剩下的50人再过10年，又要被淘汰一大半，剩下的一小部分中，能够承担雕刻艺术精品重任的，不过两三人而已。现在的雕刻技师，平均年龄已经在50岁以上，这些人正在逐年老去，由于工作难度大，而且收入并不高，所以现在的年轻人都不愿学徒……"[4]

---

4. 见http://www.huaxia.com/wh/mjwh/2005/00315979.html。

3.雕漆的设计和图样趋于固定

除了工匠的因素,雕漆产品本身也对其价格有着较大影响。以雕漆的设计和图样为例,其通常被分为三类:人物,山水与亭台楼阁,以及花鸟。(张女士)

人物是所有图样里最贵的。人物开脸比较困难,在雕漆漆层表面雕刻具有生动面部表情的人物无疑是相当困难的,需要精雕细刻,雕完还要在人物边缘进行打磨。山水与亭台楼阁排在第二位,水有河水与海水之分,它们的不同之处在于刻刀行走的方向:河水相对平稳,没有海的波澜壮阔,所以纹饰基本为平的或直的;而海水则因海浪的缘故,纹样基本是螺旋的,还要有激起的浪花。亭台楼阁则在水的上方,在中国传统文化中,山水总是与亭台楼阁相结合。花鸟排在第三位,雕刻花卉相对便宜,因为它的图样基本是传统花纹,比较固定且简单。有仿明代的栀子花,讲究富贵的牡丹花,讲究喜庆的梅花,而梅花旁有时会有喜鹊的身影,取自喜鹊登枝、喜上眉梢之意。其他小的纹饰则由缠枝莲等底纹构成。雕漆的底纹多达上百种,有回纹、缠枝莲、四方花、松球等。

尽管不同设计和图样的价格不一,但是雕漆作为一个传承千年的工艺,其设计和制作过程均是固定的,所以雕漆的生产成本也趋于稳定。

4.原材料供求关系较为稳定

"不同地区所产的生漆具有不同的功能。中国北京或越南所生产的生漆多用于绘画而非雕刻,比较便宜,所以低端雕漆多用这些材料制作。而中国湖北所生产的生漆轻盈、耐旱,更适合制作漆器。所以,我们的车间与湖北当地生产生漆的公司也有合作。"(马宁)

此外,生漆是我国特产资源,其产量占世界生漆总产量的80%以上。在我国除了黑龙江、吉林、内蒙古、宁夏和新疆之外,其他省区均有生漆产量分布,中心分布区在秦岭、大巴山、武当山、巫山、武陵山、大娄山及乌蒙山一带。(冯志坚,1984)陕西、湖北、重庆、云南、贵州、四川、甘肃等7个省(市)是生漆主产区,并有60多个重点产漆县。根据调查和不完全统计,近年来中国生漆市场的销量为500—600吨。其中,超过300吨产自陕西省,占总量的60%以上。(张瑞琴等,2014)

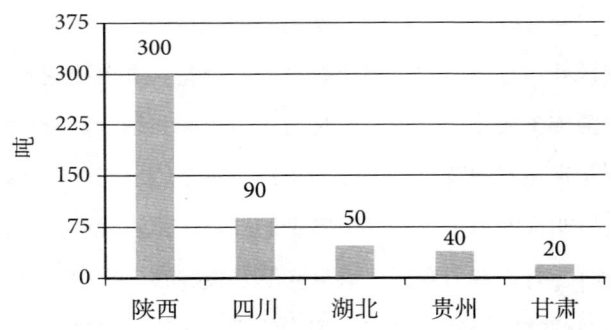

图1:生漆近年产量(张瑞琴等,2014)

漆器的原产地有很多,产量也很大。价格由需求和供给决定,当需求和供给不变时,价格也不会发生变化。因此,由于漆器的数量和产地是稳定的,所以原料成本将不会有太大改变。

除去前文详细介绍的4种影响雕漆价格的重要因素外,雕漆尺寸的大小也可以作为衡量其价值的因素之一。而漆器的厚度决定了雕漆的大小,表面漆越厚,雕漆的尺寸就越大。但由于这些都基于千年的传承,所以成本是稳定的。在这些会影响价格的因素都保持相对稳定的情况下,雕漆产品本身的价格波动就较小。

(二) 雕漆的主要消费群体

雕漆市场中影响消费的因素有很多。

1. 购买者的经济能力

消费者购买雕漆的行为取决于他们的社会地位和经济能力。通过对几位雕漆艺人的采访，我们发现，社会地位较高的人更愿意也更有能力购买一些大件的艺术品，因为他们的收入较高。而正如前文所提到的，雕漆的价格虽然稳定，但仍然较高。

> "因为自古以来，漆器和雕漆作品，实际上是不走入寻常百姓家的，自古就是皇宫贵胄所有。由于它之前的传承就是在这方面的，所以接受它的这些人群的身份也必须和消费能力要相匹配。"（权国立）

不难发现，社会地位较高的人更有能力购买雕漆艺术品。赵师傅表示："因为他们都是有消费能力的人，普通老百姓，一般是消费不起的。"中等收入的人只会购买少量可以用于日常生活的雕漆产品，因为他们负担不起大件的雕漆工艺品。

2. 购买者的知识水平

除了具有较高的购买力之外，雕漆消费者的知识水平也较高。他们对中国文化的认识更加深入，出于对中国文化的喜爱，加之对雕漆生产流程与所需材料的了解，他们能够正确评估雕漆艺术品蕴藏的真正价值，并作出购买的决定。他们不仅是雕漆艺术品的消费者，更是收藏家。当被问到雕漆的主要消费群体时，马宁表示："第一种是真正有文化、内涵、知识的收藏家。"赵师傅说："我认为还有一些喜收藏的成功人士。"马宁和赵师傅都认为,许多愿意购买雕漆艺术作品的买家都对收藏感兴趣,并且了解雕漆的艺术价值。

"所以这些人群的身份也必须和他们的消费能力相匹配。尤其像现在,很多的大师的好作品,你有钱我也不一定卖给你。我要先和你聊,我觉得第一个你要喜欢它,第二个你真的珍惜它,我才可能卖给你。"(权国立)

权国立认为,有些有经济能力购买大师制作的雕漆艺术品的人不一定有资格获得他们想要的艺术品。马宁却认为,那些足够富有的人可能对雕漆缺乏深入的了解,但他们有足够的消费能力。这将产生一种积极的消费,因为即使是那些不了解雕漆文化和工艺的消费群体,也会选择消费它们,这样雕漆市场的总收入就会增加。

很多消费者购买艺术品是基于物品材料、视觉印象、思想价值、社会价值和历史价值这几大因素。然而漆器在国际上的知名度远不及瓷器,也不像玉器那样有深厚的大众基础。制作雕漆的材料通常也不如玉等其他材料值钱。所以,购买雕漆的人并不会将材料看得非常重要,而是注重雕刻的技艺,并且这些人仅仅占据了艺术品整体消费群体的一小部分。因此,高端雕漆艺术品的主要购买者是那些有较高社会地位的、有相当高的文化修养的、喜爱并有能力购买的人。由此,最有可能购买雕漆的人将在未来几年保持稳定,购买雕漆的消费者比例也趋于稳定,所以市场在未来将不会产生很大的变化。

（三）雕漆的销售量

1. 生产时间影响销售量

马宁说："实际上雕漆艺术品目前的销量不能算是太好，但是更主要的原因是生产的数量达不到，没办法以一个正常的产品途径供应市场。但就单体的艺术品而言，它的销售是尚可以维系这个职业的存活的。"因为雕漆是一项耗时耗力的技艺，艺术家很难在短时间内完成很多艺术品。权国立说："我们都知道，雕漆里面最耗时的就是人工。我一把雕漆壶，制作周期是半年，即180天。我髹漆的时间差不多就在2个月到3个月。我晾晒的时间是1个月，雕刻的时间是2周到3周，抛光的时间是10天。"

漫长的制作过程中的每一步都需要做到位，才能产出合格的雕漆产品，而做到位便意味着无法缩短工期。这直接导致了成品制作时间长、市面上的雕漆产品偏少的现象。

2. 行业内劳动力人数影响销售量

行业内员工的缺乏限制了雕漆艺术品的产量。权国立说："中国最多有100至200人从事雕漆这个工作，算上学徒工最多300人。能拿得出手的大师级的人物可能也就是20位。"根据他所提供的信息可知，有能力制作雕漆的人较少，只有极少数人可以被称为雕漆艺术家。

3. 消费者影响销售量

作为艺术品的雕漆，需要懂它且有经济能力的人购买，而对雕漆有基本认知的人就非常少。根据本组成员的随机街头访问，在数十位受访者中，只有少数人知道雕漆是什么；有些人懂雕漆，但买不起。这使得雕漆的需求量变得很少。正因为如此，需求无法刺激生产，销量就上不去。

(四)雕漆的主要销售渠道

雕漆的销售平台分为线上和线下两种。马宁说:"我和京东这些网络平台也有合作进行销售,雕漆现在实际上已经适应了这个时代,销售是多渠道的。"

雕漆产品的线上销售平台主要是一些官方网站,如中国工艺集团有限公司[5](简称"中国工艺集团")、京东众筹等。中国工艺集团2007年由原中国工艺品进出口总公司和中国工艺美术(集团)公司两家央企联合重组成立,是由国务院国资委直接管理的中央企业。京东众筹是京东金融的业务板块之一,是互联网金融属性的业务平台。

线上销售渠道便于人们从网上购买雕漆工艺品,对于喜欢在网上购物的年轻一代来说,这些平台为他们提供了一个相对便捷的雕漆购买机会。然而,线上的雕漆销量并不好,说明这个渠道对于雕漆的销售影响很小。人们更喜欢在线下购买雕漆艺术作品。权国立说:"雕漆艺术成品的销售其实在古时候就是指线下的口口相传。用个现在特别时尚的词叫share,我们去作分享。"经过买卖双方的分享,卖家把艺术品介绍给消费者,如果消费者喜欢,就卖给他们。

"线下的销售渠道有两个,一个叫渠道性销售,一个叫口碑性销售。渠道性销售通常是有中国艺术品交易平台,还有工美集团,北京市工美集团就是中国最大的一个集散销售平台,还是推广平台和制作平台。他们会有工美大厦,会有销售窗口,然后还会有像白孔雀艺术世界这样的商厦,以及很多的艺术馆,包括像

---

5. 见http://www.cnacgc.com/。

798这样的画廊等等。"（权国立）

权国立认为，售卖雕漆工艺品的方式有很多，包括通过交谈来传播声誉。许多线下销售平台，如工美集团和画廊，可以方便人们购买雕漆工艺品，因为线下销售渠道的访问量大于线上销售渠道。"像工美、百工坊这样的机构，这些销售艺术品的较有名的平台都是有销售漆器的。"他说，"但更多的高端艺术品是直接从大师手中卖给客户的。"因此，雕漆主要的销售渠道是线下。

因为雕漆工艺品的高价值和有限的销售渠道，它的市场表现在未来几年将保持不变。人们将持续线下购买高端雕漆作品，因为他们很难从网上的图片中了解到想要购买的艺术品的真正价值。目前非常火爆的线上销售对雕漆真实销量的影响不大，因此线上的雕漆市场在未来几年可能将保持不变。

（五）雕漆的替代品

二十世纪八十年代，市场上出现了一种与北京雕漆很相似的替代品，叫注漆。它是通过注塑化学合成的树脂产品而生产出的雕漆替代品。笔者通过采访和查找文献发现，注漆只会影响低端产品市场。

丛玲玲（2008）认为，北京雕漆的主要市场已经被注漆占据。但一些雕漆大师并不认同这一看法，他们认为注漆不会对雕漆造成太大的影响。马宁认为，雕漆和注漆的客户群体完全不同，消费注漆的人永远不会成为雕漆的真正消费者。

"原则上我认为没有影响。第一不存在竞争，因为它的目标人群不一样。不识雕漆之人不是我所敬仰的,如果你本身买的是假雕漆,你还分辨不出来,那凭什么你来买我的真雕漆。第二,如果真是想买好的雕漆作品,一定会对这个领域有很深的认知,要分辨得出来真和假。喜欢真的喜欢好的人,一定不买假的东西。而辨别注漆和雕漆有非常明确的方法,也非常地简单。所以我不认为消费注漆的人群是雕漆未来的潜在客户。我相信只有具有丰富社会阅历、文化积累的人,才是雕漆的潜在客户。"(马宁)

然而,也有一些雕漆从业人士认为,注漆会对雕漆的市场产生巨大影响。

"它对雕漆有很大的影响,尤其是对那些不懂雕漆手艺的人。虽然注漆和雕漆的表面都有纹路,但是注漆没有胎,没有雕刻工艺,也没有天然漆的合成成分。它只是一种红色的东西,甚至可以被外行人区分开来。"(张女士)

所以,要确定雕漆是否会受到注漆的影响,就要考虑雕漆的层次。例如,是日常使用的低端产品还是用于收藏的高端产品。对于专攻高端艺术品的马宁、权国立来说,注漆对高端市场的影响并不大;但对于销售日常低端产品的张女士来说,注漆对低端市场的影响非常大。

(六)旺季与淡季

消费者购买雕漆的理由各不相同。他们中的一些人购买雕漆是为了日常使用，另一些人将它们作为收藏品购买。消费者在一年中的不同时间购买雕漆，这带来了雕漆销售的旺季和淡季。

雕漆销售员张女士说："大多数人都把雕漆作为礼物送给朋友或犒劳自己。"在春节、端午节、中秋节等节日，人们更愿意购买雕漆艺术品。首先，大部分雕漆都是用红漆制成的，红色是中国传统中象征喜庆的颜色。其次，艺术品上的图案通常是吉祥的象征，代表着积极的意义。例如，蝙蝠代表好运，因为"蝠"的读音同"福"。在重阳节，儿女会购买桃图案的产品送给老人，因为桃代表长寿。还有一些像结婚纪念日这样的有特殊意义的日子，人们会购买雕漆，因为有些设计适合夫妻、家人。例如，在中国文化中，孪生的树干代表爱情。此外，雕漆的漆有益健康，能够让人感到平和、放松。

然而，在采访中，有些受访者表示没有明显的旺季和淡季。马宁说："它不会有太大的区别，因为它不是那种通常在节日中出售的产品。它是一个高端艺术品，不会受到节日的影响。"雕漆工厂的经理也说："制作一件雕漆作品需要几个月的时间，所以不可能打折扣。除非它是一个小型作品，但这些不能代表雕漆。"

总而言之，旺季的产生似乎只是因为低端艺术品的销售量远高于正常水平。高端艺术品不会有同样的折扣，因为它的成本太高。每件高端雕刻艺术品都需要几年的时间才能完成。例如，马宁最自豪的艺术品之一《水月观音》花了18个月才完成。显然，这种高端艺术品不受时间和心情的影响，具有自己的生命价值。而那些被称为"行货"（仅为盈利而生产的作品）的低端作品，才有可能因为某个特殊时段的促销而取得较高的销售业绩。

五、结论

综上所述，本研究得出的结论如下。首先，雕漆的成本将会保持稳定，因为雕漆的知名度较低，但雕漆工艺品的主要价值是由雕刻人决定的。由于雕刻人成才的时间非常长，目前雕漆市场不会出现大量成熟的雕刻大师，所以雕漆的价格波动很小。从消费者的角度来看，他们的社会地位和文化素养在短期内都很难改变，因此，消费者的购买行为是相对固定的。另一个主要发现是雕漆的销量。不难看出，从生产时间、劳动力数量、消费者这三个会影响销量的方面来看，雕漆销量将会继续保持稳定。从雕漆的销售渠道来看，虽然线上销售渠道更多，但是喜欢购买高端雕漆工艺品的人，遵从一直以来的传统，倾向于在线下与大师面对面交流和购买，所以销售渠道没有重大改变。此外，雕漆的替代品注漆不能对雕漆高端市场产生很大影响。同时，雕漆工艺品的旺季和淡季也不会影响整个雕漆市场。综上所述，我们总结出雕漆市场的表现在未来会保持稳定。

参考文献：

北京雕漆走在失传边缘[EB/OL]. 华夏经纬（2005-09-05）. http://www.huaxia.com/wh/mjwh/2005/00315979.html.

丛玲玲."北京雕漆"之痛：并非只因"注漆"[J]. 美术观察，2008，（8）：92—96.

冯志坚. 漆树品种分类初探[J]. 中国生漆，1984，（3）.

张瑞琴，任端柱. 不同产地生漆质量探析[J]. 中国生漆，2014，33（3）：35—37.

中国工艺集团有限公司[EB/OL]. http://www.cnacgc.com/.

Diaoqi Market Investigation Report[1]

Gao Yijing (Margaret) Zhang Yixin (Fiona) Wang Zehua (Alex)[2]

Abstract: Through interviews with masters of *Diaoqi* and salespersons, we conclude that in the future, the market of *Diaoqi* will remain stable but unsatisfying. The consumers have two features: rich and knowledgeable. Sales channels are online and offline, but the high-end products are mainly sold via offline channels. The sales of low-end products vary in different selling seasons.

Keywords: Beijing *Diaoqi*, market development trend, cost, consumer group, sales volume, sales channels, impact of substitute (*Zhuqi*), high season and low season

1. Research Background and Objectives

Beijing *Diaoqi* (lacquer carving) is an ancient local traditional handicraft. *Diaoqi* is made by applying dozens of layers of paint to a prepared substrate and then carving with a knife. Even though the materials of *Diaoqi* do not have the same value as those of some other handicrafts, such as jade and porcelain, it is the technique and the craftsmanship that make *Diaoqi* valuable. At the same time, as a result of the high labor cost, long production time, low publicity rate, and other factors, *Diaoqi* has not achieved a high awareness in the market. We hope that through studying on the market of *Diaoqi*, we can find out its market situation, and make an appropriate judgment on its future market trend from a rational perspective.

---

1. The academic advisors of this paper are Eli Smith and Guo Minshuo, teachers of the School of International Education, Beijing Foreign Studies University.
2. The authors of this paper are the 11th grade students of International Curriculum Centre (ICC) of Beijing Foreign Studies University.

2. Literature Review

Based on the keywords of "Beijing *Diaoqi*" and "current situation of *Diaoqi* market", we searched information through academic websites such as cnki.net, etc., and only found a large number of papers on the inheritance and protection of *Diaoqi* and the art of *Diaoqi*, but no research on its market was discovered. Therefore, by reading papers about the art of *Diaoqi*, interviewing the craftsmen, and visiting stores and production studios, we further understood the impact of *Diaoqi*'s production costs, sales channels, sales volume, consumers, high season and low season, and fake product (i.e. *Zhuqi*) on its market. We concluded that despite the existing barriers, the market of *Diaoqi* will be stable in the perceivable future.

3. Research Methods and Procedures

In this paper, the primary materials are collected by interviewing the craftsmen (interview method) and visiting the production studios (field survey).

3.1 Data collection

3.1.1 Participants

Table 1: Biographical information of the participants

Name	Occupation	Years of work experience
Ma Ning	Beijing representative inheritor of Beijing *Hediao* (fruit pit carving) Beijing representative inheritor of Beijing *Diaoqi* The youngest inheritor in Dongcheng District of Beijing *Diaoqi*	10 years
Quan Guoli	One of the directors of a *Diaoqi* production studio	
Ms. Zhang	A salesperson in Baigongfang	
Zhao Haiwei	One of the craftsmen of a *Diaoqi* production studio	

3.1.2 Interview questions

We prepared the following questions:

1) Do you know the current price of *Diaoqi* in the market?
2) What factors do you think determine the price of *Diaoqi*?
3) Who are the main consumer groups of *Diaoqi*?
4) How is the sales volume of *Diaoqi* now?
5) Compared with normal time, is there any change in sales during Chinese festivals, such as the Spring Festival?
6) What are the marketing channels of *Diaoqi*?
7) As far as you know, how is the market of *Diaoqi* affected by *Zhuqi* (the fake product)?

3.2 Data analysis

The data are analyzed and coded.

Table 2: The coding system

Theme	Primary coding	Secondary coding
The market of *Diaoqi* will be stable in the perceivable future	The cost will remain stable	1. The artists charge stable prices 2. Labor costs of craftsmen are stable 3. The difficulty of carving patterns is stable 4. Prices of raw materials are stable
	The consumers are stable	1. High economic capacity 2. High level of knowledge
	The products' supply is not growing	1. It needs a long period of time to finish the products, so the supply of *Diaoqi* is low 2. Labor shortage 3. No increase in the number of consumers
	The sales channels are stable	1. Online: Small quantity, low-end products 2. Offline: Main channel, high-end products
	The substitute of *Diaoqi*	The substitute only affects the low-end market of *Diaoqi*
	High season and low season	High season: There is promotion of low-end products, but the impact is not large

4. Research findings and discussion

Through the research, the market situation of *Diaoqi* is as follows.

4.1 The cost will remain stable in the perceivable future

4.1.1 The price fluctuation of *Diaoqi* is moderate

"In comparison with the price of other Chinese historical and cultural items, *Diaoqi* is currently considered to be at a lower price, and the overall price does not fluctuate." (Ma Ning) Although *Diaoqi* is an aristocratic craft (one of the Eight Wonders of Beijing[3]) and has been passed down from ancient times, it is still not as famous as cloisonné, filigree inlays, etc., and its market is not as good as others'. It may be difficult for ordinary people to understand how *Diaoqi* can have such a high price, with its raw materials so cheap (compared with those of other crafts such as jade carving, ivory carving, etc.), because people who don't have a deep understanding of *Diaoqi* may not know what factors determine its price.

"The status and qualifications of the craftsmen are the major factors affecting the price of *Diaoqi*. For instance, the most expensive artwork of *Diaoqi* available today can be worth at least 10 million yuan. At present, the most expensive piece is probably a screen produced by Mr. Wen Qiangang, and the price of it may reach 130 million yuan. Furthermore, some top masters' works are evaluated at a price of 3 million to 5 million yuan per square meter; and for middle-level masters, like Ma Ning, the price is about 500 thousand

---

3. The Eight Wonders of Beijing are cloisonné, jade carving, ivory carving, *Diaoqi*, gold lacquer inlays, filigree inlays, imperial carpets, and Beijing embroidery, which fully demonstrate the essence of local folk crafts, and were at their peaks of Chinese traditional crafts in the Qing dynasty. Together, they have gradually formed the palace art with Beijing features.

to 800 thousand yuan per square meter. Therefore, the price range of *Diaoqi* is extremely large." (Quan Guoli)

Although the price range is large, the price of *Diaoqi* in the future will not fluctuate violently since the craftsmen have different status and qualifications. According to the research of another group of young researchers, there will not be many new masters entering the *Diaoqi* market because it takes a very long time to train a *Diaoqi* master (See "The Training Process of *Diaoqi* Inheritors").

4.1.2 The labor costs will not change too much

Craftsmen need to be trained for a long time. It is unlikely to find new craftsmen because of long working hours and the tedious nature of making *Diaoqi*; therefore the labor costs will not change too much.

> "A high-level carving technician needs more than 10 years of training. Wen Qiangang said that among 100 people learning *Diaoqi*, 2 or 3 years later, 50 people would drop out to work in the relatively easy jobs like making substrates and polishing. More than half of the remaining 50 would leave in the following 10 years, and only 2 or 3 people would persevere in undertaking the important work of carving. The average age of today's craftsmen is over 50. Nowadays young people are reluctant to be apprenticed due to the difficulty and low revenue of *Diaoqi*." [4]

4.1.3 Designs and patterns of *Diaoqi* tend to be fixed

In addition to the craftsmen, the production of *Diaoqi* also has a great impact on the price. For example, the designs of the products are usually divided into three categories: human figures; mountains, waters, and pavil-

---

4. http://www.huaxia.com/wh/mjwh/2005/00315979.html.

ions; flowers and birds. (Ms. Zhang)

Carving human figures on the surface of lacquer is the most expensive endeavor, because it is more difficult to show a character's face vividly. A craftsman has to be meticulous in carving, depict the facial expressions of the characters, and polish the edges of the characters after carving, so the price of carving human figures remains the highest. The second most expensive are those of mountains, waters, and pavilions. Water has different kinds of waves which can be horizontal or vertical, in oceans or rivers. Therefore, the carving directions of the water in the sea and in the river are totally different. The lines are relatively smooth in the carving of river water, which is not surging forward with great momentum as the sea water, and its pattern is basically flat and straight. As for sea water, the directions of the carving knives are basically spiral due to the fluctuating waves. Pavilions are placed above the waters, because mountains and waters are always put together with pavilions in Chinese traditional culture. The least expensive carvings are those of flowers and birds, because their patterns are basically traditional, relatively fixed, and easy to carve. The most common patterns are jasmines of the Ming dynasty style; peonies symbolic of richness and prosperity; and plum blossoms expressing auspiciousness, which sometimes are accompanied by magpies. (Ms. Zhang)

Despite the different prices of different patterns, as a traditional craft passed down for more than a thousand years, the designs and making process of *Diaoqi* are fixed, and therefore the production costs are stable.

4.1.4 The supply and demand of raw materials are relatively stable

"Lacquer from different regions can be used to perform different functions. The lacquer produced in Beijing or Vietnam is relatively cheap and good for painting, not for carving; so the low-end artworks of *Diaoqi* are usually produced with these materials. However, the lacquer made in Hubei province is more suitable for producing *Diaoqi* due to its lightness and drought tolerance. That's why our workshop has cooperation with the local companies producing crude lacquer in Hubei." (Ma Ning)

In addition, crude lacquer is one of China's specialties. Its output accounts for about 80% of the world's total production. In China, except Heilongjiang, Jilin, Inner Mongolia, Ningxia and Xinjiang, other provinces and regions are abundant in this resource, with the richest areas in Qinling, Daba Mountains, Wudang Mountains, Wu Mountains, Wuling Mountains, Dalou Mountains, and Wumeng Mountains. (Feng, 1984) Shaanxi, Hubei, Chongqing, Yunnan, Guizhou, Sichuan and Gansu are the main lacquer producing areas, and there are more than 60 key lacquer producing counties. According to the survey and incomplete statistics, crude lacquer sales in recent years in Chinese market are 500-600 tons, of which more than 300 tons are produced in Shaanxi province, accounting for more than 60% of the total. (Zhang et al., 2014)

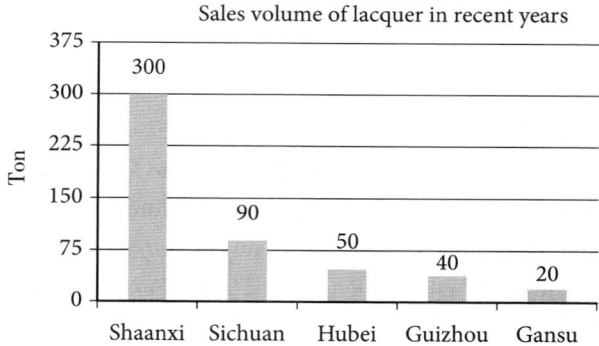

Figure 1: Crude lacquer sales in recent years (Zhang et al., 2014)

There are many production bases of lacquer with significant output. The price is determined by demand and supply. When demand and supply are constant, the price is constant. Therefore, the cost of raw materials won't change too much since the output and sources of lacquer are stable.

Furthermore, the size of *Diaoqi* is always a key factor for value. The thickness of the lacquer determines the size of the artwork. The thicker the lacquer on the surface is, the larger the size of the artwork will be. However, these are all stable due to a thousand years of practice, so the cost will be stable. Since the factors affecting the price of *Diaoqi* are relatively stable, the price of *Diaoqi* product won't fluctuate wildly.

4.2 Main consumer groups of *Diaoqi*

There are several factors that affect the consumption of *Diaoqi*.

4.2.1 The financial ability of the buyers

From the interviews, we've found that people who have higher social status are more willing and better able to buy large *Diaoqi* artworks.

> "Since ancient times, *Diaoqi* has not entered the homes of ordinary people. They have been owned by the royal families and aristocrats. Therefore, people who accept and appreciate them now are those who have matching purchasing power and social status." (Quan Guoli)

It can be easily found that the people who have higher social status have more ability to buy *Diaoqi* products. Mr. Zhao Haiwei said, "They are the people who can afford. Most people cannot afford." People of the middle class would buy a few smaller *Diaoqi* products that can be used in daily life because they may not be able to afford large *Diaoqi* artworks or do not understand the value of them.

4.2.2 The level of knowledge of the buyers

In addition, in the aspect of knowledge, consumers of *Diaoqi* are more knowledgeable about Chinese culture and some of them even know the procedures of *Diaoqi* production. It can help them evaluate the true value of *Diaoqi* and make purchase decisions. Many consumers of *Diaoqi* love collecting. Mr. Ma said, "The first type of buyers is the collectors who really understand the art." Mr. Zhao said, "I think there are some wealthy people who like to collect." Mr. Ma and Mr. Zhao both thought that many of the buyers who are willing to buy *Diaoqi* are interested in collecting and understand the artistic value of *Diaoqi*.

"Unless you have a sufficient accumulation of knowledge about Chinese culture, the *Diaoqi* masters may not necessarily sell their works to you, even if you have money. They want to talk to you first to guarantee that you are a true lover of the art and you know how to cherish it. They want their art to be in safe hands." (Quan Guoli)

Mr. Quan thought that people who are wealthy enough to buy *Diaoqi* made by masters do not necessarily meet the requirements set by the *Diaoqi* masters, and therefore they are not eligible for the purchase. Mr. Ma, however, thought that we should also sell *Diaoqi* to those who are rich enough to consume, despite their lack of knowledge. He thought this would create a positive atmosphere because the revenue would increase and it is good for the general well-being of the industry.

Many consumers buy artworks because of the materials, the visual impressions, the ideological values, the social values or the historical values. *Diaoqi* is far less famous internationally than porcelain, and the materials of *Diaoqi* are not as valuable as other materials such as jade. People who buy *Diaoqi* value the carving techniques instead of the materials. Thus, the main buyers of high-end *Diaoqi* artworks are the people who have high social status and are willing and wealthy enough to buy them. However, these people only comprise a small proportion of consumers of artworks. So, we believe the people who are most likely to buy *Diaoqi* will remain stable in the following years. In summary, the proportion of consumers who buy *Diaoqi* is stable, which leads to a stable *Diaoqi* market in the future.

4.3 Sales of *Diaoqi*

4.3.1 Production time influences sales

Mr. Ma said, "Actually, the sales of *Diaoqi* are not very high, but this is mainly because the supply cannot satisfy the demand. But with regard to individual artworks, the sales could maintain the survival of the art." *Diaoqi* products are in short supply, so that the demand in the market cannot be satisfied. *Diaoqi* is a time-consuming and energy-consuming craft. It is very hard for the artist to finish many works in a short time.

> "The longest period of time in *Diaoqi* production is the work time of craftsmen. For a *Diaoqi* teapot, the production cycle is 180 days, i.e. half a year. It takes almost 2 to 3 months to paint layers over layers of lacquer on the base, and another month to let it dry. The carving takes 2 to 3 weeks, and the polishing takes 10 days." (Quan Guoli)

As shown by the masters, for every high-quality product, each production step must be carried out meticulously with sufficient time, which leads to the shortage of supply in the market.

4.3.2 The number of workers influences sales

The lack of experienced workers in the factory restricts the output of *Diaoqi* artwork.

> "There are around 100 to 200 people who work in this field. Only about 20 of them can be counted as masters, including provincial and municipal level ones. With apprentices included, so far there are less than 300 practitioners in this field." (Quan Guoli)

According to what Mr. Quan said, it is clear that there are only a few people who have the ability to make *Diaoqi*, and only a smaller number of them can be called *Diaoqi* artists.

4.3.3 The consumers influence sales

As a kind of artwork, *Diaoqi* needs to be bought by people who can understand and afford it, while only a small number of people have basic knowledge of *Diaoqi*. According to our street interviews with dozens of passersby, only a few of them know about *Diaoqi*; furthermore, those who understand *Diaoqi* may not be able to pay for it. This limits the demand for *Diaoqi*. The demand for *Diaoqi* cannot stimulate its production, and the sales are low.

4.4 The sales channels of *Diaoqi*

There are online and offline sales platforms of *Diaoqi*. Mr. Ma said, "I'm with online shopping platforms like JD.com to sell my products. The sales of *Diaoqi* have already caught up with the new trend, and there are many ways to sell them."

The online platforms refer to some official websites, such as China National Arts & Crafts Group Corporation Limited (CNACGC)[5] and JD.com Crowdfunding. CNACGC is a central enterprise directly controlled by State-owned Assets Supervision and Administration Commission of the State Council, and jointly established by the original China National Arts and Crafts Import & Export Corporation and the China National Arts & Crafts (Group) Corporation in 2007. JD.com Crowdfunding is one of the business segments of JD.com Finance, a business platform with internet financial properties. For the younger generation who prefer to buy things online, these platforms provide an opportunity for them to get access to and even to buy *Diaoqi*.

However, sales on the online sales platforms are low. People prefer to buy *Diaoqi* offline because they think it is more reliable to see the actual work in person. Mr. Quan said, "The sales of the finished art of *Diaoqi* mean face-to-face talk, just like in ancient times. It is just like 'sharing'." The sellers should introduce the artworks to consumers and they share their joy and appreciation of the artworks.

"There are two offline sales channels: one is selling in distribu-

---

5. http://www.cnacgc.com/.

tion stores, and the other is selling via word-of-mouth recommendation. Distribution stores mainly refer to Chinese art trade platform and Beijing Gongmei Group. The latter is the largest distribution and sales platform of Chinese artworks. It has stores such as Gongmei Mall, where there is a display and sales of *Diaoqi* artworks. Others are shops and art galleries, such as 798 Art District." (Quan Guoli)

Mr. Quan thought that among the many ways to sell *Diaoqi*, art galleries and shops were effective in promoting purchases because they had more customers. But most of the high-end artworks are sold from the masters directly to the clients. So selling by word-of-mouth recommendation remains the most reliable way of sales promotion. Therefore, the main sales channel is offline channels.

The market of *Diaoqi* will not change in the future because of the high value but limited sales channels. *Diaoqi* collectors will continue to buy directly from the masters because it is hard to discern the true value of the artworks by scrutinizing the pictures on the websites. At present the popular online sales channels have little effect on the overall sales. Thus, the market of *Diaoqi* will stay stable in the following years.

4.5 The substitute of *Diaoqi*

In the 1980s, the appearance of a substitute of Beijing *Diaoqi* in the market brought forth much confusion. The new product, named *Zhuqi*, is very similar to *Diaoqi*, and is made by injecting synthetic resin into a mold. Through interviews and literature reviews, we have found that *Zhuqi* affects only the low-end market.

Cong (2008) claimed that the main market of Beijing *Diaoqi* had been occupied by *Zhuqi*. However, according to our interviews, some masters have different opinions; they believe that *Zhuqi* does not make an enormous impact on *Diaoqi*. As Ma Ning mentioned, *Diaoqi* and *Zhuqi* have totally different target groups. Those who purchase *Zhuqi* will never grow to be the genuine consumers of *Diaoqi*.

"In principle, I think there is no impact. Firstly, there is no competition. Those who don't know *Diaoqi* are not the people I respect. If you bought a fake *Diaoqi* artwork, and you can't tell the differences, then I would perceive you do not have the quality to be my client. Secondly, if someone really wants to buy valuable *Diaoqi* artworks, they must gain deep understanding of this art and learn to tell the genuine from the fake. In other words, if you really like this handicraft, you will refuse to buy a fake one. In addition, the ways to distinguish *Diaoqi* and *Zhuqi* are clear and simple. I don't think that the people who consume *Zhuqi* are the potential consumers of *Diaoqi* in the future, because *Diaoqi* is liked by people who have social experiences and knowledge, and are not easily blinded by fake products." (Ma Ning)

However, there are some *Diaoqi* practitioners who believe that *Zhuqi* may exert a huge influence on the market of *Diaoqi*.

"It has a great impact on *Diaoqi*, especially for those who don't understand the craftsmanship of *Diaoqi*. They both have carved lines on the surface. However, *Zhuqi* is just a kind of red stuff which can even be distinguished by laymen. It is simply not natural lacquer." (Ms. Zhang)

We believe that the disagreeing opinions of Mr. Ma and Ms. Zhang can be explained by the price of *Diaoqi*. The price gap between a *Diaoqi* artwork for daily use and a larger piece for collection is huge. For Mr. Ma and Mr. Quan who are working on the high-end artworks with very high prices, *Zhuqi* does not have much impact. But Ms. Zhang who focuses on the sales of daily items has witnessed the erosion of the *Diaoqi* market caused by *Zhuqi* in recent years. So *Zhuqi* has huge negative impact on low-end market but little impact on high-end market.

4.6 High season and low season

Consumers buy *Diaoqi* for different reasons, some for daily uses, and some for collection. Consumers buy *Diaoqi* at different times of the year, creating the high season and low season.

The salesperson of *Diaoqi*, Ms. Zhang said, "Most people buy *Diaoqi* as a gift for friends or for themselves." During holidays, such as the Spring Festival, the Mid-Autumn Festival, and the Dragon Boat Festival, people are more willing to buy *Diaoqi* artworks. There are several reasons for this. Firstly, most *Diaoqi* artworks are made with red lacquer, and red means prosperity and happiness in Chinese culture. Secondly, the design patterns on the artworks are usually symbols of auspiciousness, representing good fortune. For example, the pattern of a bat means a good luck, because in Chinese, the pronunciation of the word "bat" is the same as the word "happiness". The pattern of a peach is a sign of longevity, and *Diaoqi* with the design of peaches is purchased as a gift to the elderly in the Double Ninth Festival, a festival celebrating longevity. On some special occasions, like wedding anniversaries, people buy *Diaoqi* with the designs suitable for couples. For example, in Chinese culture, twinned trunks represent the love between couples. Lastly, the natural lacquer is beneficial to one's health and will make people feel peaceful and relaxed.

However, some interviewees said that there was neither high season nor low season. Mr. Ma said, "Holidays won't make a big difference, because such high-end artworks are not the kind of product sold in the festivals." Mr. Quan said, "*Diaoqi* is not like furniture. It takes several months to make a piece of work. Discount is not offered unless it is a very small piece of work. But small-sized pieces cannot represent the art."

In conclusion, the high season of the market appears because the sales of low-end artworks have become higher than normal. The high-end artworks will not be offered the same discount even on holidays. Great *Diaoqi* artworks require several years to finish. For example, one of the greatest artworks of Mr. Ma – the "Moon-and-Water-Buddha" (*Shuiyue Guanyin*) took him 18 months to finish. This work is two meters high and one meter wide. Apparently, the value of great artworks is not affected by holidays or the mood of buyers. Only low-end products will achieve high sales for certain period of time due to discount or promotion.

5. Conclusion

To sum up, we conclude that the cost of *Diaoqi* will remain stable and therefore the fluctuation of the price is very small. From the perspective of the market, the consumers' understanding and recognition of *Diaoqi* are hard to change in a short term. Thus, the consumers' buying behavior is relatively stable. We also find that the sales will remain stable as the three factors that influence it – the production time, number of workers and consumers – remain unchanged. One thing worth noticing is that although there are more online sales channels, people who prefer to buy high-end *Diaoqi* artworks are more likely to talk to masters face to face to make sure that the artworks are up to their standards. Besides, the substitute product, *Zhuqi*, cannot make huge impact on the market of *Diaoqi*. The high and low seasons of *Diaoqi* sales cannot affect the whole market neither. In conclusion, we predict the market of *Diaoqi* will be stable in the future.

References:

Beijing Diaoqi on the Verge of Extinction [EB/OL]. Huaxia (2005-09-05). http://www.huaxia.com/wh/mjwh/2005/00315979.html.

China National Arts & Crafts Group Corporation Limited [EB/OL]. http://www.cnacgc.com/.

Cong, Lingling. Pain of "Beijing Diaoqi" : Not Just Because of "Zhuqi" [J]. Art Observation, 2008, (08): 92-96.

Feng, Zhijian. Exploring the Varieties of Lacquer Trees [J]. Chinese Crude Lacquer,

1984, (3).

Zhang, Ruiqin, & Ren, Duanzhu. Exploration of the Quality of Lacquer from Different Regions [J]. Chinese Crude Lacquer, 2014, 33 (3): 35-37.

北京高中生对于雕漆认知度的调查[1]

常轩臻　王琬莹　刘　宁[2]

【摘要】 雕漆作为中国非物质文化遗产之一,虽历史悠久,但在当代社会的推广和传承却受到阻碍。本研究通过对北京高中生这一群体的结构式访谈,发现他们虽然对雕漆的认知度偏低,但却对其有着多元化的第一印象。同时,北京高中生了解雕漆的途径是多样的,其中纪录片和博物馆是两个重要渠道。另外,北京高中生认为雕漆不仅是中国文化的表达,而且具有装饰性、传承性、实用性等特征。他们还提出,需要采取多种措施来提高雕漆的认知度,从而让高中生更好地了解和传承雕漆。

【关键词】 雕漆　北京高中生　认知度　推广与传承

一、研究背景与研究目标

雕漆作为中国传统艺术形式和中国非物质文化遗产之一,有一千四百余年的历史,横跨唐、宋、元、明、清五个朝代。雕漆在明、清两朝主要用作皇家宫廷工艺器物,历来具有崇高的社会地位和艺术价值。然而,如今国内雕漆从业者仅有120余人,而且在雕漆行业拥有"中国工艺美术大师"头衔者仅有5位。中国从农业社会向工业社会转变的过程中,农业文化、手工业文化与工业文化发生了冲

---

1. 本调研报告科研指导教师为北京外国语大学国际教育集团升学规划部教师刘文婕。
2. 本调研报告的三位作者均为北京外国语大学国际课程中心十一年级学生。

撞。雕漆产业因为成本相对较高、工序烦琐、技术性强等因素，在实用领域无可阻挡地呈衰落趋势。生产企业化以后，在政府的介入下，雕漆产业于二十世纪五六十年代依赖单纯的外贸出口，曾出现过阶段性繁荣，但很快重显萎靡之势，有着悠久历史的雕漆艺术已经走到了创新与发展的紧要关头。

基于雕漆的现状，本文旨在了解当今北京高中生这一群体对于中国非物质文化遗产雕漆的了解程度与认知深度。在对北京27所高中的部分高一和高二学生的访谈中，本文调研了以下几个问题：

1）您是否听说过雕漆？
2）您认为雕漆美吗？
3）当您看到雕漆时，您的第一印象是什么？
4）您是从哪些途径了解到雕漆的？
5）看到雕漆作品，您认为它代表了中华文化的什么概念？
6）您认为雕漆有哪些用途？
7）雕漆已经被认证为中国非物质文化遗产，您觉得我们应该通过什么方式来保护和传承它？
8）如果您有机会学习雕漆，您会花费时间和精力去做这件事情吗？

二、文献检索

我们使用"雕漆""北京高中生""认知度"作为关键词，在中国知网进行检索，并没有发现任何相关内容或研究。因此可以说，我们的调查在研究年轻群体对于雕漆的认知现状这个方面有参考价值。

三、研究方法与研究步骤

本文的研究方法主要为质性研究。具体的做法是,采用结构式访谈的方式获取数据,并对数据进行分析。

(一) 结构式访谈

本调研按照访谈提纲对每位受访学生进行提问,不随意增加或减少访谈问题。

本调研样本对象为来自北京不同类型高中的中学生,共回收有效数据426条(来自63人),样本信息如下。

表1:样本的基本信息(N=63)

所在年级	样本量	人数占比
高一	50	79.4%
高二	13	20.6%
所在学校	样本量	人数占比
公立学校	40	63.5%
私立学校	23	36.5%
性别	样本量	人数占比
男	23	36.5%
女	40	63.5%

(二) 数据收集和分析

通过针对北京高中生的结构式访谈来收集数据,随后进行数据编码、数据分析和数据汇总。

四、研究发现和讨论

本次访谈所收集的数据共426条,经编码后,我们围绕北京高中生对雕漆的认知度这一研究主题,并结合上述8个具体的研究问题,将数据归纳为4个大类:对雕漆的认知程度、了解雕漆的途径、雕漆与中国文化的关系,以及对雕漆的保护与传承。

表2:4类主要发现情况(N=426)

编号	类别	条目频数
1	认知程度	191
2	了解途径	20
3	与中国文化的关系	80
4	保护与传承	135

下文将根据研究问题,详细阐述表2中各类别的具体研究发现并展开相应讨论。

(一)认知程度

认知程度的条目频数共191条,根据受访学生的回答内容,我们进一步将认知程度分为北京高中生对雕漆是否了解及他们对雕漆的第一印象。

表3对这2项分类所包含的研究发现进行了解读。

表3：雕漆认知程度下的二级分类及其解读

编号	类别	解读
1	是否了解	是否知道雕漆
2	第一印象	是否认为雕漆美
		看到雕漆，有什么第一印象

1.对雕漆的认知程度低

表4：北京高中生是否知道雕漆（N=63）

编号	是否知道	人数	百分比
1	是	19	30.2%
2	否	44	69.8%

由表4可见，在受访的63位北京高中生中，仅有19位听说过雕漆，约占总人数的30%。由此可知，受访的大多数北京高中生对雕漆没有任何了解；换言之，雕漆在北京高中生中的认知程度普遍较低。其原因可能是：雕漆在中国历史上一直是帝王使用的奢华之物，属于皇家室内家具陈设的主项，且雕漆较其他漆器的用料更加考究，工艺更加复杂，因而也更为尊贵。由于雕漆具有显赫的皇家使用功能、悠久的历史、高超的技艺、丰富的文化内涵及独特的艺术形式，一直属于奢华的工艺品或生活奢侈品，所以北京高中生与雕漆的接触机会较少，对它的了解程度自然较低。因此，在高中生中推广雕漆这一非物质文化遗产是必要和迫切的。

2.对雕漆的第一印象多样

本研究的第二个问题是通过展示一张雕漆成品的图片，询问受访学生对雕漆的第一印象。在采访数据中，大多数受访学生表示："这是一种非常美丽的工艺品。"根据受访学生对雕漆美观程度的评价，调查反馈如表5所示。

表5：北京高中生对雕漆外观的第一印象（N=63）

编号	回答	频次	百分比
1	很美	19	30.2%
2	好看	34	54.0%
3	一般	5	7.9%
4	不好看	4	6.3%
5	不确定	1	1.6%

从数据中可见，大部分受访学生都很欣赏雕漆工艺品，并被雕漆的外表所吸引，总占比约84%。同时，统计数据也表明，有一小部分受访学生对雕漆的第一印象感觉一般，甚至并不具有好感，占比约14%。此外，个别受访学生对雕漆的第一印象并不确定，占比约2%。由此可知，受访学生对雕漆的第一印象普遍良好，且绝大多数都表达出对雕漆的喜爱。

根据受访学生对接下来3个问题的回答，本文进一步将高中生对雕漆的第一印象分为象征符号、个人感受、匠人手艺和功能性。

表6：北京高中生对于雕漆第一印象的拆分

编号	类别	解读	百分比
1	象征符号	借助某人某物的具体形象，以表现某种抽象的概念、思想和情感	39.7%

续表

编号	类别	解读	百分比
2	个人感受	以观看者的角度对于雕漆的认知	30.2%
3	匠人手艺	古代匠人巧妙绝伦的工艺	15.9%
4	功能性	意指事物或方法所发挥的有利作用	14.3%

注：表中百分比相加大于100%是由保留一位小数的四舍五入所致。

表7：北京高中生对于雕漆第一印象的进一步拆分

类别	细分	百分比
象征符号	社会阶级	63.5%
	传统历史	36.5%
个人感受	作品本身	63.5%
	情绪表达	36.5%
匠人手艺	精湛的技艺	60.3%
	制作的过程	39.7%
功能性	日常用品	77.8%
	装饰用品	22.2%

首先，根据表6，北京高中生对雕漆的第一印象是多种多样的，而这种多样性主要体现在象征符号、个人感受、匠人手艺和功能性这4点。其中，很多受访学生都提到雕漆的象征意义，占总受访人数的约40%。由此可见，在北京高中生中，雕漆普遍被看作一种象征符号。而在表7对象征符号的具体分类中，63.5%的受访学生表达了雕漆与社会阶级的紧密联系，提到了"上层皇室""不像是一般老百姓

会使用的"和"皇家用品，有钱人才会买的东西"。据此推测，由于雕漆在古代作为皇家宫廷工艺器物，历来具有崇高的社会地位，因此对于了解雕漆的北京高中生来说，他们把雕漆与社会阶级联系在一起是受到雕漆历史影响的。

其次，表6显示，在北京高中生对于雕漆的第一印象中，个人感受占据了约30%，是仅次于象征符号的另一印象。而在个人感受中，有63.5%的受访学生可以对雕漆作品本身进行评论，如"精致典雅、花纹繁复、图案古老""花纹精美"和"传统古朴"。而另外36.5%的受访学生表达了其主观情绪，提及"一种震撼"和"没什么感觉"。因此得出，北京高中生对雕漆的评价更偏向于美学角度。这一发现确实超出了我们的预期，因为我们原本认为高中生没有足够的知识和能力从美学角度去评价一件艺术作品。

再者，有近16%的受访学生提到了匠人手艺，包括精湛的技艺（60.3%）和制作的过程（39.7%），受访学生具体描述为"工艺精湛""技艺高超""想到一个匠人在角落雕刻着他的作品"。另外，约14%的受访学生对雕漆的第一印象是它的功能性，包含"大盘子""碗""茶具"等日常用品，以及"窗花""艺术品"等装饰用品。

(二) 多样的了解途径

关于了解雕漆的途径，本研究共回收了20条有效数据。通过访谈得知，有一半受访学生是通过日常媒介了解到雕漆的，有四分之一的受访学生从日常对话中了解到雕漆这个概念，另有四分之一则通过展览了解到雕漆，如表8所示。

表8:北京高中生了解雕漆的途径(N=20)

调查反馈	数量	百分比
日常媒介	10	50.0%
日常对话	5	25.0%
展览	5	25.0%

在访谈过程中,受访的北京高中生有5位表示自己在与老师、家人和朋友的对话中了解到雕漆,这其中又有2位受访学生表明是通过与老师的对话来了解雕漆的。由此得出,老师在提高北京高中生对雕漆的认知度方面的作用相当大。此外,还有5位受访学生表示在博物馆里看到过雕漆作品。可见,博物馆作为一种传播载体,能给现代的高中生提供雕漆的知识与信息。

更重要的是,最普遍的雕漆了解途径是日常媒介,占比50%。其中有5人提及纪录片,另外5人分别提及书籍、电影、社交媒体、网络和新闻报道。从纪录片中看到雕漆艺术的人数和从博物馆中看到的人数是相等的(均为5人),并且都占据总体数据的较大比例(25%)。因此可得出,博物馆展出和纪录片播放是现代高中生了解雕漆最主要的2种途径。

(三)雕漆与中国文化的关系

1.雕漆是中国文化的表达

经过对数据的编码以及分析,本研究发现北京高中生认为雕漆是一种文化的表达。

赵旭东(2009)提道:"如果说文化包括了人类存在的各个方面,

那么人的表达就是通过文化而得以实现的，也可以径直而简略地说，人的表达就是文化的表达，人借助文化的表达而实现自我的表达。"

关于雕漆与中国文化的关系，本文收集了共80条有效数据，将其具体分为4个大类，分别是：工匠精神、文化精神、象征意义和情感寓意。其中，大多数受访学生提到了雕漆所体现出的工匠精神，占比37.5%，其次是雕漆体现的文化精神（26.3%）、象征意义（18.8%）和情感寓意（17.5%），如表9所示。

表9：北京高中生对于雕漆与中国文化关系的认知（N=80）

编号	文化	解读	百分比
1	工匠精神	工匠对自己的产品精雕细琢、精益求精，具有完美的精神理念	37.5%
2	文化精神	精神文化是人类在物质文化基础上产生的一种人类所特有的意识形态，它是人类各种意识观念的集合	26.3%
3	象征意义	用具体事物表现某些抽象意义	18.8%
4	情感寓意	寄托或蕴含某种思想感情表达	17.5%

注：表中百分比相加大于100%是由保留一位小数的四舍五入所致。

表10显示，受访学生反馈的工匠精神主要包括工匠精细的技艺手法（46.7%）、追求完美和富有耐心的匠心精神（46.7%）和在雕漆上凝聚的工匠智慧（6.7%），例如受访学生提到的"精致考究""严谨的精神"和"智慧结晶"。在文化精神方面，大多数学生提及文化传统（76.2%），如"天人合一"和"兼容并蓄"，但也有学生表达"雕漆和传承的精神有关"，而且"雕漆不仅仅是外表美丽，更是中华传统文化多样性的体现"。雕漆还有一定的象征意义。受访学生提到最多

的是龙的象征（53.3%），还用"皇宫贵族""皇权"等词来表述其与皇室的历史关联（46.7%）。另外，雕漆也是情感寓意表达的一种方式，85.7%的受访学生提到了它所蕴含的美好寓意，如"喜庆""吉祥"和"美好生活的向往"；而14.3%的受访学生直接提到雕漆具有情感表达作用。

表10：北京高中生对于雕漆与中国文化关系的认知细分

类别	细分	百分比
工匠精神(N=30)	技艺手法	46.7%
	匠心精神	46.7%
	工匠智慧	6.7%
文化精神(N=21)	文化传统	76.2%
	民族传承	14.3%
	文化多样性	9.5%
象征意义(N=15)	龙的象征	53.3%
	皇室皇权	46.7%
情感寓意(N=14)	美好寓意	85.7%
	情感表达	14.3%

注：部分类别中的百分比相加大于100%是由保留一位小数的四舍五入所致。

2.雕漆用途的多样性

面向对雕漆有一定了解的学生，我们进一步询问了其对雕漆用途的认知。其中，受访学生主要有3种说法：雕漆的装饰性、雕漆的实用价值、雕漆的继承与传承。

表11：北京高中生对雕漆用途的认知（N=31）

回答	数量	百分比
装饰性	13	41.9%
实用价值	13	41.9%
继承与传承	5	16.1%

注：表中百分比相加小于100%是由保留一位小数的四舍五入所致。

在受访学生中，近42%的学生认为雕漆可以作为家中的一种装饰品，比如"花瓶""屏风"等等；同时，还有近42%的学生认为雕漆具有一定的实用价值，建议将其制作成实用产品，其中有3名学生提到了"珠宝盒子"，2名学生提到了"手机壳"，还有"茶壶""手镯""盘子"和"器具上的防滑材料"。此外，约16%的学生认为雕漆是国家文化的一种传承形式，可以用来继承。更具体地说，受访学生认为雕漆是一种"精神传承""中华文化传承"或"手工业传承"。总而言之，在大多数受访的北京高中生心目中，雕漆不仅实用，而且富有文化意义。

(四)雕漆的保护与传承

1.对雕漆的多种保护措施

雕漆现已成为国家非物质文化遗产之一，北京高中生认为应该更好地保护和传承这项技艺。根据受访学生的反馈，我们把他们提出的保护和传承措施分为5个大类：公众意识提高、线上宣传、线下宣传、应用性实践和政府机制建立。本研究一共收集到73条有效数据。

表12：北京高中生认为保护雕漆的措施（N=73）

编号	保护措施	数量	百分比
1	公众意识	31	42.5%
2	线下宣传	18	24.7%
3	应用性实践	10	13.7%
4	政府机制	7	9.6%
5	线上宣传	7	9.6%

注：表中百分比相加大于100%是由保留一位小数的四舍五入所致。

由表12可见，提高公众意识这一项占比最大（42.5%），可通过舆论的宣传和监督，引起大众对雕漆的普遍关注。例如，有受访学生提到，通过培训中小学教师来创造和提供学习雕漆的机会，而学生是公众保护意识的"继承者"，通过提高非物质文化遗产保护者的保护意识和文化知识水平，可以提高非物质文化遗产保护的质量。

相较之下，占比最小的是政府机制和线上宣传，均为9.6%，而这一结果出乎我们的预料。政府作为具有官方权威性和影响力的机关，可以通过制定政策对非物质文化遗产的继承机制给以优惠，或通过发动大众保护非物质文化遗产的举措来提高雕漆的普及度与认知度。另外，线上宣传，如利用网媒等载体进行宣传，具有受众广、传播快、信息量大的特点和优势，网媒已成为公众接收信息的主要渠道。因此，通过开展雕漆的线上宣传，媒体可以让传统文化更贴近大众，走进大众的生活，且更有利于让年轻人传承传统文化。

2．对雕漆不同的传承态度

在针对北京高中生对雕漆传承态度的调查中，高中生总体呈现出

2种截然不同的观点：一是有意愿去学习雕漆，二是没有意愿去学习雕漆。本研究共收集了62条有效数据，如表13所示。

表13：北京高中生学习雕漆的意愿（N=62）

编号	意愿	数量	百分比
1	愿意	43	69.4%
2	不愿意	19	30.6%

可以看出，大多数受访学生（69.4%）都愿意学习雕漆。显然，雕漆作为国家非物质文化遗产之一，具有很强的吸引力和魅力。

对于有意愿学习雕漆的学生，我们总结了3个主要原因：时间管理、个人对于雕漆的认知，以及雕漆所散发的魅力。本研究一共收集了43条有效数据，如表14所示。

表14：北京高中生愿意学习雕漆的原因（N=43）

编号	原因	数量	百分比
1	个人认知	28	65.1%
2	时间管理	8	18.6%
3	雕漆的魅力	7	16.3%

可以看出，个人对雕漆认知所占的百分比（65.1%）大于其他两个原因的总和，这意味着北京高中生一旦对雕漆的认知达到一定程度，就会自觉自愿地去学习和保护雕漆这门古老的中国艺术。例如，一些受访学生认为他们有责任保护和传承雕漆，因为雕漆是老祖宗留下来的东西；也有受访学生表示把雕漆当作一种信仰。

表15：北京高中生不愿意学习雕漆的原因（N=19）

编号	原因	数量	百分比
1	个人认知	13	68.4%
2	时间管理	6	31.6%

表15显示了北京高中生不愿意学习雕漆的原因。其中，最主要的原因是个人认知，占68.4%。这表明现在的一部分北京高中生对历史悠久的雕漆技术兴趣不大。随着科技发展和社会进步，北京高中生对更新奇的事物感兴趣，比如人工智能。例如，有受访学生说道："大概也不太想学习雕漆，因为兴趣不在这一块儿。"

此外，北京高中生没有任何额外的时间去做其他事情，包括学习雕漆。采访中有同学表示："不会学习雕漆，因为现在学习很忙。"的确，对于北京高中生来说，他们面临着相对繁重的学业压力，入学考试和未来的挑战使得他们无暇他顾。

五、总结

随着现代市场的兴起，雕漆这种制作周期长、技术人才稀缺的传统技艺似乎难以适应时代的要求。技艺精湛的雕漆大师大部分已经逝去，而当今的年轻人对雕漆没有足够的认知，这使得雕漆逐渐衰落。因此，本文的研究目的是探究雕漆在北京高中生这一群体中的认知度。

通过研究，本文发现北京高中生对于雕漆的认知度偏低，但他们对雕漆的第一印象却是多元化的，主要体现在象征符号、匠人手艺、个人感受和功能性。同时，高中生了解雕漆的途径也是多样化的，其中有很大一部分高中生都是通过纪录片和博物馆这2个主要的传播渠道去了解雕漆。

本文另一个重要发现是北京高中生认为雕漆是中华文化的表达，他们从工匠精神、文化精神、象征意义和情感寓意这4个方面来阐述雕漆蕴含的中华文化。另外，雕漆不仅有装饰性，还有传承性、实用性等多种特征。因此，采取多种保护措施来提升雕漆的认知度是非常重要的。我们可以通过提高公众意识、线上线下宣传、应用性实践、建立政府机制等方式，让当代高中生更加了解雕漆的内涵，了解非物质文化遗产，让雕漆传承下去。

参考文献：

赵旭东.文化的表达：人类学的视野[M].北京：中国人民大学出版社，2009.

Beijing High School Students' Cognition of *Diaoqi*[1]

Chang Xuanzhen Wang Wanying Liu Ning[2]

Abstract: As part of Chinese intangible cultural heritage, *Diaoqi* has a long history, but its promotion and inheritance in contemporary society has been hindered. Through a structured interview of high school students in Beijing, this paper finds that they have diversified first impressions of *Diaoqi*, although they have a low cognition of it. At the same time, the channels through which they get access to *Diaoqi* are diversified, with documentaries and museum exhibitions the two important ones. In addition, high school students in Beijing believe that *Diaoqi* not only is an expression of Chinese culture, but also has a variety of characteristics including decorativeness, inheritability and practicality. They also propose to take a variety of measures to popularize the cognition of *Diaoqi*, so that contemporary high school students can better understand and pass on *Diaoqi*.

Keywords: *Diaoqi*, Beijing high school students, awareness, promotion and inheritance

1. Research Background and Objectives

As one of the traditional Chinese national arts, and as part of the Chinese intangible cultural heritage, *Diaoqi* has a history of more than 1400 years, spanning five dynasties including the Tang, Song, Yuan, Ming and Qing dynasties. In the Ming and Qing dynasties, *Diaoqi* was mainly used as royal palace handicrafts, which always had high social status and artistic

---

1. The academic advisors of this paper are Liu Wenjie, from the Counselling Division of BFSU International Education Group; and Dana Melchior, a teacher from EPlus of BFSU International Group, Beijing Foreign Studies University.
2. The authors of this paper are the 11th grade students of the International Curriculum Centre (ICC) of Beijing Foreign Studies University.

value. However, nowadays there are only about 120 domestic *Diaoqi* practitioners, among whom only 5 hold the title of "Chinese Master of Arts and Crafts" in the *Diaoqi* industry. During the transformation from agricultural society to industrial society, the Chinese agricultural culture and handicraft culture collided with the industrial culture. Due to factors like relatively high cost, complicated process, and demanding techniques, the *Diaoqi* industry showed an inexorable decline in the practical field. After the industrialization of production and intervention by the government in the 1950s and 1960s, depending on pure export, the *Diaoqi* industry appeared to be at a stage of prosperity, but soon fell back into the trend of depression. Chinese *Diaoqi* art, with all of its long history, has now come to a critical point of innovation and development.

Based on the status of *Diaoqi*, this paper aims to understand the comprehension and cognitive depth of Beijing high school students regarding Chinese intangible cultural heritage, *Diaoqi*. The following questions were investigated in interviews with the 10th and 11th grade students of 27 high schools in Beijing:

1) Have you ever heard of *Diaoqi*?

2) Do you think *Diaoqi* is beautiful?

3) What was your first impression when you saw *Diaoqi*?

4) In what ways did you learn about *Diaoqi*?

5) What Chinese cultural concepts do you think *Diaoqi* represents?

6) What purposes do you think *Diaoqi* has?

7) *Diaoqi* has been certified as Chinese intangible cultural heritage. How do you think we should protect and inherit it?

8) If you had the opportunity to learn the skills of *Diaoqi*, would you spend time and energy doing it?

2. Literature Review

We used "Diaoqi" "Beijing high school students" and "cognition" as keywords to search CNKI, but did not find any relevant content or research. Therefore, we think this research is of reference value in terms of the current situation of young people's understanding of *Diaoqi*.

3. Research Methods and Procedures

The research method of this paper is mainly qualitative research, which applies the method of structured interview to obtain and analyze data.

3.1 Structured interview method

In this survey, structured interview was applied, and each participant was asked questions in accordance with the interview outline. Interview questions were not added or reduced at will.

The participants of this survey are secondary students from different types of high schools in Beijing, and 426 valid pieces of data were collected from 63 participants. Their biographical information is as follows:

Table 1: Biographical information of the participants (N=63)

Grade	Number of participants	Percentage
10th	50	79.4%
11th	13	20.6%
School type	**Number of participants**	**Percentage**
Public School	40	63.5%
Private School	23	36.5%
Gender	**Number of participants**	**Percentage**
Male	23	36.5%
Female	40	63.5%

3.2 Data collection and analysis

Data were collected through structured interviews with Beijing high school students, followed by data coding, data analysis, and data aggregation.

4. Research Findings and Discussion

The research collected a total of 426 pieces of data (from 63 students of responses) and focused on the topic of Beijing high school students' cognition of *Diaoqi*. By coding and combining with the above 8 specific research questions, we classified the data into 4 categories: degree of cognition of *Diaoqi*, ways of knowing *Diaoqi*, the relationship between *Diaoqi* and Chinese culture, as well as the protection and inheritance of *Diaoqi*.

Table 2: Four major findings (N=426)

Number	Category	Item frequency
1	Degree of cognition	191
2	Approach of knowing	20
3	Relationship with Chinese culture	80
4	Protection and inheritance	135

The specific findings of the different categories in Table 2 will be elaborated and discussed below according to the research questions.

4.1 Degree of cognition

There was a total of 191 items on degree of cognition. According to the answers of the students interviewed, we further divided the degree of cognition into whether Beijing high school students know about *Diaoqi* and their first impressions of it. Table 3 illustrates the two categories.

Table 3: Secondary classification and interpretation of *Diaoqi* cognition

Number	Category	Interpretation
1	General knowledge	Do you know *Diaoqi*?
2	First impression	Do you think *Diaoqi* is beautiful?
		What is your first impression of *Diaoqi*?

4.1.1 Low awareness of *Diaoqi*

Table 4: Whether Beijing high school students know about *Diaoqi* (N=63)

Number	Answer	Number of participants	Percentage
1	Yes	19	30.2%
2	No	44	69.8%

It can be seen from Table 4 that only 19 out of 63 Beijing high school students interviewed in this survey have heard of *Diaoqi*, accounting for about 30% of the total number of respondents. Therefore, the majority of students interviewed did not know anything about *Diaoqi*. In other words, the degree of cognition of *Diaoqi* in Beijing high school students is generally low. The reasons may be, *Diaoqi* had belonged to the luxury of Chinese emperors throughout Chinese history, being the main items of furniture display in the emperors' interior. As *Diaoqi* is more exquisite than other lacquerware, and its craft more complicated, *Diaoqi* is also more honorable. Because *Diaoqi* has exclusive royal usage, profound history, superb craftsmanship, rich cultural connotation, and distinctive art form, it is a costly handicraft or luxurious indulgence. As it is, Beijing high school students' opportunity of accessing *Diaoqi* is limited, which leads to their poor understanding of *Diaoqi*. Therefore, it is necessary and urgent to popularize the intangible cultural heritage of *Diaoqi* among high school students.

4.1.2 First impressions of *Diaoqi* are varied

The second question of this survey was to show a picture of a finished piece of *Diaoqi* work and ask respondents their first impressions of it. In the interview data, most respondents said, "This is a very beautiful artifact." The survey feedback is shown in Table 5 according to the respondents' evaluation of the beauty of *Diaoqi*.

Table 5: First impressions of *Diaoqi* among Beijing high school students (N=63)

Number	Answer	Frequency	Percentage
1	Extraordinary	19	30.2%
2	Good	34	54.0%
3	So-so	5	7.9%
4	Not good	4	6.3%
5	Uncertain	1	1.6%

It can be seen that most of the participants appreciate *Diaoqi* very much and are attracted by the appearance of it. At the same time, the statistics also show that a small number of students surveyed have a so-so or even unfavorable impression of the beauty of *Diaoqi*, accounting for about 14%. In addition, some of the participants are uncertain about their answers, accounting for about 2%. It is found that *Diaoqi* generally has a good reputation among the surveyed Beijing high school students, and a significant majority of respondents expressed their affection for *Diaoqi*.

According to the students' answers to the next 3 questions, the first impressions of *Diaoqi* are diversified. This paper further divided the first impressions of *Diaoqi* among high school students into symbolic significance, personal feelings, craftsmanship, and functionality.

Table 6: Diversified first impressions of *Diaoqi* among Beijing high school students

Number	Category	Interpretation	Percentage
1	Symbolic significance	To express an abstract concept, thought or emotion by means of the concrete image of someone or something	39.7%
2	Personal feelings	Perception of *Diaoqi* from the perspective of the viewer	30.2%
3	Craftsmanship	Exquisite craftsmanship	15.9%
4	Functionality	Beneficial functions of something	14.3%

Note: The sum of the percentage exceeds 100% because of the rounding off.

Table 7: Further analysis of the first impressions of *Diaoqi* among Beijing high school students

Category	Specification	Percentage
Symbolic significance	Social hierarchy	63.5%
	History of tradition	36.5%
Personal feelings	Exquisite art work	63.5%
	Sentiment expression	36.5%
Craftsmanship	Consummate skills	60.3%
	Time-consuming process	39.7%
Functionality	Daily commodity	77.8%
	Decoration	22.2%

Firstly, according to Table 6, Beijing high school students have different impressions and views on *Diaoqi*, and this diversity is mainly reflected in the following four aspects: symbolic significance, personal feelings, craftsmanship, and functionality. Most of the students surveyed mentioned symbolic significance, accounting for nearly 40% of the total. It can be seen that in Beijing high school students' cognition, *Diaoqi* is generally regarded as a symbol. In the specific classification of symbolic significance in Table 7, 63.5% of the participants expressed the close connection between *Diaoqi* and social classes. The students mentioned "upper royal family" "not likely that ordinary people can use" and "royal supplies, only those with money can buy". It can be inferred that, because *Diaoqi* was predominately a craft implemented by the royal court and possessed a lofty social position, Beijing high school students' comprehension of *Diaoqi* will begin with this historical reality, and consequently they connect *Diaoqi* with social classes.

Secondly, Table 6 shows that in the participants' first impressions of *Diaoqi*, personal feelings account for about 30%. Among those, 63.5% of the students surveyed made rational comments on *Diaoqi* itself, such as "delicate and elegant pieces of work, complicated and ancient patterns" "exquisite patterns" and "traditional simplicity". Another 36.5% of the respondents expressed their subjective feelings, saying "astonishing" or "no feelings". Therefore, high school students in Beijing tend to be more rational in their evaluation of *Diaoqi*. The findings did exceed our expectations, as before the survey, we had thought that Beijing high school students do not have enough knowledge and ability to rationally evaluate an art work from the perspective of aesthetic criticism.

Furthermore, nearly 16% of the respondents mentioned craftsmanship, including consummate skills (60.3%) and time-consuming process (39.7%). In addition, nearly 14% of the respondents noted *Diaoqi*'s functionality, mentioning daily items such as "large plates" "bowls" and "tea sets", as well as decorative items such as "window flowers" and "art works".

4.2 Various approaches of getting to know *Diaoqi*

Regarding the approaches of getting to know *Diaoqi*, our research collected 20 pieces of valid data. According to the interview, half of the participants learned about *Diaoqi* through daily media, and a quarter of the participants mentioned that they learned about the concept of *Diaoqi* from daily conversations and another quarter through museum exhibitions, as shown in Table 8.

Table 8: Beijing high school students' approaches of knowing about *Diaoqi* (N=20)

Results	Frequency	Percentage
Daily media	10	50.0%
Daily conversations	5	25.0%
Museum exhibitions	5	25.0%

During the interview, the surveyed high school students in Beijing mentioned they learned about *Diaoqi* in conversations with teachers, family members, and friends, wherein learning about it through conversations with teachers takes up 40%. It is concluded that the role of teachers in promoting the cognition of *Diaoqi* is quite significant. In addition, 5 students interviewed also reported that they had seen *Diaoqi* art works in museum exhibitions. Therefore, *Diaoqi* museum exhibitions, as a carrier of communication, can provide knowledge and information to modern high school students.

Most importantly, the most common way to learn about *Diaoqi* is daily media, accounting for 50%. Five students mentioned documentaries, while the other five mentioned books, movies, social media, the Internet, and news reports. The number of students who saw *Diaoqi* art from a documentary was the same as those who saw it in a museum exhibition (5 students), and both accounted for a large proportion (25%) of the overall number. Therefore, it can be concluded that museum exhibitions and documentaries are the two most important ways of popularizing *Diaoqi*.

4.3 The relationship between *Diaoqi* and Chinese culture

4.3.1 *Diaoqi* is an expression of Chinese culture

Through data coding and analysis, this paper finds that Beijing high school students regard *Diaoqi* as a kind of cultural expression. Zhao (2009) mentioned, "If culture is said to include all aspects of human existence, then human expression has to be realized through culture; to put it directly and simply, human expression is cultural expression, and human beings rely on cultural expression to realize the expression of self."

As for the relationship between *Diaoqi* and Chinese culture, this paper collected a total of 80 pieces of valid data, and divided them into 4 categories: craftsman spirit, cultural spirit, symbolic meaning, and emotional meaning. A large number of students surveyed mentioned the craftsman spirit embodied in *Diaoqi*, accounting for 37.5%, followed by cultural spirit (26.3%), symbolic meaning (18.8%), and emotional meaning (17.5%), as shown in Table 9.

Table 9: The relationship between *Diaoqi* and Chinese culture (N=80)

Number	Culture	Interpretation	Percentage
1	Craftsman spirit	The craftsman strives for perfection in one's product elaboration and has the perfect spiritual idea	37.5%
2	Cultural spirit	Spiritual culture is a kind of special ideology of human beings produced on the basis of materialistic culture	26.3%
3	Symbolic meaning	To express some abstract meaning with concrete things	18.8%
4	Emotional meaning	To express or convey some thoughts or feelings	17.5%

Note: The sum of the percentage exceeds 100% because of the rounding off.

Table 10: Subdivisions of the relationship between *Diaoqi* and Chinese culture

Category	Subdivision	Percentage
Craftsman spirit (N=30)	Exquisite skills	46.7%
	Originality spirit	46.7%
	Craftsman's wisdom	6.7%
Cultural spirit (N=21)	Cultural tradition	76.2%
	National heritage	14.3%
	Cultural diversity	9.5%
Symbolic meaning (N=15)	Symbol of the dragon	53.3%
	Royal power	46.7%
Emotional meaning (N=14)	Beautiful implication	85.7%
	Emotional expression	14.3%

Note: The sum of the percentage in some category exceeds 100% because of the rounding off.

Table 10 shows that the craftsman spirit indicated by the participants mainly includes the exquisite skills of the craftsmen (46.7%), the originality spirit of striving for perfection and keeping patience (46.7%), and the craftsman's accumulated wisdom on *Diaoqi* (6.7%). For example, the participants mentioned "exquisite craftsmanship" "rigorous spirit" and "fruit of the wisdom". In terms of cultural spirit, most of the students mentioned cultural tradition (76.2%), such as "integration of nature and people" and "compatibility and inclusiveness", but some students claimed that "*Diaoqi* is related to the spirit of inheritance", and "*Diaoqi* is not only the beauty of appearance, but also the embodiment of the diversity of Chinese traditional culture". *Diaoqi* also has a certain symbolic meaning. Most frequently mentioned by students in the survey was the symbol of the dragon (53.3%). "Palace" and "royalty" are also used to describe the historical connection between *Diaoqi* and royal power (46.7%). In addition, *Diaoqi* is also an expression of emotional meaning. 85.7% of the students interviewed mentioned the implied beautiful meaning of *Diaoqi*, such as "happy" "auspicious" and "longing for a good life". Two students interviewed directly mentioned that *Diaoqi* had emotional expression.

4.3.2 Diverse usages of *Diaoqi*

For students who had a certain understanding towards *Diaoqi*, we asked a question to find out their cognition of *Diaoqi*'s usages. Among them, 3 views have been mentioned: some think *Diaoqi* can be used as decorations, some think it has practical values, while others view it as an inheritance.

Table 11: The usages of *Diaoqi* (N=31)

Answer	Frequency	Percentage
Decorations	13	41.9%
Practical values	13	41.9%
Inheritance	5	16.1%

Note: The sum of the percentage is less than 100% because of the rounding off.

Of the students surveyed, nearly 42% thought *Diaoqi* could be used as decorations in their homes, such as a "vase" or a "screen". Meanwhile, nearly 42% of the students thought *Diaoqi* had some practical values and suggested making it into practical products. Among them, 3 students mentioned "jewelry box" and 2 students mentioned "mobile phone case", followed by "teapot" "bracelet" "plate" and "anti-slip material on utensils". In addition, about 16% of the students believed *Diaoqi* was a form of inheritance. More specifically, they believed that *Diaoqi* was a kind of "spiritual inheritance" "Chinese culture inheritance" or "handicraft inheritance". To sum up, in the minds of most Beijing high school students interviewed, *Diaoqi* can not only perform practical usages, but is also full of cultural significance.

4.4 The protection and inheritance of *Diaoqi*

4.4.1 Various approaches to protect *Diaoqi*

Diaoqi has been certified as part of the national intangible cultural heritage. According to the interview data, there are 5 main categories of answers: public awareness, online publicity, offline publicity, practical application, and government support. A total of 73 pieces of valid data were collected.

Table 12: The protective measures for *Diaoqi* mentioned by Beijing high school students (N=73)

Number	Protective measures	Frequency	Percentage
1	Public awareness	31	42.5%
2	Offline publicity	18	24.7%
3	Practical application	10	13.7%
4	Government support	7	9.6%
5	Online publicity	7	9.6%

Note: The sum of the percentage is less than 100% because of the rounding off.

From Table 12, we know that public awareness was mentioned most frequently in the protection of *Diaoqi* (42.5%). Media publicity and supervision can draw public attention to *Diaoqi* and public awareness will rise. For instance, some participants mentioned that we needed to train primary and secondary school teachers to create and provide opportunities for students to learn about *Diaoqi*, as students are the "inheritors" of our culture. Only by improving the mindset of people on the protection of intangible cultural heritage can the protection of traditional art works be improved.

To our surprise, the fewest students mentioned government support and online publicity (both at 9.6%). The government, with official authority and influence, can improve the popularity and cognition of *Diaoqi* by making policies which set up inheritance mechanisms of intangible cultural heritage, and promulgating measures which call on the public to protect it. In addition, online publicity, such as Internet promotion, with characteristics and advantages of a wider range of audience, faster transmission, and a larger amount of information, has become the main channel for the public to receive information. Therefore, through online publicity of *Diaoqi*, the media can make traditional culture closer to the public, and ultimately make it accepted by the public, which is more conducive to young people for their inheritance of traditional culture.

4.4.2 Attitudes towards the inheritance of *Diaoqi*

Concerning the attitudes of Beijing high school students towards the inheritance of *Diaoqi*, by and large, our data show two contrasting points of view: willingness and lack of willingness to do this work. A total of 62 pieces of valid data were collected.

Table 13: The degree of willingness to learn the technique of *Diaoqi* (N=62)

Number	Degree of willingness	Frequency	Percentage
1	Willing	43	69.4%
2	Unwilling	19	30.6%

From the results of the data, we can see that most of the participants are willing to spend time learning it. Apparently, *Diaoqi* as part of the national intangible cultural heritage has the charm to attract students to know or comprehend it.

For those who are willing to spend time on it, there are 3 reasons: time management, personal cognition, and the charm of *Diaoqi*. A total of 43 pieces of valid data were collected.

Table 14: The reasons why Beijing high school students are willing to learn *Diaoqi* (N=43)

Number	Reason	Frequency	Percentage
1	Personal cognition	28	65.1%
2	Time management	8	18.6%
3	The charm of *Diaoqi*	7	16.3%

As we can see in Table 14, the percentage on personal cognition (65.1%) is greater than the sum of the other two reasons, which means that Beijing high school students have their own ideas about *Diaoqi*. For instance, some thought that they had the responsibility to protect and inherit *Diaoqi*. Or maybe it's a kind of faith that makes people want to learn it.

Table 15: The reasons why Beijing high school students are unwilling to learn *Diaoqi* (N=19)

Number	Reason	Frequency	Percentage
1	Personal cognition	13	68.4%
2	Time management	6	31.6%

Table 15 shows the reasons why students are unwilling to learn *Diaoqi*. The most important reason is personal cognition, which accounts for 68.4% and shows that nowadays teenagers are not very interested in ancient techniques like *Diaoqi* and paper-cut. Because with the development of technology, society is improving; they may be interested in more novel things like artificial intelligence. For example, one participant said, "I probably don't want to learn it because I'm not interested in this area."

In addition, many high school students do not have any extra time to do other things, including the study of *Diaoqi*, because they need to study. One participant mentioned, "I will not study *Diaoqi* because I'm very busy every day." Indeed, for high school students, they have a relatively heavy load of homework and face the challenges of entrance exams. The physical and psychological pressure keeps them away from other things except study.

5. Conclusion

Diaoqi is a carving technique. With the rise of the modern capital market, *Diaoqi*, with its long production cycle and scarce raw material, cannot adapt to the modern and industrialized world. With older generations of *Diaoqi* artists passing away, and today's young people with too little an understanding of the art, *Diaoqi* has gradually declined. Therefore, the purpose of this survey is to explore the degree of cognition of *Diaoqi* among Beijing high school students, a special and specific group.

Through research, this paper has found that Beijing high school students have a low awareness of *Diaoqi*, but their first impressions of it are diversified. They explore *Diaoqi* through symbolic significance, craftsmanship, personal feelings, and functionality. At the same time, the students learn about *Diaoqi* through various channels, among which a large number of them learn about it through documentaries and museum exhibitions, the two important communication channels to spread *Diaoqi* among students.

A more important finding is that high school students believe that *Diaoqi* is the expression of Chinese culture. It demonstrates the Chinese culture from four aspects: craftsman spirit, cultural spirit, symbolic meaning, and emotional meaning. Additionally, *Diaoqi* still has a variety of utilities; it has not only the application of decoration, but also inheritance values and practical values. Therefore, it is very important to take a variety of protection measures to popularize the cognition of *Diaoqi*. Through the improvement of public awareness, online and offline publicity, application practices, the establishment of government support mechanisms, etc., contemporary high school students can better understand the connotation of

Diaoqi, understand intangible cultural heritage, and most importantly, pass it on.

References:

Zhao, Xudong. Expression of Culture: From the Perspective of Anthropology [M]. Beijing: China Renmin University Press, 2009.

评书篇

浅析北京评书的艺术特征

梁 彦[1]

关于评书的表演特色,从一首广为人知的《西江月》中可以看出些许端倪:"世间生意甚多,惟有说书难习。评叙说表非容易,千言万语须记。一要声音洪亮,二要顿挫迟疾。装文装武我自己,好似一台大戏。"其中,"评叙说表"指的是表演手法细腻而多样,"声音洪亮"指的是语重声洪、悦耳动听,"顿挫迟疾"指的是口齿清晰、节奏多变,"装文装武"指的是刻画人物生动形象,而最终要达到的效果是"好似一台大戏"。对于北京评书而言,说演细腻、人物传神,尤为重要。

从剖析本质的层面探寻到的评书艺术特色,首先是虚拟。传统戏曲和曲艺艺术都是虚拟写意的,评书也不例外。这里所说的虚拟写意是广义的,并不局限于某些具体的表现手法,而是指完整的表演程式和体系。其次是变化。既有叙事结构上的变化,或"倒插笔",或"花开两朵,各表一枝",或"有话则长,无话则短";又有表现手法上的变化,或叙述,或说明,或描写,或议论,或抒情,甚或五者并举;还有句式和遣词用字上的变化;以及在表演层面上的手(手势)、眼(眼神)、身(身段)、法(程式)、步(脚步)的节奏变化。再次是灵活。虽然情节内容、诗词赋赞等表演程式相对固定,但"书外书""现挂"都属于灵活这一范畴,尤其是在书馆现场表演,一部书每说一遍都不

---

1. 本文作者为中华书局编辑,评书名家连丽如的弟子,宣南书馆评书演员,曲艺研究者。

同，或是一遍拆洗一遍新，或是"把点开活"，或是随机应变、见景生情。最后是幽默。相较于前三者，幽默在评书中只是起到穿插、点缀、锦上添花的作用，更像是调味品，看似可有可无，但只要有，演出效果就会迥然不同。评书中的幽默来自或情节、人物出其不意的巧合，或谲智机巧且耐人寻味的讽刺议论，或惟妙惟肖且诙谐风趣的表情动作。而灵活、幽默这两点，北京评书尤为看重。

将上述四方面内容归结起来，评书，尤其是北京评书的艺术特征便呼之欲出，即以夹叙夹议为基本程式，情节跌宕、说演细腻、人物传神、灵活幽默。

一、情节跌宕

情节跌宕是北京评书，乃至评书最基本的艺术特征。比如连阔如先生《东汉演义》中的"贾复闯营拖肠大战"：贾复头次闯营，误失密箭；二次闯营，力胜巨无霸；换马取箭，三闯敌营，遭人暗算，受伤进城；进昆阳取回文，带重伤四闯敌营，身中数箭，又被巨无霸追赶；郅君章及时赶到，逼走巨无霸，救下贾复……故事曲折离奇，情节跌宕起伏，令人心潮澎湃，如醉如痴。

对于北京评书而言，情节跌宕在表演方面的另一种体现是结构严密、语言紧凑。构建情节如同盖房子，梁柱檩椽，榫卯扣合，不能出现任何偏差；亦即脉络清晰、层次分明、逻辑严密、丝丝入扣，否则书一散，观众的神就散了。语言紧凑是对演员很严格的要求，字斟句酌，准确到位，切忌谈吐迟钝、叙述拖沓、冗词赘句，正所谓"一句不到，观众发躁"。紧凑的语言能够抓住观众，带动观众随着故事情节的发展而前进。

比如《三侠五义》中"五鼠闹东京"一节,从耀武楼展昭献艺,得号"御猫"开始,引出白玉堂独奔东京寻衅,开封府寄柬留刀,石惊赵虎,猫鼠争锋,白玉堂夜进皇宫,杀人题诗,四鼠进京,开封府盗三宝等故事,形成了一波未平一波又起、环环相扣的严密结构。所谓长江后浪推前浪,前浪未平,后浪即至,否则气断而神散,情节的跌宕性荡然无存。当然,上述是主线情节,演员实际说书时,其中还穿插了许多小故事,如展昭比剑联姻、三吃鱼、花园赠金、大闹花神庙等。这些小故事看上去似乎游离于主要情节之外,实际不然。所谓结构严密、语言紧凑,不等于主线情节的飞快发展。说长篇评书要"人断书不断,事多条不乱",这些小故事恰恰是紧扣人物行动的,它们是主线或副线上的枝叶,交代了人物的成长,推动了情节的发展。像颜查散的出场与之后的经历,作为与主线并行的副线,至关重要,对于后文起到了重要的铺垫作用。

所以,主线与副线的交叉,故事与故事间的衔接,要求丝丝入扣、入情入理、顺理成章、一气呵成。这既要求结构上的严密,又要求演员说书语言的紧凑,两者缺一不可。

二、说演细腻

老舍先生在《谈〈武松〉》一文中曾谈道:"评书演员似乎可分为两类:一类是真给书听,一件事紧接一件事,不多费力气去详述细节,或旁征博引。这是尽职的演员。可是我所见过的第一流名手,都是第二类的——把书中每一细节都描绘得极其细腻生动,而且喜欢旁征博引，离开正题，说些闲书。"所谓"细腻生动"，正是北京评书的风度和气质所在。北京评书的说演细腻，不是为细腻而细腻，而是有艺术表达方面的三个作用，即细腻蕴含形象性，细腻蕴含知识性，细腻蕴含合理性。下面就以连阔如先生传本、连丽如先生口述的《评书三国演义》为例，对这三点作逐一分析。

细腻蕴含形象性。比如"辕门射戟"一段对于拉弓射箭的描写：

> 咱们中国射箭跟外国射箭用的功力不一样，中国射箭八个字：撑、拔、拐、抹、托、捋、刁、合。九斤十二两为一个劲儿，十三把半这张弓算是拉开。拉弓的人都得背着手往这儿一站，拔脯子调脸儿，练这个站功。站功练好了，吊膀子。膀子吊好了，才能拉硬弓。……左手攥着弓背儿，右手攥着弓弦儿，举过脑门儿，往下落。弓一撑，前把推，后把一拉，前把托住，后把捋住，一拔脯子，拐胳膊肘儿，一调脸儿。吕布左手攥弓背儿，右手箭认扣，左手手指头还要掐着箭杆儿，箭杆儿这儿叫扣门儿。箭杆儿翎毛尾巴这儿有一道深沟儿，还把弓弦搁在里头，这就叫填弦。

（《评书三国演义》上册，中华书局2006年版，160页）

交代清清楚楚，既生动形象，又翔实可信。此段较之一般的套语，如"弓开如满月，箭走似流星，前把如推泰山，后把如抱婴孩……"等等，哪个更好，不言而喻。

细腻蕴含知识性。比如"借东风"一段对于七星坛的"摆切末儿"描写：

这座七星坛一共三层，每层高三尺，方圆一共二十四丈，在下面一层插二十八宿旗。东方是七面青旗，按东方七宿，角木蛟、亢金龙、氐土貉、房日兔、心月狐、尾火虎、箕水豹，总名叫苍龙，布出苍龙之形；北方是七面皂旗，按北方七宿，斗、牛、女、虚、危、室、壁，总名叫玄武，有的说是龟，有的说是蛇，还有一种说法是龟蛇合体，是北方的神，所以布出玄武之势；西方是七面白旗，按西方七宿，奎、娄、胃、昴、毕、觜、参，总名叫白虎；南方是七面红旗，按南方七宿，井、鬼、柳、星、张、翼、轸，布成朱雀之状。第二层周围黄旗六十四面，按八八六十四卦，分八位而立。上边一层用的是四个人，这四个人头戴束发冠，身穿皂罗袍，凤衣博带，朱履方裾。前方左边这个人，手里拿着长竿，长竿的尖上用鸡羽为葆，就是扎上鸡毛，以观察风的动静；后方左边立着一个人，捧着宝剑；前方右边立着一个人，手里也挑着长竿，竿上系着一条七星号带，以表示风的方向和强弱；后方右边站的人手里捧着香炉。七星坛下还有二十四个兵士，各持旌旗、宝盖、大戟、长戈、黄钺、白旄、朱幡、皂纛，在四周环绕。

（《评书三国演义》中册，中华书局2006年版，838页）

京剧《群英会·借东风·华容道》中鲜有实体布景，唯独诸葛亮七星坛借风，台上高搭法坛，再现典型环境，皆因为它是"戏核儿"，必须与众不同。评书中这一段也如是，属于"有话则长"，必须细致描述，否则不仅会失去细腻的特色，而且也会削弱诸葛亮借东风的形象性。而这种细腻笔法本身是蕴含着充足知识性的。

细腻蕴含合理性。理,指人物性格的逻辑性和情节的可信性,所谓"顺理成章"。比如对于小说《三国演义》中诸葛亮的塑造,鲁迅说:"至于写人,亦颇有失,以致欲显刘备之长厚而似伪,状诸葛之多智而近妖。"而在《评书三国演义》中,作者设身处地,揆情度理,扬小说之长,藏原作之拙,为这场赤壁大战中运筹帷幄的实际主帅恢复了"人"的光彩。比如"草船借箭"一段:

> 诸葛亮事先早就算好了,一支箭估计有多大分量,船两边幔帐都是草束,一条船一面受箭受多少支时杯中的酒倾斜到什么程度。如果一条船一边受箭,得了七八千支,你拔下来后得有折的、坏的,剩下的好箭五六千支,所以二十一条船才能得上六七万支箭。调过头来,两面都射匀了,船也能摆平了,十万支雕翎箭绝不会少一根。
>
> (《评书三国演义》中册,中华书局2006年版,785页)

如果说罗贯中笔下对诸葛亮将空船逼近曹营,面对骤雨飞蝗似的乱箭,"只顾酌酒取乐"的描写是表现其镇定自若、成竹在胸、稳操胜券的气概,而评书中通过对椅子、杯盘、筷子、酒壶的细节描述和上述分析,确实把诸葛亮所以能"稳操"的未尽之情展示出来,表现了诸葛亮并非仅是知奇门、晓阴阳的"不全之态",而且是学识渊博的"心"机妙算家。此后的"借东风"和"华容道",无一不是如此。这就是细腻笔法中蕴含的合理性。

三、人物传神

在北京评书中，生动传神的人物形象是很重要的艺术特征之一。刻画人物形象的一种手段是介绍人物时因势利导，从而生趣，凭借会心之幽默加深观众对人物的理解，这也是演员在表演中一种淡出淡入的技巧。连丽如先生《评书三国演义》"诵赋激瑜"一段，在介绍周瑜出场时，为了加深观众的印象，书里这样说：

> 周瑜不但文武全才，风流倜傥，而且精通音乐，是个大音乐家。这在《三国志》上有记载："曲有误，周郎顾。"如果现在举行歌手比赛，周瑜在这儿当评委，他闭着眼睛听，这歌手有个小音符、音节唱错了，他立刻能听出来。一抬头，把眼睛睁开，他得瞧这歌手一眼。
>
> （《评书三国演义》中册，中华书局2006年版，710—711页）

此处巧妙地将周瑜的性格爱好与时下流行的唱歌比赛相结合，观众眼前势必会浮现出电视里歌手比赛评委打分时的情景，而周瑜的形象亦牢牢地印在观众脑海中了。

另一种手段是在人物出场时，通过先声夺人的"开脸儿"（外貌描写）描摹人物，从而给观众留下深刻的印象。比如连丽如先生《评书三国演义》中对大将典韦的"开脸儿"，生动细致，人物形象如在眼前：

> 看将军，八面威，人又大，马又肥。腰圆膀阔三山配，身高

丈二晃巍巍。铜铃怪眼一字眉，翻天鼻孔獠牙嘴，一部红髯颔下垂。红耳毫，尖似锥，红发根根背后披。头上戴，錾金盔，焦黄抹额金丝垒。黄绒球，绕四围，雉鸡翎，白狐尾，五杆黄旗背后背。紫火焰，金铃坠，上绣金狮把云吹。黄金甲，连线缀；金牛犀带花纹碎，护心宝镜明秋水。杏黄袍，绣红葵；鱼褟尾，苫两腿，大红中衣露微微。虎头靴，黄云绘；坐下马，虎皮被，四蹄蹬翻土雨飞。手中拿，戟一对，八十斤，力不费；大红缨，嵌草穗，峨嵋尖，戟枝锐。抛戟能将敌命追，当年大战濮阳内。黄幡乍下天堂路，黄魔离去蜀江湄。有人若问名和姓，五路救应是典韦。

（《评书三国演义》上册，中华书局2006年版，111—112页）

洋洋洒洒一大段"贯口"，朗朗上口，韵味十足，极富语言美感。

再有一种手段是通过描写人物的思想活动，刻画生动传神的人物形象，并产生打动人心的力量。但评书不习惯采用大段的内心描写，而是结合人物的行动过程，使思想活动成为故事的组成部分。比如袁阔成先生《舌战小炉匠》中说到杨子荣在巡山过程中，见土匪押着小炉匠进山时的心理活动是：

他怎么能到这儿来呢？难道说我军宽大，把他释放了？不能啊！这家伙罪大恶极。要不就是这小子越狱逃跑了？不管怎么说，这家伙是来啦，我得马上把他除掉，不然，我们俩人一见面他立刻就会认出我来。想到这儿，子荣心里是万分紧张！这位独胆英雄所怕的不是自己的安危，而是怕整个灭匪计划遭到破坏。

子荣越想越觉得刻不容缓，干脆我以司宴官的身份毙了他吧。想到这儿，子荣的右手紧紧地抓住了枪柄，又一想，慢着，这样会不会引起敌人对我的怀疑？暗暗命令自己，先别忙，要镇静，二〇三首长经常教导我们：一个无产阶级的革命战士，越遇到大的变故，越应当冷静。当前这个局面应当怎么对付呢？……

　　他想事儿这工夫，小炉匠已被押进威武厅去了。子荣忽听背后有脚步声，噔，噔，噔，跑来了一个小土匪，走到跟前一呲牙，说："九爷，咱山上来人了，三爷请您去一趟，说有要紧的事儿和您商量。""知道了，你回禀三爷，说我马上就到。""是！"杨排长一转身，用手把帽子往后一推，啪，大氅一甩，高挺胸膛就奔威武厅来了。

　　（刊于《革命故事（第2集）》，春风文艺出版社1964年版，50—51页）

这段对杨子荣心理活动的描写，既说明杨子荣对敌人有了足够的思想准备，又为接下来的"舌战小炉匠"作了必要的铺垫，更重要的是让杨子荣这个人物的形象跃然眼前，丰满而生动。

四、灵活幽默

　　灵活幽默是北京评书另一个重要的艺术特征。所谓灵活，指的是表演的灵活、随意。表演灵活不可绝对化，存在好、坏两种可能。如果灵活得当，得到观众的认可，就等于为北京评书增加了表演手段和风格，有助于其丰富和发展；反之，则需从中吸取教训，得到启示，这同样是艺术发展不可或缺的一面。表演随意指的并不是信口开河，想怎么来就怎么来，而是不拘一格、别开生面的艺术创造，必须服从艺术的需要，目的是创新发展，更富艺术魅力。

所谓幽默，就是制造评书的笑料。北京评书一种常见的手法是从书中塑造的滑稽人物身上找笑料。传统评书《隋唐演义》中的程咬金、《三侠剑》中的贾明，都属于这样的人物。另一种常见的手法是通过演员的批讲议论找笑料。如连阔如先生《东汉演义》中，小将耿耳活捉奸臣朱鲔、胡殷，将二人押到囚车旁。囚车内已然关住奸臣同党陈本、曹宣，他们一看朱、胡，说："才来呀，二位。"在此，说书人不失时机地加入一句："好嘛，改成对口相声了。"巧妙戏谑，观众会心。

评书中还有一种幽默手法是"现挂"，多为在书馆说书，古事今说，即兴发挥，或针砭时弊，或现场抓哏。因为来得突然，加之演员的聪明机智，"现挂"往往收到出人意料的火爆效果。

二十一世纪北京评书的艺术特色与创新[1]

<u>童双雯　顾　婷　李仡文</u>[2]

【摘要】 北京评书有着鲜明的艺术特色。促进北京评书的艺术创新，是新一代北京评书演员的社会责任。北京评书不仅具有鲜明的语言韵味，也具有深厚的文化韵味。北京评书表演艺术不仅要立意正直，还要形式灵活、表演生动。北京评书演员在艺术创作过程中要注重形式、语言、审美等方面的创新，并从现实生活、听书观众和时代特色中汲取营养。只有这样才能增强评书的艺术特色，拓宽评书的受众面，更好地促进北京评书艺术的创新。

【关键词】 北京评书　艺术特色　艺术创新

一、研究意义

北京评书有着非常鲜明的艺术特色，深入挖掘这些艺术特色，并在此基础上融入二十一世纪鲜明的时代特色，促进北京评书艺术的创新发展，是新一代北京评书表演艺术家的神圣使命。从这个意义上来讲，研究北京评书的艺术特色和创新发展途径，对于北京评书艺术的传承具有重要的社会意义。

---

1. 本调研报告科研指导教师为北京外国语大学专用英语学院副教授仵胜奇。
2. 本调研报告的三位作者均为北京外国语大学附属中学高中部十一年级学生。

二、文献综述

目前，学界对于北京评书艺术特色和创新的研究有一些初步成果。例如，北京评书年轻表演艺术家梁彦在《北京评书》一书中表示："在漫长的发展历程中，北京评书有着属于自身的独特魅力，如情节跌宕，说演细腻，人物传神，灵活幽默等。"（梁彦，2015）中国戏曲学院副研究员李小红将评书和小说的艺术特色进行对比，她认为评书具有如下鲜明的艺术特色：一是鲜活的口语表达，二是善于运用对话叙事，三是动态化的说演以及多度创作（李小红，2017）。在目前中国评书艺术出现断层的背景下，研究北京评书的艺术特色，促进北京评书的艺术创新，就显得尤为重要。

三、研究方法

本研究采用访谈方法收集数据。研究小组成员从2018年7月16—28日对四名评书演员——马剑平、唐柯、汤凡、贾林——进行了实地采访，并对采访内容进行科学分析，得出如下结论。

四、发现与讨论

(一) 数据分析

表1：北京评书的艺术特色

研究主题	编码	定义
北京评书对说书人的特殊意义	行业传承	将评书或者评书的某一派别传承下去：子承父业，徒承师业
	文化传播	传播中华传统文化
	社会责任	运用评书去教人向善，即"高台教化"
	兴趣使然	出于热爱评书才去学习评书、表演评书
北京评书的特点	语言韵味	北京方言的音韵
	文化韵味	北京评书还原或再现了老北京人的生活方式、生活结构、生活节奏和生活习惯
说书人在评书演绎上的特色	立意正直（立意正）	无论是评书内容还是评议都朝着客观、正确的方向
	形式灵活	面对各类观众时，评书衍生出了各种表演形式（如砸挂、现挂等），并需要演员灵活运用、临场发挥
	能力多样	了解并掌握书内、书外，或者评书话本领域内、话本领域外的事物
	代入感强	以细致、精致的描绘使人物、情节完美再现，吸引观众
	忠实传承	传统评书的思想内容保持不变，但形式上有所创新
说书人与其师父演绎方式的差异	风格差异	每位评书表演艺术家都有其特有的风格，差异或多或少，但肯定有差异
	水平差异	跟老师们相比，学徒在经验、知识、功底等方面肯定存在不足
	改编创新	为了迎合社会潮流而对经典评书进行改编，将现代文化融入其中，形成一种特有风格
	严谨传承	模仿师父的风格，进行传承

续表

研究主题	编码	定义
当代北京评书的创新之处	形式创新	主要是指双语评书，用中英对照(或中文与其他语言对照)的方式表演评书
	语言创新	将一些当今社会不用或少用的语言改为流行语言
	审美创新	将与当今社会冲突的审美观念更改为大部分现代人能接受的审美观念
北京评书的创新来源	源于生活	艺术源于生活而高于生活
	源于观众	适应观众审美需求
	源于时代	适应时代变化和进步
北京评书未来的发展方向	艺术高度	增强评书的艺术特色
	受众广度	拓宽评书的受众面
	时间长度	传承评书，推动其发展
	保护力度	加大评书保护力度

(二) 发现

1. 北京评书对说书人的特殊意义

在2018年7月16—28日期间，我们对唐柯、贾林、汤凡和马剑平老师进行了采访。通过概括分析可以看出，北京评书对说书人具有非常特殊的意义。正因为如此，新一代年轻评书表演艺术家就肩负着传承、推广评书艺术的社会责任。在此，我们将从行业传承、文化传播、社会责任和兴趣使然四个方面加以讨论。

行业传承是指将评书或者评书的某一派别传承下去。评书传承人通过子承父业、徒承师业的方式促进北京评书的传承和发展。正如唐柯老师所说："评书具有一个完整的传承体系。"评书要想得到延续与发展，传承是必不可少的。

文化传播是指传播中华传统文化。作为中华传统文化的杰出代表，评书"具有深刻的内涵，以及深厚的文化底蕴"（唐柯）。因此，评书首先应扩大在中国的传播范围，然后再逐步走向世界。正如双语评书人马剑平老师所说："我觉得作为一个中国人，必须要了解自己的文化，才能走出去。"

社会责任是指运用评书去教人向善，即说书人常说的"高台教化"。评书不单单是一门艺术，也不单单是讲故事，它蕴含着道理。唐柯老师说："它是劝善的，是通过讲故事给老百姓讲清楚一些道理，并且教他们去做一个好人。"可以看出，评书能够教人们如何为人处世，这一点是十分重要的。

兴趣使然是指出于对评书的热爱或者因喜爱评书表演而决定学习评书、表演评书。大多数北京人都把听北京评书当作一种童年记忆，而从小培养这方面的兴趣爱好，会使他们更加热爱评书文化。评书传播不应区分年龄，甚至更应该从小就接触评书，这样才能激发兴趣。马剑平老师就提到自己演绎时的感受："一个词，过瘾！"正因为热爱评书，评书人才能够享受其中，乐意去表演，去评述，去传承这份文化。

2. 北京评书的特点

北京评书有两个鲜明的特点：一是语言韵味，二是文化韵味。评书作为一种语言艺术，它既包含了北京方言的音韵特色，也还原了老北京人特有的生活方式和文化特色。这两种韵味在北京评书中贯穿始终。

语言韵味是指语言（特别是方言）的音韵之美。正如唐柯老师所说:"北京评书的韵味来自自然韵味。"虽然评书语言的细致、精致是比较容易达到的,但字、词、句之间的音韵把握是十分困难的。马剑平老师也提道:"北京评书有很多北京的古话和官腔。"这种特殊的语言之美是北京评书中最精致的一笔。

文化韵味是指评书对老北京人的生活方式、生活结构、生活节奏、生活习惯进行了还原、再现,将曾经各个时代的北京保存在人们的记忆中。正如唐柯老师所言:"它是北京人的一种生活方式,它背后是深厚的北京文化基础。"

评书人因从事评书表演艺术而感到骄傲自豪,这是另一种文化韵味。它的含义更多的是对于中国文化的自信和骄傲。评书具有自己的民族特性,它根植于民族文化的土壤之中。

3. 说书人在评书演绎上的特色

对于一个说书人来说,自己在演绎上的特色是十分重要的,它关系到是否有能力吸引大众,进而传承评书文化。通过对四位说书人的采访,我们了解到,他们大致的特点包括立意正直、形式灵活、能力多样、代入感强和重视传承。

立意正直是指无论是评书内容还是评议都本着客观、公正、教人向善的原则。"出人、出书、走正路"是陈云同志对曲艺发展提出的要求,曲艺发展需做到"崇德尚艺"。在采访中,唐柯老师也说道:"我们行业里有这样一句话,'说书唱戏劝人方',我们是劝善,你在台上必须得是一个很正的形象,而不是油嘴滑舌,哗众取宠。"所以,这个特点便可以用一个"正"字概括。

形式灵活是指面对不同的观众群体,评书衍生出各种表演形式(如砸挂、现挂等),并需要演员灵活运用、临场发挥。说书人运用自己擅长的表演形式，生动地将情节、细节演绎出来，吸引观众的注意力。通过与唐柯老师的交谈，我们知道他先前学习过鼓书，所以有"唱"的功底。他说："这就是一个活，表现手段必须要灵活。"由此可见，针对不同的观众，采取不同的形式也是十分重要的。

能力多样是指为了能够吸引大众，说书人要对书内、书外，或者评书话本领域内、话本领域外都有所了解并尽可能熟练掌握。以唐柯老师为例，他提道："我涉猎比较广泛，如唱、弦、音、述等。"唐柯老师通过学习不同的技巧，增强自己多领域的能力，从而让评书有更大的魅力。

代入感强是指以细致、精致的描绘使人物、情节完美再现，并以此吸引观众。马剑平老师提到了一个关键词——人物鲜明。如果有生动的情节，鲜明的人物特征，再加上灵活的演绎，评书就能给观众带来直观的感受和体验。

也有一些说书人更加注重传承，也就是对于传统评书不予改变。贾林老师提道："目前来说没什么太大的特色，就是老老实实地传承。"这不仅是一部分说书人的特点，更是一种以保护为主的传承方式。

4.说书人与其师父演绎方式的差异

在这个问题上各位说书人的回答有所不同。风格差异、水平差异、改编创新、严谨传承是回答这个问题的关键词。

风格差异是指每位艺术家都有自己特有的风格，艺术风格一般同个人因素有关。唐柯老师提道："如果说我跟老先生不一样的地方，那就是，他专说西河大鼓书，他一辈子就说西河大鼓；但是我不一样，我学过京韵大鼓、三弦、南方的评弹、台湾的小曲，这些东西我可能都会借鉴。"双语评书演员汤凡和马剑平说道:"说评书,一个人一个风格。评书里面没有说每个人就是一模一样的风格,不可能有。"

水平差异是指与老师相比,学生还是会有些地方(如经验、知识、功底等)相对欠缺,他们需要通过长期积累来丰富自己的表演艺术。"人家(老一辈评书表演艺术家)的底蕴要深厚得多。"(马剑平)我们可以看出,四位说书人对于自己的表演一直保持谦虚态度,这也是他们能够一直进步的一个原因。

改编创新是指为了迎合社会潮流而对经典评书进行改编,去除糟粕并将现代文化融入其中,从而形成一种特有的风格。这种创新实践是需要勇气的。评书毕竟是一种传统艺术,这种创新有着打乱评书结构的风险。唐柯老师提到自己的创新经验,他认为创新在于与时俱进:"每次说书说下来,我都请老先生给点拨。但点拨完了,我不是盲目地把老先生的意见拿过来马上就用,我要通过我自己的分析,决定这些东西什么时候能用,能不能反复用,用的时候要作什么变通。有些可以变通,有些不能变通;可以变通的,就是对传统的进一步丰富和发展。"

严谨传承是指模仿师父的风格,进行传承。贾林老师提道:"我最早是从模仿开始,也没有形成自己的风格或者特色。"这是一种比较保守的做法,也确保了评书的演绎可以传承下去。

5. 当代北京评书的创新之处

评书要想得到发展,就一定要跟上时代的脚步,要与时俱进。因此评书的创新之处有:形式创新、语言创新、审美创新。

形式创新主要是指双语评书,用中英对照(或中文与其他语言对照)的方式表演评书。评书是中国传统文化,它不会止步于中国,会向世界传播,更多人会了解这门艺术。因此要在语言上有所改进和创新。正如汤凡和马剑平两位老师所说:"双语评书就是创意。"评书艺术不能仅限于中文观众,要加强在外语方面的传播,要让更多人能听得懂评书内容,让更多人接受并喜爱这门艺术。

语言创新是指将一些当今社会不用或少用的语言改为流行语言。北京评书历史悠久,其中的一些老话或专业词语都不易被观众理解。所以,"要用现代人能听得懂的语言,讲述他们没有听过的故事,让现代观众感受历史人物的喜怒哀乐、爱恨情仇"(汤凡、马剑平)。为了让观众更好地理解评书内容,更有兴趣听下去,评书人也在不断更新自己的语言表达方式。例如,在马剑平老师的评书演绎中,"现话(如当今流行语)会更多一些"。在评书表演过程中,融入更多现代流行的词汇,把历史故事与当今流行语相结合,会让观众对传统文化的认知有所改观。这样,评书就不再枯燥乏味,而变得生动有趣、贴近生活。

审美创新是指将与当今社会冲突的审美观念更改为大部分现代人能接受的审美观念。正如汤凡和马剑平两位老师所说:"有很多年轻的观众,还有小孩,他们要接受一些老的事物,可能会有点隔阂感。"评书具有年代感,很多老一代的审美观念,对现代人来说都是无法接受的,所以评书要与时俱进,与当今社会的审美观念接轨。正如马剑平老师所说:"审美创新就是对评书内容适当取舍,取其精华,去其糟粕,让它适应现代人的审美观念和认知习惯。"适当取舍,使之为大部分现代人所接受,也有利于评书艺术更好地发展与传承。

6. 北京评书的创新来源

北京评书要想传承,创新是必不可少的。但如何创新,正是每一个说书人和听书人最关注的问题。通过采访我们认为，北京评书创新有三个主要来源：一是源于生活，二是源于观众，三是源于时代。

例如，马剑平老师特别强调了生活对于评书艺术的重要意义，他说："艺术源于生活而高于生活，是从生活中点点滴滴积累下来的。"评书虽然没有大范围普及，但是也有一部分人通过听评书来消遣娱乐。只有将评书扎根于生活，才能汲取生活中最朴素的元素，让观众在听书过程中身心放松，使评书成为一种真正的娱乐方式。

评书源于观众是指迎合观众的审美需求。说书人要根据大众的兴趣设计内容，设计演绎形式，以确保观众对评书时刻保持新鲜感。这些都是因为说书人"时刻面对的都是观众"（唐柯），所以一切都要建立在观众喜欢的基础之上。"你说的不吸引观众，观众必然不听；观众不听你，那你说给谁听？"（唐柯）只有老观众支持，新观众关注，说书人才有动力和条件去保护和传承评书。所以，观众也是北京评书发展的一个重要因素。

源于时代是指要适应时代的变化和进步。唐柯老师提道："与时俱进，所有的事情不要墨守成规，你要跟上时代，因为你面对的群体是跟着时代往前走的。"传统的事物固然有它的好处，但时代在变化，人的理念也在变化，不创新必然遭到时代淘汰。墨守成规，不懂得变通，就是停滞不前，更无法进步。所以，评书要想不断发展，紧随时代变化就是必然趋势。

7. 北京评书未来的发展方向

在有关评书发展方向的问题上，受访者主要从艺术高度、受众广度、时间长度和保护力度这四个维度作出回答。

艺术高度是指提高了评书的艺术特色，评书就能在更大范围内推广,从而更好地达到保护的目的。但是盲目创新是不对的,维持传统的方式是一种具有保护性质的发展方式。这也就是唐柯老师提到的,"不随意性恰恰是确保你发展正确轨迹的一个约束"。

受众广度是指拓宽评书的受众面,也就是把评书大众化,这很考验评书演员的能力。北京是著名的历史名城,具有深厚的文化底蕴,流传着无数传奇故事,这也为北京评书积累了宝贵的素材;北京方言趣味性强,也非常容易引起观众的兴趣。所以,只要作品吸引人,就一定能够获得更多观众的青睐。

时间长度是指长久地把北京评书传承下去。唐柯老师表示:"传承北京评书是我们这一代人的使命。我们不能让老祖宗传下来的艺术在我们手上断了。"

保护力度是指加大评书的保护力度。唐柯老师说:"现在的首要任务是要让评书至少'寿终正寝',而不要'死于非命'。"评书要想更好地发展,就需要国家、政府、人民的联动配合。"我们要保护它的积极因素,让它积极的一面发挥得淋漓尽致。"(唐柯)

五、结语

北京评书的艺术特色和创新,对评书表演艺术家具有重要意义;它是一种兴趣,一种传播文化的方式,一种派别传承的责任感。北京评书之所以能够吸引一部分人的兴趣,不仅因为它有独具特色的语言韵味和文化韵味,还因为它有丰富生动的表演形式,这就十分考验说书人的功底和能力。评书演员需要先明确自己的演绎形式,然后从生活、观众、时代中收集素材,改编内容。这样的创新方式,不仅能够增强评书的艺术特色,拓宽评书的受众面,还能加大评书的保护力度,从而促进评书艺术更好地发展。

参考文献:

李小红. 论评书的艺术特征 —— 与小说作对比[J]. 中国古代小说戏剧研究(第十三辑), 2017: 366 — 374.

梁彦. 北京评书[M]. 北京: 北京美术摄影出版社, 2015.

The Artistic Features and Innovations of Beijing *Pingshu* in the 21st Century

Shen Yiwen[1] Tong Shuangwen Gu Ting Li Yiwen[2]

Abstract: Beijing *Pingshu* is characterized by its distinctive artistic features. To promote its artistic innovation is the social responsibility of the new generation of *Pingshu* performers. Beijing *Pingshu* not only has a distinctive flavor of language, but also a profound cultural background. It should not only be ethical in content, but also flexible in form and vivid in performance. In the process of artistic creation, the performers should make changes in form, language, and the sense of aesthetics, and draw inspiration from life, audience, and modern society. Only in this way can *Pingshu* improve its artistic characteristics, broaden its audience, and better its future.

Keywords: Beijing *Pingshu*, artistic features, artistic creation

1. Research Significance

Beijing *Pingshu* has very distinctive artistic features. It is of great significance to explore and integrate them with the new mode of entertainment in the 21st century, so as to promote the innovative development of *Pingshu*. In this sense, studying the artistic features and innovations of Beijing *Pingshu* is a vital step to preserve this cultural inheritance.

2. Literature Review

At present, some preliminary achievements have been made in the research on the artistic features and innovations of Beijing *Pingshu*. For

---

1. Associate professor of English, Beijing Foreign Studies University.
2. The other authors of this paper are the 10th grade students of the 1+3 program of The Affiliated High School of Beijing Foreign Studies University.

example, Liang Yan, a young *Pingshu* performer, said in his book *Beijing Pingshu*, "In the long course of development, Beijing *Pingshu* has its own unique charm, such as the exciting stories, the fine performance, the vivid characters, and the humorous language." (Liang, 2015)

Li Xiaohong, an associate research fellow at the National Academy of Chinese Theatre Arts compared the artistic features of *Pingshu* with those of novels and pointed out that *Pingshu* has the following distinctive artistic features: the lively oral expressions; the excellent use of dialogues for plot development; the dynamic performance and improvisation. (Li, 2017)

At present, there exists a gap of inheritance in this art, so it is of great importance to study the artistic features of Beijing *Pingshu* and to promote its artistic innovation.

3. Research Methods

This study used structured interviews to collect data. The team conducted field interviews with four performers, Mr. Ma Jianping, Mr. Tang Ke, Mr. Tang Fan, and Mr. Jia Lin, from July 16 to 28, 2018, and made a detailed and scientific analysis of the interview contents. The findings are as follows.

4. Findings and Discussion

4.1 Data analysis

Table 1: The artistic features of Beijing *Pingshu*

Research Subject	Code	Definition
The special significance of Beijing *Pingshu* to its performers	Industry inheritance	To carry on the culture and characteristics of *Pingshu*: family or master-apprentice inheritance
	Cultural transmission	Dissemination of traditional Chinese culture
	Social responsibility	*Pingshu* educates people to be kind and civilized; that is the function of "Stage Education"
	Enthusiasm	Out of love and interest

continued

Research Subject	Code	Definition
Features of Beijing *Pingshu*	Linguistic charm	The charm of Beijing dialect
	Cultural charm	Beijing *Pingshu* revitalizes or reproduces the old Beijing lifestyle, life structure, pace of life, and living habits
The performance characteristics	Moral integrity	Both the content and the comment of *Pingshu* are morally upright
	Flexibility in form	For the wide range of audience, *Pingshu* gives rise to a variety of forms of performance (such as humor and improvisation, etc.) and requires the performers' ability to play on the spot
	Extensive knowledge	To understand and master the context within and beyond the stories
	Vivid description	To attract the audience by a detailed and exquisite description of the characters and the plot
	A strong sense of inheritance	The ideological content of the traditional *Pingshu* should remain unchanged, but innovation is carried on constantly in the form of performance
The differences in performance between the performers and their teachers	Differences in style	Each performer, though varying in degrees, has their own unique style
	Differences in ability	Compared with their teachers, apprentices are certainly short of experience, knowledge, and competence
	Adaptation and innovation	In order to follow the social trend, classic *Pingshu* pieces are adapted and integrated with modern culture to form a unique style
	Faithfulness in inheritance	To imitate the masters' style and to carry on the tradition
The innovations of contemporary Beijing *Pingshu*	Form innovation	It mainly refers to bilingual *Pingshu*, which are performed in Chinese and English (or other languages)
	Language innovation	To change the terms that are not used or less used into popular expressions
	Aesthetic innovation	To change the sense of aesthetics that are in conflict with today's society to the one that most modern people can accept

continued

Research Subject	Code	Definition
Sources of innovation	From life	Art comes from life and is beyond life
	From audience	To follow the aesthetic needs of the audience
	From the times	To follow the changes and progress of the times
The future development	Artistic height	To improve the artistic features of *Pingshu*
	Audience breadth	To broaden the audience
	Time length	To carry on and to develop *Pingshu*
	Protection strength	To strengthen the protection of *Pingshu*

4.2 Findings

4.2.1 The special significance of Beijing *Pingshu* for its performers

From July 16 to 28, 2018, we interviewed Mr. Tang Ke, Mr. Jia Lin, Mr. Tang Fan, and Mr. Ma Jianping. Analysis of these interviews suggests that Beijing *Pingshu* has a great significance to the performers. This is why the new generation of young *Pingshu* artists shoulders the social responsibility of inheriting and promoting *Pingshu*. This paper will discuss the special significance of Beijing *Pingshu* from the following four aspects: the industry inheritance, the cultural transmission, the social responsibility, and the enthusiasm of the performers.

The industry inheritance of *Pingshu* refers to the passing down of *Pingshu* or its branches. *Pingshu* is inherited from either father to son or master to apprentice. As Mr. Tang Ke said, "*Pingshu* has a complete heritage system." To continue and develop *Pingshu*, inheritance is essential.

Cultural transmission refers to the dissemination of Chinese traditional culture. As an outstanding cultural symbol, *Pingshu* "has profound connotation and cultural background" (Tang Ke). Therefore, the dissemination of *Pingshu* should first focus on spreading among Chinese people and then gradually to the world. As Mr. Ma Jianping, a bilingual *Pingshu* performer said, "I think as Chinese people, we must first understand our culture before presenting it to the world."

Social responsibility refers to using *Pingshu* to educate people to be virtuous. Just as the *Pingshu* performers often say, "*Pingshu* is educational and enlightening." *Pingshu* is not just for fun, or simply telling stories; it is telling stories with embedded truths. Mr. Tang Ke said, "It advises people to be nice, presents truth through stories, and teaches them to be good people." *Pingshu* attempts to convey a moral lesson, which can benefit society.

Enthusiasm refers to the love of *Pingshu* or the interest in it, which inspires the performers to learn and perform *Pingshu*. People in Beijing regard listening to *Pingshu* as a childhood memory, and developing interest and hobbies in this field from an early age will probably make them love more of *Pingshu*. The dissemination of *Pingshu* should not be age-sensitive; people should even be exposed to *Pingshu* from an early age in order to stimulate interest. Mr. Ma Jianping expressed how he felt about *Pingshu* when he performed himself, "One word, addictive!" He claimed that it was because of their love of *Pingshu* that they enjoyed it and were willing to perform it, comment on it, and pass on the culture.

4.2.2 The characteristics of Beijing *Pingshu*

Beijing *Pingshu* has two distinctive features: linguistic charm and cultural charm. As an art of language, Beijing *Pingshu* not only possesses the phonological features of the Beijing dialect but also evokes the unique lifestyle and cultural characteristics of old Beijingers. These two aspects of charms are consistently evident in Beijing *Pingshu*.

Linguistic charm refers to the phonological beauty of a language (especially a dialect). As Mr. Tang Ke said, "The charm of Beijing *Pingshu* comes from its natural taste." Although it is relatively easy for Beijing *Pingshu* to achieve finesse and delicacy in language, it is very difficult to grasp the rhymes and tones between words and sentences in the Beijing dialect. Mr. Ma Jianping also pointed out, "There are many ancient Chinese languages and accents in Beijing *Pingshu*." The unique expression of this language is a defining aspect of Beijing *Pingshu*.

Cultural charm refers to the restoration and revivification of the life style, living structure, pace of life and living habits of the old Beijingers that *Pingshu* brings. And thus, the images of Beijing in various times have been preserved in people's memory. As Mr. Tang Ke said, "It is a way of living for Beijingers, and behind it lies a deep cultural foundation of Beijing."

4.2.3 The characteristics of *Pingshu* performers

For *Pingshu* performers, their distinct performance characteristics are very important as they affect the performers' ability to attract the public, and subsequently inherit the culture of *Pingshu*. From the interviews with the four *Pingshu* performers, we have learned that their characteristics mainly include moral integrity, flexibility in form, extensive knowledge, vivid description, and a strong sense of inheritance.

Moral integrity means that both the content and the comment of *Pingshu* are based on the principles of objectivity, justice and virtue, impartiality and benevolence. Comrade Chen Yun, who was the vice General Secretary of the Communist Party of China, once put forward the request for the development of *Quyi*, "Train artists, publish books, and take the right path", which calls for "advocating morality and art". In the interview, Mr. Tang Ke said, "There is a saying in our industry, which is, 'the entertainment is for education'. If you are to advise audience for good, you must have a very positive image on the stage, not a slippery and sensational one." So this characteristic can be summarized with one word, "integrity".

Flexibility in form refers to different *Pingshu* performing skills, such as humor and improvisation, which will be used differently in front of different audience groups. And performers need to use them appropriately, based on the context. The performers use the acting skills that they are good at to vividly present the plot and details to attract the audience's attention. In our interview with Mr. Tang Ke, we were informed that he learned *Gushu* before, which is a one-person opera, emphasizing singing skills. He said, "*Pingshu* emphasizes adaptability, so the means of expression must be flexible." It is also very important to use different expressions for different audiences.

Extensive knowledge means that each performer should know and master as much knowledge as possible about *Pingshu* and the world, i.e. the nature and the society, so as to attract the public. Let's take Mr. Tang Ke as an example. He mentioned, "I have a wide range of interests, such as singing, instruments, pronunciation, narration, etc." By learning different skills, Mr. Tang Ke strengthens his ability in many fields, so that he can make *Pingshu* even more attractive.

Vivid description refers to the representation of characters and plots with detailed descriptions. Mr. Ma Jianping mentioned a keyword, "vivid characters". If there is a lively plot, vivid characters, and attractive performance, *Pingshu* can bring the audience intuitive feelings and experience.

There are also some *Pingshu* performers who pay more attention to inheritance. They refuse to make any changes to the traditional *Pingshu*. "At present, I'm not thinking of developing any special features of my own," said Mr. Jia Lin, "I just want to honestly inherit this traditional art." This is not only a characteristic of part of performers, but also a way of inheritance for the purpose of protection.

4.2.4 The differences in performance between the performers and their teachers

Each performer gave different answers to this question. The differences in style, ability, innovation and faithfulness in inheritance are the keywords of this question.

The difference in style refers to that each artist has his or her own unique style. Artistic style is generally related to personal factors. Mr. Tang Ke mentioned, "My style is different from my teacher's. He specialized in and performed *Xihe Dagu* (a kind of musical form with drum) all his life. But I have learned various oral performance arts such as Beijing opera, *Sanxian*, southern *Pingtan* and *Xiaoqu* from Taiwan. I integrate the skills and make my own style." Mr. Tang Fan and Mr. Ma Jianping, the two bilingual *Pingshu* performers said, "Everyone has his or her own *Pingshu* performing style. In *Pingshu*, no two performers have exactly the same style. It cannot be possible."

The difference in ability is that compared with teachers, apprentices still have some relative deficiencies (such as lack of experience, knowledge, and skills). They need to enrich their performing arts through long-term accumulation. "Older generation of *Pingshu* performers has a much deeper foundation." (Ma Jianping) We can see that the four *Pingshu* performers we interviewed are modest about their performances, and this is one of the reasons why they are making progress.

Adaptation and innovation refer to adapting the classic *Pingshu* plays in order to cater to the social trend. By discarding the inappropriate factors, maintaining the classic beauty, and incorporating modern culture, we can form a unique modern *Pingshu* style. This kind of innovation needs courage, because the innovation risks disrupting the inner structure of *Pingshu*, a traditional art. Mr. Tang Ke mentioned his experience in innovation. He believed innovation "lies in keeping pace with the times". "Every time I finish my performance, I ask my teacher to give me advice. But I don't blindly take all of his advice and apply them immediately. I will make an analysis to decide whether these suggestions can be used, whether they can be used again and again, and what adaptations should be made when they are used. Some of the things can be changed, some cannot; what can be changed is to further enrich and develop the tradition." (Tang Ke)

Faithfulness in inheritance means to imitate the style from the teacher strictly. Mr. Jia Lin mentioned, "I started with imitation and have not formed my own style or characteristics yet." This is a more conservative approach and it ensures that the tradition of *Pingshu* can be passed on.

4.2.5 Innovation of contemporary Beijing *Pingshu*

In order to develop, *Pingshu* must keep pace with the times. Therefore, the innovations of *Pingshu* include form innovation, language innovation, and aesthetic innovation.

One of the innovations so far we have observed is bilingual *Pingshu*, performed in both Chinese and English (or other languages). It is hoped that *Pingshu*, as a traditional Chinese culture, will spread to the world and more people will become familiar with it. Therefore, there must be improvements and innovations in its language. As the two performers, Mr. Tang Fan and Mr. Ma Jianping said, "The bilingual *Pingshu* is innovation." *Pingshu* should not be limited to Chinese audiences. The spread of *Pingshu* to other parts of the world by foreign languages should be strengthened, so that more people can understand the content of *Pingshu* and more people will accept and love this art form.

Language innovation refers to the transformation of some terms that are not used or less used into popular expressions in today's society. Beijing *Pingshu* has a long history, and many of the old sayings or jargons are not easy for the audiences to understand. "In a language that modern people can understand, we should tell stories that they have never heard, so that modern audiences can feel the joys, sorrows, love and hatred of historical figures." (Tang Fan and Ma Jianping) In order to facilitate the audiences' understanding of the content of *Pingshu*, and to cultivate their interest in *Pingshu*, the performers are constantly updating their expressions. For example, in Mr. Ma Jianping's *Pingshu* performance, "there will be more modern words, such as today's catchphrases" (Ma Jianping). In the process of the performance, more modern, popular vocabulary will be incorporated, and historical stories will be combined with contemporary words, so that the audiences' understanding of traditional culture will be boosted. In this way, listening to *Pingshu* is no longer boring, but becomes lively and interesting, and more authentic.

Aesthetic innovation refers to changing the old aesthetic ideas that are in conflict with modern society to the ones that are acceptable to most modern people. As the two performers, Mr. Tang Fan and Mr. Ma Jianping, said, "Many young audiences and children may feel estranged from accepting the old ideas." Beijing *Pingshu*, appealing to the old generation, may not be welcomed by modern people. Therefore, we should keep pace with the times and conform to the aesthetic concepts of today's society. As Mr. Ma Jianping said, "Aesthetic innovation is the proper choice of the content of *Pingshu*, taking the essence and removing the dross so that it can adapt to the modern aesthetic concepts and cognitive habits through a process of selection and adaptation." Appropriate choices and trade-offs will be accepted by most modern people, which will also be conducive to the better development and inheritance of the art of *Pingshu*.

4.2.6 Sources of innovation for Beijing *Pingshu*

Innovation is essential for the passing on of *Pingshu*. But how to innovate is the most important concern for every *Pingshu* performer and audience. Through the interview, we learned that there are three main sources of innovation: from life, from the audience, and from the times.

For example, Mr. Ma Jianping emphasized the importance of daily life in *Pingshu* innovation. He said, "Art comes from life but is beyond life. It is accumulated piece by piece from life." Even though *Pingshu* is not widely popularized, there are some people who entertain themselves by listening to *Pingshu*. Only when *Pingshu* is rooted in life can it absorb the most essential elements from life, so that the audience can relax in the process of listening, and make *Pingshu* a real way of entertainment.

Pingshu rooted in the audience means catering to the aesthetic needs of the audience. The performer should design the content and presentation form according to the public's interest, so as to ensure that the audience keeps fresh all the time. "We face the audience all the time" (Tang Ke), so everything must be based on the preference of the audience. "If what you say is not attractive to the audience, they will not come back. Without audience, who do you perform for?" (Tang Ke) Only with the support of old audiences and the attention of new audiences can we have the motivation and conditions to protect and inherit Beijing *Pingshu*. Therefore, the audience is also an important factor in the development of Beijing *Pingshu*.

Being rooted in the times means adapting to the social changes and progress of the era. Mr. Tang Ke mentioned, "Keep up with the times and don't stick to the rules, because the audiences you face are moving forward with the times." Traditional things have their advantages, but as time passes, people's ideas are changing. So non-innovation will inevitably be eliminated by the times. Therefore, in order to develop continuously, it is an inevitable trend to keep abreast of the changes of the times.

4.2.7 The future development of Beijing *Pingshu*

In terms of the development of Beijing *Pingshu*, the interviewees mainly answered this question from the following four dimensions: artistic height, audience breadth, time length, and protection strength.

Artistic height refers to enhancing the artistic characteristics of *Pingshu* so that it can be spread to a wider audience and achieve the goal of protection. But blind innovation is wrong, and maintaining and adhering to its traditional character at this time is a protective development direction. This is what Mr. Tang Ke mentioned, "Uncertainty is a constraint to ensure that you are developing on the right track."

Audience breadth means to popularize *Pingshu*. This is a great challenge to the *Pingshu* performers, and a test on their ability. Beijing is a famous historical city with a deep cultural background and numerous legends which provide the richest materials for Beijing *Pingshu*. Beijing dialect is fun to the ear and is easy to arouse interest of the audience. Therefore, as long as the *Pingshu* performances are attractive, they will surely be favored by more and more audiences.

Time length refers to the inheritance of Beijing *Pingshu*. Mr. Tang Ke said, "It is the mission of our generation to pass on *Pingshu*. We must not let this art, which has been handed down from our ancestors, die in our hands."

Protection strength means to promote the protection of *Pingshu*. Mr. Tang Ke said, "The premier task now is to prevent a premature death of *Pingshu*". We need the joint efforts from the nation, the government and the people to achieve these goals. "We must protect *Pingshu*'s positive factors and let them play their full and vivid roles." (Tang Ke)

5. Conclusion

The artistic characteristics and innovations of Beijing *Pingshu* are of great significance to the performers. To them, *Pingshu* is an interest, a way of spreading culture, and a sense of responsibility for the inheritance of factions. The reason why Beijing *Pingshu* can attract some people is not only that it has unique linguistic and cultural charm, but also that it has rich and vivid forms of performance, which test the ability and foundation of the performers. The performers need to define their own storytelling form first, then collect material from life, audience and era, and adapt the content. Such an innovative way can not only improve the artistic characteristics of *Pingshu*, broaden the art form to the crowd, but also promote the protection of *Pingshu*, so as to better the development of the art of *Pingshu*.

References:

Li, Xiaohong. The Artistic Features of Pingshu – in Comparison with Novels [J]. The Study of Ancient Chinese Novels and Drama (13th Vol.), 2017: 366-374.

Liang, Yan. Beijing Pingshu [M]. Beijing: Beijing Arts and Photography Press, 2015.

北京评书说书人的培养[1]

孙泽萌　程　曦　王　颂[2]

【摘要】 北京评书是老北京人中流传的一种喜闻乐见的娱乐形式。但遗憾的是，目前北京评书传承出现严重断代的问题。大力培养评书传承人就显得尤为重要。在传承人培养过程中，候选人本身的资质固然重要，但更要把着眼点放在提高传承人的专业素养上，特别是要鼓励传承人在努力吸收评书思想内容和师父表演风格的同时，做到融会贯通，形成自己鲜明的表演风格。当然，传承人的培养也离不开政府和社会各界的大力支持。

【关键词】 北京评书　说书人　专业素养　表演风格

一、研究意义

评书是中国民间优秀的口头文学之一，深受老百姓喜爱。但是，目前北京评书的发展遇到了前所未有的瓶颈——北京评书艺术家的数量十分有限。因此，大力培养说书人，对于评书艺术的传承和发展具有重要意义。遗憾的是，目前学界对于说书人培养的研究十分有限。本文希望能够填补这个空白。

---

1. 本调研报告科研指导教师为北京外国语大学专用英语学院副教授仵胜奇。
2. 本调研报告的三位作者均为北京外国语大学附属中学高中部十一年级学生。

二、文献综述

学界对于说书人的培养有零星的一些研究成果。例如，上海大学文学院的李小红认为，近年来研究者的目光集中在对评书艺术家的关注上，这些研究有助于我们了解著名评书艺术家的成长历程。他们的出身、经历、对人生磨难的正确对待等，都对后人有着重要的启示。(李小红，2010)评书艺术家宝贵的经验往往会对后世说书人起到模范作用。鞍山人民广播电台的杨佩琴在《单田芳评书的艺术风格》(1995)一文中，从干净利落的快节奏、融汇情理的知识、跌宕起伏的情节和通俗简练的语言四个方面高度评价了单田芳先生的艺术才华。

三、研究方法

本研究采用结构式访谈和田野调查的方法收集数据，并通过案例研究对数据进行分析，取得了一些发现。研究小组成员在2018年7月16—28日对四名北京评书演员——梁彦、马剑平、唐柯、贾林——进行了实地采访，并对采访内容作了科学分析，得出如下结论。

四、发现与讨论

（一）数据分析

表1：北京评书说书人培养的具体内容

研究主题	编码	定义
学习北京评书必备的基本素质	地道的北京话	有着老北京的语言特色和文化特色
	良好的形象	形象端正、着装大方、言谈得体、举止典雅、气质不凡
	出众的能力	语言表达能力：发音清晰、说话利索、善于表达
		逻辑思维能力：合理思考、灵活使用
		学习能力：有强烈的求知欲、好奇心，以及学习新知识的能力
		舞台技巧能力：具备舞台表演经验、随机应变能力
	勤奋的精神	认真踏实、坚持不懈
说书人必备的专业素养	热爱评书	发自内心喜爱并且能用心学习、表演评书
	知识丰富	博览群书、涉猎广泛、文化素养高
	表现形式现代化	表现形式丰富、灵活，在表演中融入更多的时代元素
	具有深厚的中华传统文化底蕴	认真阅读中国经典，领略中华文化的精髓，培养自己深厚的文化底蕴
培养一名说书人需要经历的阶段	吸收	接受评书的思想、内容和师父的表演风格
	融通	在师父的讲解中融入自己的想法，并在此基础上做到"活用"
师父的传授方式	口传心授	师父口头传授，徒弟内心领会

续表

研究主题	编码	定义
政府和社会对说书人提供的帮助	政府扶持	政策支持：国家倡导人们多学习传统文化，帮助评书表演艺术家开拓评书市场
		场地支持：免费提供特定场地，供评书传承人开展评书教学、练习、表演、讨论、交流等活动
		经费支持：通过国家非遗项目提供一定的活动经费
		教育支持：开展"评书进校园"活动
	社会扶持	观众到书场听书，社会慈善家为国家非遗项目提供赞助

(二) 发现

1. 学习北京评书必备的基本素质

北京评书是北京人的评书，有着老北京的语言和文化特色，所以在选择和培养说书人时，"北京人"几乎成了硬性条件。对此，马剑平老师给出了原因，他说："因为北京评书说的很多内容都跟北京城的风土人情有关，如果说让一个从外地来京的孩子去现学现积累的话，恐怕是来不及的。北京评书有很多古话，也有一些北京的官腔，如果不是生长在北京环境里，恐怕很难有机会学到。"

北京评书候选人不仅要是北京人，他们的形象也是说书人选拔的一个重要条件，即形象端正、着装大方、言谈得体、举止典雅、气质不凡。用评书里的行话讲，就是"书风要正"。正如唐柯老师所说："第一个字，正。首先，我们有一句话叫'说书唱戏劝人方'。我们是'劝善'，意思是你在台上必须得是一个很正的形象，而不是油嘴滑舌，哗众取宠。我们当然要讲幽默，因为幽默是我们的表现手段之一。总之一句话，你说书必须正，你的书风必须正。"唐柯老师对于形象方面，提出了一个"正"字，而马剑平老师提出的是"精气神"三个字。他说："'精气神'这三个字就够了。也就是说，说书人的精神是非常高昂的，他的气息够，功夫也就更强。"

在能力方面，我们采访的各位老师也都提出了不同的要求。首先，说书人应具备良好的语言表达能力。例如，梁彦老师说："要口齿清晰，表达清楚；大舌头和卷舌肯定不行。"马剑平老师也认为："要成为一个良好的评书艺术家，必须要吐字清楚。如果说话说不清楚、不利索，这儿'啊'，那儿'啊'，'打磕巴'等，这些都不行。"

其次，说书人应具备很强的逻辑思维能力。马剑平老师说："你要给观众讲的话，首先你自己需要明白；你要不明白，你就无法和观众互动。而这就需要说书人的语言组织能力强，逻辑思维清晰。"

再次，说书人应有强烈的求知欲、好奇心，以及学习新知识的能力。正如唐柯老师所说："求知欲、好奇心是学习新知识的基础，学习评书表演也不例外。"

最后，说书人应具备一定的舞台技巧。在舞台上要有很强的随机应变能力，能轻松化解各种突发状况。例如，马剑平老师说："说书人反应一定要快，在现场会有很多的突发状况。那么你要根据当时的情景、当时的作品、当时的语言环境，创造出一些语言，把这个事情给抹过去，或者是抖个包袱之类的，我们行话叫作'现挂'。"梁彦老师也表示："舞台上临场发挥的一些经验，包括道具（如扇子、手绢等）怎么样使用，都需要反复练习才能掌握。"

说书人还应拥有勤奋的精神，做到认真踏实，坚持不懈。例如，马剑平老师说："想要掌握说书的技巧就需学而不断，因为学习北京评书就如逆水行舟，不进则退。如果你放下几天，再上台那感觉完全不一样，这就要求学习不能间断。我们要是想说一部书，至少得通读五遍，通读五遍以上才能够达到说书的要求。"贾林老师也持有相同的观点。他说："如果训练普通观众一个十分钟的小段落，那可能强化突击训练三天，甚至于只要把词背会了，在台上不忘词就可以说小段落了。但成为一个真正在台上说书的人，那可不是三天就能练就的，那是毕生无止境的追求。"

2. 说书人必备的专业素养

要想成为一名合格的说书人，不仅要真心喜欢评书，还要拥有广博的知识，掌握丰富的表现手法，具备深厚的文化修养、勤奋刻苦的意志品质和必要的说书技巧。

首先，说书人要真心喜欢评书，热爱评书事业，只有这样，才能坚持不懈地学习并长期静心钻研评书表演艺术。正如唐柯老师所说："必须要热爱这项艺术，肯为这一艺术付出。因为评书是很难学的，尤其是学习传统艺术，都是需要下功夫、用心钻研的，而不是图一时之利，让它马上达到一个什么效果，这是不可能的。"只有说书人对评书充满兴趣，他们才愿意投入全部的精力和感情，通过刻苦钻研和长期积累去更深入地了解评书、充实自己，从而实现传承。这是学习评书艺术的基础。对此，唐柯老师的感受也非常深刻，他说："你投入感情就像你喜欢你的爱好一样，你喜欢才会对它投入。说书也是一样，你也得投入，把你的一切奉献给它，这是一种奉献精神。为它奉献，你无怨无悔，你才能去传承。只有用心，你才能扎根去研究。"

其次，说书人应该博览群书，不断地汲取知识的营养，具备一定的文化素养。唐柯老师说："说书人要有博闻强记的本事。广泛阅读，要把文案印到脑子里面，因为上台说书和作报告是不一样的，不能在台上拿着稿子讲内容。你必须把它消化在你的骨子里头，然后再将文案运用到表演中。"此外，说书人应通过收听、观察、熟悉评书不同流派的表演风格，增加知识储备。梁彦老师说："想学书要先听书。"因为只有听的书足够多，说书人才会有丰富的知识储备，思维也才能更活跃。而且随着时代的变化和社会的发展，观众的知识水平也在不断提高。在这种情况下，评书演员扎实的知识结构和广博的知识储备就显得尤为重要。

再次，说书人的表现形式也应丰富、灵活，要在表演中融入更多的时代元素，从而形成自身鲜明的评书风格。正如唐柯老师所说："表现手段必须要灵活多样，你要根据观众的不同需求去设计。由于我的评书表演涉及面比较广，如弹、唱、乐、述，我要花大量时间思考书以外的这些东西，久而久之，就熟练了，形成了我个人的说书风格。"

最后，说书人要认真阅读中国经典，领略中华文化的精髓，培养自己深厚的文化底蕴。也就是说，"评书艺术要有深刻的内涵，它有非常深厚的文化底蕴在里面，这些是新一代评书从业者首先需要理清的思路。所谓'书风必须正'，就是说评书艺术要根植于博大精深的中华文化"（唐柯）。

3.培养一名说书人需要经历的阶段

说书人的培养需要经过吸收和融通两个阶段。

吸收是指认真学习评书的思想、内容和师父的表演风格。对于评书的内容，要熟记于心；对于师父的表演风格，要潜心钻研，从简单模仿开始，到掌握处理技巧、领悟处理思路，都要细致入微，最终做到融会贯通。马剑平老师认为，学评书就需要通过多听老师的评书表演来吸取知识的营养。他说："'听'是基础。'听'这个阶段可能需要一到两年时间,快的可能也得要十个月左右。"唐柯老师认为,在听的过程中,要特别注意领会不同评书表演艺术家的表演思路。他说:"学评书的第一手段是坚持听。听书是第一步,想学评书必须要多听,长时间听,甚至听一辈子,学无止境。在听的过程中,要琢磨不同评书表演艺术家的思路和风格。"唐柯老师提到了评书入门常说的一句行话,即"评书初学者先要'死学'"。他说:"所谓'死学',是将学习的知识全盘接受,师父怎么做你就怎么做。通过'死学',领会师父对特定文本的处理思路。这个过程中必须有一个从量变到质变的过程,通过量的积累来实现质的飞跃。"

融通是指在师父的讲解中融入自己的想法,并在此基础上做到"活用"。通过不断练习,在熟练掌握师父传授知识的基础上,创造属于自己的鲜明的评书风格。唐柯老师认为,融通需要勤学苦练。他说:"只有上台前不断地练习,才能将评书的学习活用到表演中。"马剑平老师谈了他对"活用"的看法:"'活用'指在思路正确的基础上,将自己的辨别能力运用到艺术实践过程中,找到适合自己的表达方式;能根据故事情节、自己的理解、自己积攒的词汇和自己储备的知识去讲解评书内容。"

4. 师父的传授方式

师父的传授方式一般为口传心授,这是现阶段最普遍也是最传统的一种传授方式。正如马剑平老师所说:"就是师父说你听,然后你把师父的技巧融会贯通。师父会帮你作一些总结,还会有一些文本记录,这些都是在帮你积累经验,但是最主要还是靠面对面讲授。在听了师父说的大量评书后,你便要自己去尝试说书。你每次说完书以后,师父会帮助你分析——你哪儿说得好,哪儿说得不好,应该怎么改进——这样你才能有大幅度的提高。"

在口传心授的过程中，师父真心传授，徒弟真诚接受，这种方式有助于徒弟与师父建立深厚的感情，也有利于更好地传承中华传统文化。正如唐柯老师所说："我们称师父'三年为师，终身为父'。你对你父亲怎么孝敬，你就对师父怎么孝敬，因为他给你的是一辈子都让你受益的东西。他对你的呵护，他对你的关爱，甚至他对你的批评，都是促进你长进的，是切实有效的手段。他是真心对你，那么你也应该真心去回报。中国传统艺术的传承更多的是要靠感情的维系，所以口传心授是目前甚至更长时间内的学习传统。"

5.政府和社会对说书人提供的帮助

政府对说书人的帮助主要体现在提供政策支持、场地支持、经费支持和教育支持。

政府会在政策方面提供支持。正如唐柯老师所说："政府会倡导人们多学习传统文化，帮助评书表演艺术家开拓评书市场，进而让更多的人了解评书。"同时，国家领导人也会号召大家学习中华传统文化。"例如，习近平总书记号召大家学习中华优秀传统文化，传承优秀传统文化，这些都给我们这些说书人很大的鼓舞。"(唐柯)

政府也会在场地和经费方面提供支持。一些书馆的建立离不开政府的资金支持。梁彦老师说："宣南书馆能坚持到现在，就是得到了政府的经费扶持，就比如演出过程中需要的水电费用全部减免，演出的场地费进行相应的减免或全免。这样的支持对我们评书演员来说很重要。"

此外，社会各界也会为评书艺术发展提供一定的帮助。例如，观众亲自到书馆去支持评书演员的表演、社会慈善家为国家非遗项目提供赞助等，都为说书人提供了宝贵的支持。

五、总结

总体来看，本文在说书人的培养方面主要介绍了说书人必备的基本素质、必备的专业素养、所需经历的阶段、师父的传授方式、政府和社会对说书人提供的帮助这五方面。要想学习评书表演艺术，说书人首先应掌握地道的北京话，拥有良好的形象、出众的能力和勤奋的精神；而要想成为一名合格的说书人，则需要热爱评书，获得一定的知识储备，掌握灵活多样的表现形式，具备深厚的中华传统文化底蕴等。培养说书人需要经历吸收和融通两个阶段。吸收是指认真学习评书的内容、思想，以及师父的表演风格，评书的内容要熟记于心，师父的表演风格要潜心钻研。融通是指在师父的讲解中融入自己的想法，并在此基础上做到"活用"，创造属于自己的鲜明的评书风格。在传授的过程中，师父口传心授，徒弟心领神会。培养说书人离不开政府的支持和社会提供的帮助；国家大力支持评书的发展，鼓励人们去了解传统文化。

参考文献：

李小红.中国评书研究的现状与思考[J].艺术百家，2010，(3)：150—154.
杨佩琴.单田芳评书的艺术风格[J].现代广播–北京广播学院学报，1995，(3)：75—76.

The Training of Beijing *Pingshu* Performers

Shen Yiwen[1] Sun Zemeng Cheng Xi Wang Song[2]

Abstract: Beijing *Pingshu* is a popular form of entertainment among Beijingers. However, the shortage of performers is one of the critical factors that hinder its inheritance and development. Therefore, it is particularly important to cultivate the younger generation of performers. In the process of training, the focus is on enhancing both the personal and professional qualities. In particular, the young performers are encouraged not only to imitate the masters' performance but also to integrate their own features and form their distinctive styles. Furthermore, the training of young performers depends on the strong support of the government and the community.

Keywords: Beijing *Pingshu*, *Pingshu* performers, professional qualities, performance styles

1. Research Significance

Beijing *Pingshu* is an outstanding example of popular oral literature in Chinese folk arts. However, the development of Beijing *Pingshu* has hit an unprecedented bottleneck, and the number of *Pingshu* performers is very limited. Therefore, taking great efforts to cultivate *Pingshu* performers is of great significance for the inheritance and development of this art. However, there is only a limited amount of research on the training of *Pingshu* performers. We hope this paper can, to some extent, fill the gap.

---

1. Associate professor of English, Beijing Foreign Studies University.
2. The other authors of this paper are the 11th grade students of The Affiliated High School of Beijing Foreign Studies University.

2. Literature Review

We have found a limited number of articles on the training of *Pingshu* performers. For example, Li Xiaohong, from Shanghai University, stated the following:

> "In recent years, researchers have focused their attention on the famous *Pingshu* performers, and these studies help us understand the growth of these famous artists. Their family backgrounds, career experiences and hardships and sufferings in their lives have important implications for future generations." (Li, 2010)

The valuable experience of famous *Pingshu* performers will often serve as a role model for later generations. In the article "The Artistic Features of Shan Tianfang's Pingshu Performance", Yang (1995) highly praised Mr. Shan's artistic talent from four aspects, namely the rolling plot, the understanding of the society, the clean and fast-paced expressions, and the simple language.

3. Research Methods

The study used structured interviews and field surveys for data collection. From July 16 to 28, 2018, the team conducted field interviews with four *Pingshu* performers, Liang Yan, Ma Jianping, Tang Ke, and Jia Lin, and made a detailed analysis of the data. The following results have been drawn.

4. Results and Discussion

4.1 Data analysis

Table 1: The training of *Pingshu* performers

Theme	Code	Definition
Basic qualities necessary for learning *Pingshu*	Authentic Beijing dialect	A master of Beijing dialect and cultural characteristics
	Good personal image	A good personal image of dressing, speech, manner, and temperament
	Outstanding ability	Interpersonal communication: clear pronunciation, fluency, good expression
		Critical thinking: rationality, applications of knowledge
		Learning ability: thirst for knowledge, curiosity, and the ability to learn new knowledge
		Skills on stage: rich experience on stage and the ability to improvise
	Diligence	Earnest and persistent
Necessary professional qualities for a performer	Devotion to *Pingshu*	Love *Pingshu* and study and perform *Pingshu* with commitment
	Knowledgeable	Extensive reading, wide range of interest, high cultural awareness
	Modern performance style	Rich and flexible in performance style; modern elements incorporated in the performance
	Profound Chinese traditional culture	A thorough study on Chinese classical masterpieces, appreciation for the essence of Chinese culture and cultivation for profound cultural background
The stages of training a performer	Absorption	Learn the stories of *Pingshu* and the master's performance style
	Integration	Integrate one's own thoughts with the master's teaching and apply appropriately
The method of teaching	Word of mouth	Masters teach orally, and learners understand and learn by heart

continued

Theme	Code	Definition
Government and community assistance to *Pingshu* artists	Governmental support	Policy support: the government encourages people to learn more about traditional culture and helps *Pingshu* artist and performer to explore markets
		Performing venue support: providing free sites for performer to carry out *Pingshu* activities such as teaching, practice, performance, discussion, and interaction
		Financial support: funding through National Intangible Cultural Heritage Program
		Educational support: carry out *Pingshu* activities in schools
	Social support	Audience attending *Pingshu* performance; funding and charities sponsor the National Intangible Cultural Heritage Program

4.2 Research findings

4.2.1 Basic qualities necessary for learning *Pingshu*

Beijing *Pingshu* originated from Beijing and is a form of entertainment for local Beijingers. So the primary requirement for a *Pingshu* performer is being a Beijinger. Mr. Ma Jianping gave reasons for this:

> "Many contents in Beijing *Pingshu* are related to the local customs and traditions in Beijing. I am afraid that it will be too late for a child from other places to learn and accumulate such a sense of locality. There are a lot of ancient Chinese language uses and some formal Beijing tones in Beijing *Pingshu*. It would be really hard to learn if the person did not grow up in Beijing." (Ma Jianping)

To learn Beijing *Pingshu*, the performers also need to have a decent personal image in the style of dressing, speech, manner, and temperament. In the jargon of *Pingshu*, it says that "the style of the performance must be upright". As Mr. Tang Ke said, "The first key word should be upright. In our profession, we have a saying called '*Pingshu* advises people on the ethical conscientiousness'. As *Pingshu* performers, we 'exhort for the good', meaning that we must have a morally upright and trustworthy image on the stage. Of course, we need humor in the performance, because humor is one of our means of expression, but there is no place for glibness and grandstanding. In a word, *Pingshu* and its style must be upright." Mr. Tang proposed the word "upright" to describe *Pingshu* performers while Mr. Ma mentioned the word "spirit". Mr. Ma said, "The word 'spirit' means a lot. When a *Pingshu* performer's spirit holds high, he is well-prepared."

In terms of outstanding abilities, the *Pingshu* performers that we interviewed talked about different requirements. Firstly, *Pingshu* performers should have a good ability of language expression. For example, Mr. Liang Yan said, "The performers must speak clearly and must not have a thick tongue or retroflexion." Mr. Ma also said that "to be a good *Pingshu* performer, a person should speak clearly. It is not acceptable to speak unclearly or incoherently, or to have a stutter".

Secondly, *Pingshu* performers should have strong logical thinking. "To let the audience understand your story, you need to understand the logic of the story first; if you don't even understand them, you won't be able to interact with the audience. *Pingshu* performers should know how to organize their language and think logically". (Ma Jianping)

Thirdly, *Pingshu* performers should have a thirst for knowledge, curiosity, and the ability to learn new knowledge. As Mr. Tang said, "Curiosity is the basis for learning all new knowledge, and it is the same for *Pingshu* performance."

Lastly, *Pingshu* performers should have certain stage skills. They need to have the ability to improvise and be able to cope with emergencies on stage. For example, Mr. Ma said, "*Pingshu* performers must quickly respond to the temporary emergencies on stage and create some new lines to cover up the emergencies. In our jargon, it is called '*Xiangua*'." Mr. Liang also said, "Some of the experience on stage, including how to use props such as Chinese fans, handkerchiefs and so on, needs repeated practice for full mastery."

Pingshu performers should also be diligent, conscientious, and persistent. Mr. Ma said:

> "You need continuous learning if you want to master the skills of *Pingshu* performance. Learning Beijing *Pingshu* is like sailing against the current. If you don't go forward, you will lag behind. If you stop performing continuously for a few days, you will feel raw when you get back on stage again. This requires you to keep on learning and practicing. If you want to perform a story, you must read it at least five times. Only by reading it more than five times can you meet the requirements of performing *Pingshu*." (Ma Jianping)

Mr. Jia Lin has the same opinion. He said, "If you teach an amateur a ten-minute *Pingshu* piece, it may need an intense training session of three days. The time is even shorter if one can learn the words by heart and perform on stage without stage fright. But if you want to be a real *Pingshu* performer, it's a life-long pursuit."

4.2.2 Necessary professional qualities for a performer

In order to become a qualified *Pingshu* performer, one should not only love *Pingshu*, have extensive knowledge, master rich expression techniques, but also have a high cultural awareness, a strong will, and necessary *Pingshu* skills.

First of all, a *Pingshu* performer should love *Pingshu* wholeheartedly and enjoy the career. Only in this way can the performer continue to study the art for a long period of time. As Mr. Tang said, "We must love this art and be willing to sacrifice everything for it. It is impossible for anyone to achieve the skills immediately." Mr. Tang felt deeply about this. He said, "You put your heart into it just as you do for your passion. The same is true of *Pingshu*, and it is a kind of dedication that you have to put in, giving it everything you have. If you are dedicated, then you will have no regrets, and you can pass it on. Only with your heart can you study diligently."

In addition, *Pingshu* performers should read many books, constantly learn new knowledge, and be culturally cultivated. Mr. Tang said, "It is necessary for *Pingshu* performers to learn more and remember fast. *Pingshu* performance, unlike presenting a report, cannot be done by reading scripts on the stage. You must digest the stories and tell them in your show." In addition, *Pingshu* performers should increase their knowledge by listening to different schools of *Pingshu*, and observing and familiarizing themselves with the performance styles. Mr. Liang said that "if you want to learn a new story, you should first listen to how other people present it". Only by listening extensively to different *Pingshu* performances from other artists, can one have abundant knowledge and active thoughts. With the change of times and the development of society, the audience is becoming more knowledgeable. In this circumstance, *Pingshu* performers should learn as much as they can.

What's more, *Pingshu* performers should have rich and flexible expressions, and incorporate more modern elements into their performances, thus forming their own distinctive styles. As Mr. Tang said, "The means of expression must be flexible and varied. You have to design them according to the needs of different audience groups. I've spent a lot of time thinking about things beyond *Pingshu*, such as playing musical instruments and singing; and over time, I've become more skilled and formed my own *Pingshu* style."

Finally, *Pingshu* performers should earnestly read Chinese classics, appreciate the essence of Chinese culture, and cultivate their own cultural understanding. In other words, "The art of *Pingshu* should have a profound connotation, and it has a very deep cultural background. These are the things that we as younger generation of *Pingshu* performers need to realize first. The art of *Pingshu* must root itself in the profound Chinese culture."

(Tang Ke)

4.2.3 The stages of training a performer

The training of *Pingshu* performers includes two stages: absorption and integration. Absorption refers to the study of the stories' contents and the master's performance style. Remembering the content of the story is the basis. As for the master's performance style, a *Pingshu* performer should study it carefully. From simple imitation to the mastery of performing techniques and the understanding of performing ideas, all should be analyzed in detail and learned gradually, and finally be integrated.

Mr. Ma believed that learning *Pingshu* required one to absorb the essence through watching the master's performances. He said, "Watching is the basis. The stage of watching may take one to two years, and the minimum would be about ten months." Mr. Tang said that "in the course of watching masters' performances, special attention should be paid to their performing ideas". The fundamental way to learn *Pingshu* performance is to watch. Mr. Tang said, "Watching is the first step. You have to watch more, watch for longer periods of time, and watch even for a lifetime. While watching, one should learn different ideas and styles from different performers." Mr. Tang mentioned an old saying: "The beginners start with 'blind watching'. That is, to accept the knowledge as a whole, and follow whatever the master does. There must be a process of accumulation and assimilation. Only through quantitative accumulation can one achieve a qualitative leap."

Integration means to integrate one's own thoughts into the master's explanation and to apply it appropriately, which is called "active application". On the basis of mastering all the basic skills, one can create his own distinctive performing style. Mr. Tang believed that it all depended on hard work and practice. He said, "Only through continuous practice can one integrate his or her own thoughts into actual performance." Mr. Ma also talked about his view of "active application": "On the basis of correct thinking, performers can apply their critical analyses on artistic practice, find their own ways of expression, use their own vocabulary and knowledge, and tell the story and give comments."

4.2.4 The method of teaching

In *Pingshu* performance, masters teach through oral instructions, which is the most common and traditional way. As Mr. Ma said, "Your teacher instructs you and you listen and watch, and then you digest the skills through practice. The master will help you by making comments and summaries, and there will be some recorded texts, which is the empirical experience. But the most important method is to teach face to face. After watching a lot of *Pingshu* performances, a learner has to perform live himself. Every time a learner finishes performance, the master will point out the merits and weaknesses; and this is the best way to improve."

In the process of oral instruction, both the master and the learner are sincere to each other, and through this way a firm emotional bond is established. This benefits the inheritance of traditional Chinese culture. As Mr. Tang said, "We regard our masters as our parents, because they have given us something that benefits our whole life. The care, love and even criticism they give are beneficial to our career. In fact, the inheritance of Chinese traditional arts is somehow sustained by this kind of love and respect between the masters and learners."

4.2.5 Government and community assistance to *Pingshu* artists

The government supports *Pingshu* performers mainly in the following aspects: policy support, performing venue support, financial support, and educational support.

The government provides support at the policy level. As Mr. Tang mentioned, "The government encourages people to learn more about traditional culture, helps *Pingshu* performers explore the markets, and makes more people know about *Pingshu*." Meanwhile, the national leaders also exhort people to learn more about Chinese traditional culture. "For example, President Xi Jinping called on all of us to learn the splendid traditional Chinese culture. His words give us *Pingshu* performers great encouragement." (Tang Ke)

The government also provides support in venues and funding. The establishment of some *Pingshu* theaters cannot be realized without financial support from the government. Mr. Liang said, "The survival of the Xuannan Pingshu Theater depends on the financial support from the government. For example, the use of utility is free and the rental fee for the venue is partly or even completely covered by the funding. This kind of support is very important to *Pingshu* performers."

In addition, the community also provides assistance to the development of *Pingshu*. For example, some audiences come to watch *Pingshu* performance regularly. Funding and charities sponsor the National Intangible Cultural Heritage Program. These all provide great support for *Pingshu* performers.

5. Conclusion

Overall, the training of *Pingshu* performers includes the following five aspects: the basic qualities, the professional qualities, the different stages of training, the method of teaching, and the support from government and society. To learn the art of *Pingshu*, one should speak Beijing dialect, obtain a good personal image, have outstanding ability, and most importantly, be diligent. In order to be a qualified performer, one needs to love *Pingshu*, be erudite and flexible in the performance, and have a profound Chinese traditional culture background.

The training of *Pingshu* performers includes two stages: absorption and integration. New performers should absorb the contents of the stories and the performance styles of their masters. Integration means that new performers should incorporate their own ideas into the master's demonstration and create their own distinctive styles of performance. The instruction process usually carries on through oral instruction. The government's support and the help from society are indispensable in the process of training new *Pingshu* performers. The government supports the development of *Pingshu* and encourages people to understand this traditional culture.

References:

Li, Xiaohong. The Research and Thinking on Chinese Pingshu [J]. Hundred Schools in Arts, 2010 (3): 150-154.

Yang, Peiqin. The Artistic Features of Shan Tianfang's Pingshu Performance [J]. Modern Communication – Journal of Communication University of China, 1995, (3): 75-76.

书场说书和电视说书的区别[1]

杨京晶　郭云笛　花朵朵[2]

【摘要】 北京评书是一种传统的说唱艺术。本研究通过对北京市西城区宣南书馆评书演员进行采访并经过分析发现，对于北京评书演员来说，书场说书在感受上优于电视说书。他们认为，书场说书和电视说书遇到的困难是不同的：在书场说书比在电视上说书困难更大、更多，对演员的各种能力要求也更高；电视说书相较于书场说书的困难在于演员要适应新的表演环境。北京评书演员认为，书场听书的观众质量优于电视听书的观众，他们对于书场说书和电视或新媒体说书的发展前景也有不同看法。

【关键词】 北京评书　书场　电视　感受　观众　区别　发展

一、研究意义

北京评书是北京人传统的休闲娱乐方式之一，以其表演形式简单、内容通俗易懂而为普通民众所喜闻乐见，被称为"成年人的童话"。"古事今说，佐以评论"是评书艺术的重要特征。评书贵在"评"，也精在"评"。演员通过评论可以将人物刻画得更加生动细致，将背景交代得更加清楚。可以说，以北京评书为代表的中国评书艺术，是最具中国民族特点、最富中国审美特色的艺术类型之一（梁

---

1. 本篇论文辅导老师为北京外国语大学国际教育集团升学规划部教师郭倩。
2. 本篇论文的三位作者均为北京外国语大学附属中学高中部十一年级学生。

彦，2015)。

当今大多数人没有进过书场，不了解真正的评书是如何表演的，甚至认为广播中播放的就是评书(杨旭东，2013)。"进入二十一世纪以来，由于娱乐的多元化和新媒体的发展，评书渐渐淡出电视，在广播中也是勉强支撑。然而此时网络评书使得评书这门传统艺术和新媒介产生了交集，一直持续至今。"(梁彦，2015)现在人们更愿意在网络上听评书，而不是在书场中感受评书。同时，在众多其他娱乐方式的冲击下，评书逐渐淡出人们的视线，受众大量缩减(杨旭东，2013)。这种状况严重影响了北京评书的发展，致使评书从业者减少，书场评书近乎消失，曾经辉煌一时的优秀民间艺术后继乏人，其传承工作正面临巨大困难(梁彦，2015)。

电视说书是最接近书场说书的表演形式，同时它又与现代数字技术相结合。为了了解书场说书与电视说书的区别，我们展开研究，希望通过了解当今环境下书场说书和电视说书的差异，使传统评书文化通过多种渠道得以传承。

二、文献综述

二十世纪八十年代，电视评书呈现短暂的繁荣景象。这一时期，电视进入了普通百姓家。"过去在书场、茶馆说书，听众充其量不过千人左右，如今评书进入电视屏幕，观众动辄数以亿计，评书空前普及。"(汪景寿等，1997)由此可见，在评书艺术的发展中，电视起到了不可替代的作用。"在网络出现之前，电视是传播速度最快、覆盖面最广的传播媒介。而评书是根深蒂固的传统艺术，二者之间的矛盾是无法避免的。"(梁彦，2015)其矛盾的一个表现就是二者的结合部分限制了各自特色的发挥。电视能带来视听的盛宴，而评书演员仅凭一个人、一张嘴讲故事，无法充分发挥电视这一媒体与生俱来的特点和魅力。评书怕短不怕长，评书越长演员越能发挥，越体现演员的积累和功夫。但电视对于节目时长有严格的限制，要求评书故事精练，少有发挥，这样就降低了评书的精彩程度和吸引力。电视评书不同于广播评书，保留了传统书场的背景设置，但仍然没有改变新媒体割断说书人与观众的连接和互动这一弊端。矛盾的另外一个表现就是电视与评书的结合虽然丰富了评书的传播方式，但同时也致使传统书馆愈发不受关注。

从画锅撂地到书场，再到电视，评书的表演场所几经变迁，各有利弊。但在说书人心里，书场才是评书表演的最佳场所，在这里有评书特有的表演氛围。说书人从现场观众的反馈中得到启发，激发自己的表演潜能和创作欲望，这会带来更好的即兴发挥；说书人在观众的检验和评价中不断成长和提升。观众也能在与说书人和其他观众的互动中充分获得艺术享受。很多演员都是从书场观众的支持中成长起来的，书场也培养出懂评书、懂评书文化的观众。书场在时空设置方面的局限性注定使评书成为小众艺术，但是只有在书场才能实现评书演员和观众对评书的真正传承(杨旭东，2013)。"书场的优势在于能够给艺人和观众提供一个互动的平台，在互动的环境中，艺人的表演更加的灵活、生动，艺术与生活之间的跳跃给评书以无限的生命力，且有利于培养受众群体和评书的传承人，它的不足在于，无论书场多么的兴旺，它的受众群体仍然是非常有限，而且受时空设置的约束极大。"(杨旭东，2013)

电视、网络等新媒体的发展不可阻挡。如何在保有评书的舞台表演艺术特性和书场最佳生态环境的同时，利用新媒体手段帮助评书更好地传承和发展是我们亟待探究和解决的问题。现有文献并未在这个方面作深入探究。

三、研究方法

(一) 数据收集

1. 采访对象

2018年7月16—28日，我们对四位评书演员进行了采访，他们是梁彦、唐柯、马剑平和贾林。

表1：采访对象

姓名	年龄	从业时间	擅长表演内容	特点
梁彦	37岁	12年（2007年6月2日正式拜连丽如老师为师）	善于讲述逸闻典故	广泛涉猎，博闻强记，传统文化功底扎实；语言优美，口齿清晰
唐柯	38岁	20年	擅京韵大鼓、西河鼓书及鼓曲伴奏	口齿清晰，声情并茂
马剑平	35岁	8年	擅相声、评书	声音洪亮，表情丰富
贾林	41岁	28年（2007年6月2日正式拜连丽如老师为师）	擅京剧武生、评书	身手矫健，动作干净利落

2. 数据收集

本研究采用结构式访谈形式，询问四位评书演员以下问题：

您参与过电视说书吗？

参与过：

1）您在书场说书和电视说书的感受有什么不同？

2）您在书场说书和电视说书的观众有什么不同？

3）您在书场说书和电视说书遇到的困难是否一样？如不一样有什么区别？

4）您认为哪一种说书的方式更有前途？为什么？

只参与过书场说书：

1）您对电视说书有什么了解？能具体说说吗？

2）您觉得书场说书和电视说书有哪些区别？

3）您认为哪一种说书的方式更有前途？为什么？

（二）数据分析

我们通过反复阅读、分析数据，最终获得以下编码。

表2：数据分析研究结果

研究主题	编码	定义
说书人感受	说书氛围	评书演员和台下观众的交流与互动程度：评书舞台表演艺术的特点和魅力在于与观众的交流与互动，所以它的最佳表演场所是在书场，而非电视镜头前
	表演的自由度	评书演员的表演发挥空间
	对口误的容忍度	如何解决演员表演出现口误的问题
听书观众	兴趣	观众听书的意愿
	熟悉度	观众对于评书内容和演员表演技巧的熟悉程度
	年龄结构	评书观众的年龄层次

续表

研究主题	编码	定义
遇到困难	对自身失误及时补救的能力	评书演员在书场与电视镜头前在表演出现差错时补救能力的差别
	适应现场观众和随机应变的能力	评书演员在书场与电视镜头前现场适应和随机应变能力的差别
	现场发挥和创作的能力	评书演员在书场与电视镜头前现场发挥和创作能力的差别
	适应电视说书时间和空间要求的能力	电视说书与书场说书的时间和空间要求不同，习惯了书场说书的演员要适应电视说书的环境
发展前景	电视/新媒体说书好	电视及新媒体说书传播量大，传播速度快，受众人群广，发展前景好
	书场说书好	书场说书可以保持传统书场文化，书场说书发展前景好
	都好	各有千秋，两者皆为媒介：电视或新媒体说书在传播方面有优势，但受到收费模式的制约，可能会丧失观众基础；书场说书在传播方面有劣势，但照顾了特定的观众基础，保持了传统的书馆文化

四、发现与讨论

通过对采访数据进行概括分析，我们可以看出，在书场和电视这两种不同环境下，说书人在表演中会产生不同的感受，拥有不同的观众，面对不同的困难。同时，说书人对于书场说书和电视或新媒体说书的发展前景也有不同看法。

(一) 书场说书对于北京评书演员来说，在感受上优于电视说书

说书人的感受主要集中在说书氛围和表演自由度上。他们认为在这两个方面，书场说书的感受明显优于电视说书。

1. 书场说书在氛围上优于电视说书

评书艺术的特点和魅力在于与观众的交流与互动，所以它的最佳表演场地是在书场，而非电视镜头前。

首先，由于评书本身"需要说书人和观众现场沟通互动"（唐柯），而这种互动是每一个舞台艺术从业者所最渴望、最期待的。唐柯老师说："书场说书是和人交流，……台上台下心灵沟通是别的东西替代不了的，那也是冷冷的镜头替代不了的。"说书人要用心灵感受到在座的观众在听，从观众的反应来获得认同感。这种认同感不仅有观众对说书人能力的肯定，还有观众对评书艺术发自内心的喜爱与尊敬。唐柯老师说："电视说书面对的是三个玻璃镜头。那我面对死的东西和面对活的东西，这个感觉是不一样的。"即使在电视台，如果有些平时不听评书的大妈来评书录制现场充当观众，对于梁彦老师来说，"有大妈坐着就比没人强"。

其次，观众的呼应是演员表演的灵感和动力。调动观众与其互动，是对评书演员能力的考验。马剑平老师说："现场说书气氛能把演出的情绪调动得更好一些，更饱满一些。"梁彦老师说："如果说书就面对摄像机，几个角度都是摄像机，没人，这说出来什么感觉？没有这种交流，没有反应啊。看见人呢就有反应，这对于演员当时的思维创作就有好处。"

由此，几位说书人都认为评书艺术应该回归书场。在书场和电视镜头前都说过书的唐柯老师是这样比较两者的："北京评书是舞台艺

术。我个人认为北京评书排位第一的施展空间是舞台和书台，而不是电视和广播。"梁彦老师生动地描述了书场的日常和其特有的文化：

> "在书场，您可以买茶、嗑瓜子、吃花生米，这都是书馆文化。听音乐会你喝茶、你嗑瓜子行吗？不可能。看电影，最好还是吃那没声的东西，对不对？只有书馆允许。而且这样跟说书人的表演，是相辅相成的，不影响。没听说过会影响我让我忘了下句词的，相对来说这还促进。听这声我高兴，我文思泉涌了，我说得更好了，这也是台上台下的一种互动。因为你这不吃瓜子了，那会觉得哟他不爱听了，快睡着了，连瓜子都不吃了嘛。你这嗑瓜子喝茶，这品头论足，到我们这儿就是一种好的反应，我们高兴得很呢。"

他认为，"曲艺这个艺术是必须要在小剧场里，要在书馆里"。文化没有贵贱之分，但其健康的传承需要自身土壤支持它的成长。"没有什么阳春白雪、下里巴人之分。但是因为它本身就是中国传统曲艺艺术，它是在这个土壤上形成的，那么它就有它合适的演出场所。"（梁彦）

相较于电视说书沉闷、安静的录制氛围，书场说书观众反响热烈、互动性强。习惯了书场说书的演员面对电视镜头时自然会有不适感，说书人会自动把任务从"给观众说书"转变到"说完这段书"。这种单一的目的性会使气氛低迷冷淡，使说书人创作热情缺失，从而降低说书人的心理满足感。

2. 电视说书在时间和内容上对评书演员的表演都有较大限制，演员发挥的自由度小

首先，电视台对节目时长有严格管控，电视评书时长一般限制在二十六七分钟。而书馆说书通常一个人有一个小时的时间，而且对开始和结束时间也没有严格的限制。所以，评书演员感觉电视说书时间紧张，还没有说多长时间，就要找机会收尾了。马剑平老师说："电视说书时间没有那么长，导演会掐很多的章节。"梁彦老师也表示："电视不可能多给你播一分钟，那么对演员的要求在于抓紧抢时间，演员就要在说的过程中找'扣子'。"

其次，电视说书相比书场说书，演员在内容选择和发挥方面更为拘束，自由度小，发挥空间小。梁彦老师说："书馆呢，相对来说随意一点。一些书你在电视台没法说，在书馆说没有问题。你比方我这回录《西汉》，大家都知道项羽屠城，后来火烧阿房，这些我都一笔带过，重点说鸿门宴斗智。"评书演员认为，由于电视覆盖面广，观众人群年龄多样，因此电视对评书内容要求高，要求老少皆宜。因此在电视上说书没有在书场说书放松和痛快。

3. 电视说书对表演错误的容忍度高

电视说书，演员如果出现失误可以重录，所以电视最终会把完美无误的结果展现给观众。马剑平老师说道："电视说书不会出错，它一定要把最好的一面展现给观众。而书场说书更要功夫，因为现场说书的话，一个小时的书不能有错。"评书演员认为书场说书要求更高，因为是现场，所以表演不能出错。

(二) 书场说书的观众质量优于电视说书

电视说书有两种情况：一种是没有观众，演员面对镜头讲；另一种是面前有观众，但这些观众与书场观众不同，通常是为了配合录制电视节目临时找来的。这里我们只讨论有观众的情况。

1. 书场说书和电视说书的观众对评书的热爱程度不同

多数来书场的观众对评书有兴趣，有些甚至是几十年的评书迷；而有些电视说书的现场观众对评书基本没有了解，更谈不上有兴趣。

唐柯老师说道："（电视说书的现场观众是）50块钱一个人请来的，他不一定爱听评书。台底下坐着50个不爱听评书的人和台底下坐着2个爱听评书的人，给台上演员的感觉是不一样的。"相对于被动邀请来的电视现场观众，来书场的观众是自己花钱买票进馆听书的，一些老观众甚至是十几年如一日地听书，他们对评书的兴趣已经转变成为一种生活习惯，他们在生活中已经离不开评书了。

书场里长期听书的老观众，被称为"书座"，对现场说书最为热爱。书座常在同一书场听书，与台上演员和周围书座长期相处，并成为朋友，他们的座位也就相对固定下来。书座们互相礼貌交谈，添茶续水；书座与演员形成观演默契，逢年过节还会给演员赠礼物，以示抬爱。"整个书场逐渐转化为一个相对的内部人关系群体。"（杨旭东，2013）书座们有演出必到，因此书场会给他们留着常坐的位置。梁彦老师解释，书馆里为老观众留前排固定位置的文化是这样形成的：

"书场文化包括什么？自打你一进书馆开始，文化就到了。买完票你一进书馆，得有人领你到座位上去。大家看了我们书馆的票，不对号入座，不像电影院，你可以选座。你们为什么坐不到头一排？这就是文化。我11点半我就去了，他1点半才到，凭什么他坐第一排我坐不了？第一，因为人家来10年了，您第一次去。这是书馆文化。老观众他就是坐那个座位，因为人家捧我们10年，他可以有固定座位。如果您也这样，那好，您也可以有这个机会。咱对不起您，这次您是第一次来，我们一定是先照顾老观众。"

2. 书场说书和电视说书的观众对评书内容和表演技巧的了解程度不同

书场听书的观众对评书内容与表演技巧的认知度比电视说书的观众高。书场听书的观众比在电视录制现场看评书的观众更懂评书，对评书特点、故事内容及表演技巧有更深刻的了解。马剑平老师介绍："书场说书的观众都是常年听书的观众，他们比较有经验，知道哪里鼓掌哪里叫好。而且现场听书的观众，他们的素质要更高一些，更懂得观众和演员之间的互动。电视观众没有什么太多的沟通，或者是他们也不熟悉评书的一些关键诀窍之类的地方。"因为常听评书，了解评书，书场观众才会听得更有兴致，更投入；听到精彩和过瘾之处就会自然而然地鼓掌和叫好，与演员互动。

3. 书场说书和电视说书的观众年龄层次不同

书场说书的观众主要为中青年，电视评书的观众多为老年。梁彦老师对书场和电视评书的观众作了比较："电视台坐的都是大妈，是专门组织来的，都是退休在家，没事干啊，到这还能吃两顿盒饭。……(宣南)书馆这十年大家看到了，都是青年人，或者家长带孩子。现在是三四十岁的这些人，他们带着十几岁的孩子。"唐柯老师也说道："那你到宣南书馆来看，你看台下坐着的老人多还是年轻人多?恐怕中青年占绝大多数,当然还有我们的老观众,一辈子多少年都在听书的观众。"

说书人指出,电视评书录制现场的观众普遍是老年人,而书场的观众多为中青年人。中青年人对评书艺术的传承起到了关键作用,因为评书艺术是一定要有观众的,没有观众,这一脉就死了。中青年观众带着他们的下一代来书场听书就是一种建立观众传承的举动,为新时代评书发展奠定了观众基础。

很多评书艺人都是由书座转为职业艺人的。年轻观众中有一类熏陶学艺型的书座,他们目的明确,就是为了从艺人表演中学到表演技能,积累曲艺知识,之后成为评书演员。他们常在知名度低的非正式场合得到演出机会,去练习、实践;同时在书场结识其他书座和艺人,交换行业知识。这些年轻书座在书场长期捧场,甚至以礼物馈赠的方式来进一步增进与艺人的关系,从而获得艺人的指点和传授。(杨旭东,2013)

(三)电视说书与书场说书遇到的困难

被采访的评书演员表示,电视说书和书场说书遇到的困难是不同的。在书场说书比在电视上说书遇到的困难更大更多,对演员的各种能力要求更高。

1. 对表演中出现的错误及时补救的能力

电视说书,不怕出错,也不会出错。因为观众看不到电视录制过程中演员出现的失误和重复录制、纠错的过程,观众看到的是最终的完美版本。而在书场说书就不一样了,演员如果在表演时出现失误,因为是现场表演,问题一下子就暴露在观众面前了,所以演员具备及时补救的能力就非常重要。对此,马剑平老师发表了他的观点:"我们现场说书的话有可能会有口误,或者是失误之类的东西,我们尽量避免,也难免。但电视台说书会把最好的一个面貌展现给观众。"马剑平老师认为,如果在表演中出现失误,在电视台可以进行反复录制,而在书场说书就一次机会,所以评书演员只能随机应变,将说错的话圆回来。所以电视说书相对容易,书场说书更需要功夫。杨旭东(2013)提到,演员在台上出错,观众就会给他挑毛病,用行话说叫"摘毛",甚至起哄、喝倒彩。这就要求演员有承压能力和好的心理素质,临场不乱,从容面对;同时要讲究方法,不正面回复纠正,而是找机会,在接下来的表演中巧妙回应。演员在观众不断"摘毛"中积累经验和成长。

2. 对现场观众的适应能力和随机应变的能力

相比电视说书,书场说书要求演员的现场把控能力更强。唐柯老师根据经验,给出了这样的解释:"书馆人更杂。一百、三百多人的场子,同时坐在这儿。每个人的欣赏角度,每个人要的,都不一样,你等于面对三百种需求。你要善于总结这些需求的共性,你去为这个共性走一个方向。"在书场说书,为了满足不同需求,获得更多观众的现场回应和认可,说书人需要具备很强的综合概括能力和敏感细致的体察能力,随时调整自己的表演路数和内容,适应现场需要。梁彦老师也提道:"书场说书,临时有突发情况:谁孩子哭了?谁手机掉地上了?谁茶杯摔了?这考验你的随机应变、见景生情的能力。这是说它的难点,就是它是活的艺术。其他艺术都不是这样。"在书场,观众更多更杂,环境也相对嘈杂,还会出现各种意想不到的状况。为了应对这些意外状况,实现最好的演出效果,评书演员需要具备在一个比较嘈杂的环境中清晰明了地将自己要表达的内容传达给观众并且能够牢牢抓住观众注意力的能力。

3. 现场发挥和创作的能力

在评书表演中，一个评书演员能否成功的关键就在于他是否讲得精彩。所以为了能把观众熟知的、书座烂熟于心的书讲得有趣，评书演员通常会在其中加入自己合理的联想，使"每一次表演，都是一次故事的再创作和人物形象的再塑造"（杨旭东，2013）。这是对评书演员技术和积累的很大考验。而这种创作和现场发挥的能力在电视说书时是很难表现的。唐柯老师说："电视说书不需要你的一些个临场发挥，你按着故事往下说就行。而现场说书的难点就在于你现场的发挥，是在技术层面对演员的考验：你的积累够不够，你能不能满足现场观众的需求。"

从某种程度上说，电视评书改变了评书的性质：没有了评，只有书，变成了讲故事。新观众和不了解评书的人，以为评书就是讲故事，对评书的性质产生了误解。唐柯老师认为："电视评书的要求和舞台的要求不一样。真正的评书是舞台上那样的说法，不是电视上那样一味地讲故事，一个故事没完没了地讲，而不加入演员自身的点评。电视评书恰恰对观众有一个误导，观众现在就认为评书就是电视上的样子。"

4. 电视说书相较于书场说书的困难在于要适应新的表演环境

电视说书与书场说书最大的区别就在于场地不同，所以说书人要面对的环境就有很大差别。评书演员最早都从书馆说书出身，对于书馆这样有着一个小舞台和一群坐在台下喝着茶、嗑着瓜子听书的观众的环境相对熟悉，并感到舒服，而在电视台有的只是几个冷冰冰的摄像头。唐柯老师根据自己的经验，给出了这样的解释："在电视面前就是非技术层面，你去适应一个不该你去适应的节奏；那你不去适应，你就被电视淘汰。"评书演员认为，如果要在电视上说书，说书人需要具备适应新节奏和与书场说书迥然不同的新环境的能力。

（四）书场说书与电视或新媒体说书的发展前景对比

如今传统的书场说书与新时代的电视说书或新媒体说书共存，这两种不同媒介使评书艺术不断发展。当被问到哪种方式可以使评书艺术发展得更好，几位老师的反馈不同。

有人认为从传播角度来讲，电视或新媒体说书的发展前景更好。贾林老师说："要说传播的话，恐怕还是电视说书，它的传播量更大。不说前途，只说传播。"梁彦老师也表明："新媒体的传播速度明显是惊人的，虽然电视电台受到一定冲击，但毕竟它群体还是很大。自媒体力量也不容小觑，而且今后会越来越发达。"两位老师都认为一项非物质文化遗产要想发展下去，就必须要让大众更多地了解它、认识它。这也就需要将评书艺术进行传播，而传播是发展的必要条件。电视和新媒体的传播量更大，传播速度更快，受众人群更广。

唐柯老师则持不同意见："当然是书场说书（发展前景更好），电视说书是一个特殊媒体环境下的特殊现象，它并不能完全代表最真的那种评书艺术。"唐柯老师认为书场说书的前景要比电视或新媒体说书更好，因为书场说书可以保持传统的书场文化，保持评书最本真的样子。

还有人认为书场说书与电视或新媒体说书从传承和观众选择的角度来讲，发展前景各有千秋。梁彦老师在以上观点的基础上还补充道:"对于评书这门艺术来说,我不否认自媒体的传播速度、传播范围、传播空间都有优势,但是我们现在立足的首先来说是传承,而不是大范围传播。"客观来说,电视或新媒体说书的发展前景确实很好,但梁彦老师作为传承人,更希望评书艺术能保持着自己最本真、最传统的样子传承下去,而不是一味地求发展。所以两种方式各有各的好处。马剑平老师认为:"(两种方式)都有前途,电视其实是一个载体,是一个媒体;现场说书是阵地。这两个都是评书,只是不同的媒介而已,没有哪个好哪个不好,只不过是观众适于听哪种,你有时间可以来现场听,没有时间可以在家看电视。"

五、总结

总体来看,书场说书和电视或新媒体说书的主要区别在于评书演员的说书感受和需要具备的能力。相较于电视说书的录制现场,评书演员更倾向于回归书场,在互动气氛活跃、能够激发灵感的书场说书;但这同时也意味着面对真实观众对评书演员能力的要求更高、更全面。而电视说书对评书演员的能力要求在于要适应这种对演员的发挥和创作没有支撑的新环境和新节奏。由于评书本身的性质,观众是必不可少的。访谈结果显示,书场说书的观众普遍为中青年,且部分为常年听书的老观众;而来到电视说书录制现场的观众大多为没有听书经验、为拿报酬和打发时间而来的老年观众。可见书场说书作为评书最原汁原味的现场舞台表演形式,在观众传承方面有望持续发展。但是电视或新媒体评书凭借当今时代的潮流与科技手段,具有传播速度快、传播范围广的优势,会吸引大量屏幕前的观众。书场说书立足于根本，电视或新媒体说书谋求变革出路，今后应该研究如何将二者有效地结合，帮助评书更好地传承和发展。

最后，本研究的局限性在于没有真正实地考察电视说书，只是根据被采访者的叙述对电视说书有了一定的了解；且本研究也只是针对电视说书的录制现场进行分析，没有调查电视机前评书观众的感受与想法。此外，由于访谈对象少，笔者没有机会更多地参与书场听书，所以本研究未能从研究者的角度切实考察书场说书和电视说书的差异。但本研究的调研方法、对评书现状和未来发展的探究仍具有参考价值。

参考文献：

梁彦.北京评书[M].北京：北京美术摄影出版社，2015.
汪景寿，王决，曾惠杰.中国评书艺术论[M].北京：经济日报出版社，1997.
杨旭东.当代北京评书书场研究[M].北京：民族出版社，2013.

The Differences between Performing in a *Pingshu* Theater and on TV

Shen Yiwen[1] Yang Jingjing Guo Yundi Hua Duoduo[2]

Abstract: Beijing *Pingshu* is a traditional oral performing art. This study, through interviews with the *Pingshu* performers from Xuannan Pingshu Theater in Xicheng District of Beijing, finds that Beijing *Pingshu* performers feel better when performing in a *Pingshu* theater than on TV. The performers thought that the difficulties of performing in a *Pingshu* theater were different from those of performing on TV. Performing in a *Pingshu* theater is more difficult than on TV as the former requires more comprehensive abilities, while the latter requires adaption to a new performance environment. They also believed that the quality of audience in a *Pingshu* theater was better than that of TV audience. Besides, they shared different opinions on the prospects of live *Pingshu* performance in a theater, TV *Pingshu*, and new media *Pingshu*.

Keywords: Beijing *Pingshu*, *Pingshu* theater, TV, feeling, audience, distinction, development

1. Significance of the Study

As a traditional entertainment for the locals in Beijing, Beijing *Pingshu*, known as "fairy tales for adults", gains its popularity because of its simple form and interesting stories. It mainly features "comments on ancient stories". Through comments, the performers can describe the characters more vividly and more accurately, and give a detailed account of the background. It can be said that the Chinese *Pingshu* art, represented by Beijing *Pingshu*, is one of the art types with the richest Chinese national

---

1. Associate professor of English, Beijing Foreign Studies University.
2. The other authors of this paper are the 11th grade students of The Affiliated High School of Beijing Foreign Studies University.

and aesthetic characteristics (Liang, 2015).

Most people today don't know how traditional *Pingshu* is performed because they have never been to a *Pingshu* theater. They think that what they hear on the radio is *Pingshu*. (Yang, 2013) "Since the beginning of the 21st century, *Pingshu* has gradually disappeared on TV and radio due to the diversity of entertainment and the development of new media. At this time, however, the online *Pingshu* has brought about the integration of the traditional art and the new media, which has been going on ever since." (Liang, 2015) People are more willing to listen to *Pingshu* on the Internet than enjoy it in a *Pingshu* theater. At the same time, in the face of many alternative ways of entertainment, people are less attracted by *Pingshu* (Yang, 2013). This situation has seriously affected the development of Beijing *Pingshu*, resulting in a decrease in the number of people engaged in *Pingshu*, and *Pingshu* theaters are close to extinction. The inheritance of Beijing *Pingshu*, once a very popular folk art, is facing great difficulties. (Liang, 2015)

TV *Pingshu*, combined with modern digital technology, is close to theater *Pingshu* in the performing way. In order to understand the differences between performing in a *Pingshu* theater and on TV, we have interviewed some Beijing *Pingshu* performers, in the hope of helping pass on *Pingshu* via multiple channels.

2. Literature Review

TV *Pingshu* was popular for a short time in the 1980s when TV became a household commodity. "The number of audience was no more than a thousand in a *Pingshu* theater in the past. However, now the number is usually over hundreds of million. With the help of TV, *Pingshu* is more popular than ever." (Wang et al., 1997) This shows that TV has played an irreplaceable role in the development of *Pingshu*. "TV is the fastest and most widely spread medium before the advent of the Internet, while *Pingshu* is a kind of deeply rooted traditional art. The contradictions between the two are inevitable." (Liang, 2015) One of the contradictions is that the combination of the two partially limits their respective characteristics. TV is an audio-visual feast, but *Pingshu* is a storytelling solo performance set in a background which cannot give full play to the inherent charm of the TV. *Pingshu* tends to be long, as the longer it is, the more the performers can show their ability and experience. However, there is a strict limit on the length of TV programs, so it requires the story to be refined and limits performers' performance, reducing the attractiveness of *Pingshu*. TV *Pingshu*, unlike radio *Pingshu*, retains the background of traditional *Pingshu* theaters, but still cuts off the connection and interaction between performers and audience, which is the common disadvantage of new media. Another contradiction is that though it enriches the access channels of *Pingshu*, the combination of TV and *Pingshu* reduces people's enthusiasm of attending live *Pingshu* performances at *Pingshu* theaters.

From streets to *Pingshu* theaters, then to TV, the performance venue of *Pingshu* has changed over time, and each has its advantages and disadvantages. However it changes, the *Pingshu* theater is the best one in the minds of *Pingshu* performers. In the special atmosphere of a *Pingshu* theater, performers can draw inspiration from the feedback of the audience and give wonderful improvisation. Their abilities are improved through the evaluation of the audience. The audience can also better enjoy the performance through sharing his opinions with others. In the theaters, many performers grow, and audience learns more about *Pingshu*. Theater *Pingshu* is bound to be a kind of niche art for its limitation on time and space. However, only in the *Pingshu* theater can the culture of *Pingshu* be passed on to the audience and performers. (Yang, 2013) "The *Pingshu* theater provides both performers and audience a platform where performers can give more vivid and flexible performances, and where the audience and *Pingshu* enthusiasts can be cultivated. However, no matter how popular it is, the theater, bound by space and time, has limited audience." (Yang, 2013)

The development of new media such as TV and the Internet is inevitable. How to use new media to popularize and develop *Pingshu* and at the same time to retain its performing features and natural environment are urgent problems for us to explore and solve. The existing literature does not delve into this aspect.

3. Research Methods

3.1 Data collection

3.1.1 Participants

From July 16 to 28, 2018, we interviewed four *Pingshu* performers, Liang Yan, Tang Ke, Ma Jianping, and Jia Lin.

Table 1: Biographic information of the participants

Name	Age	Years of Working	Specialties	Characteristics
Liang Yan	37	12 years (He formally became a student of Lian Liru on June 2, 2007)	Good at telling anecdotal and classical stories	With a good memory and extensive experience, he has a profound knowledge of traditional culture, and tells stories in a literary and clear way
Tang Ke	38	20 years	Good at other forms of oral performing arts, such as *Xihe Gushu*	He tells stories in an articulate and emotional way
Ma Jianping	35	8 years	Good at crosstalk and *Pingshu*	He is articulate and has a very expressive face
Jia Lin	41	28 years (He formally became a student of Lian Liru on June 2, 2007)	Good at playing *Wusheng* (a martial role in Beijing Opera) and *Pingshu*	He is agile and good at using body language

3.1.2 Data collection

The study used structured interviews and asked the four *Pingshu* performers the following questions:

Have you ever performed *Pingshu* on TV?

Yes.

1) How do you feel about performing in a *Pingshu* theater and on TV?

2) What's the difference between the audience in a *Pingshu* theater and in TV studio?

3) Do you have the same difficulties as performing in a *Pingshu* theater and on TV? If there are differences, what are they?

4) Which performing way do you think is more promising? Why?

No, I only perform in the *Pingshu* theater.

1) What do you know about TV *Pingshu*? Can you tell more about it?

2) In your opinion, what are the differences between performing in a *Pingshu* theater and on TV?

3) Which performing way do you think is more promising? Why?

3.2 Data analysis

After reading and analyzing the data, we finally get the following results.

Table 2: Data analysis results

Topic	Code	Definition
Performers' feelings	Atmosphere	The atmosphere includes the interaction and communication between *Pingshu* performers and the audience: the charm of *Pingshu* lies in the interaction and communication with audience, so it's best to perform *Pingshu* in a theater instead of on TV
	Flexibility	The flexibility of the performers' performances
	Tolerance to slips of the tongue	How to solve slips of the tongue in the performance
Audience	Interests	The audience's willingness to listen
	Familiarity	The audience's familiarity with the performing content and performing skills
	Age structure	The age structure of the audience

continued

Topic	Code	Definition
Abilities of solving problems	The ability of making up for mistakes	The difference in a performer's ability of making up for mistakes which occur when he performs in a *Pingshu* theater and on TV
	The ability of adapting to the audience's reaction and other situations	The difference in a performer's ability of adaption in a *Pingshu* theater and on TV
	The ability of improvised performance	The difference in a performer's improvised performance in a *Pingshu* theater and on TV
	The ability of adapting to time and space requirements of TV *Pingshu*	TV *Pingshu* and theater *Pingshu* have different requirements on time and space, so the performers who are used to performing in a *Pingshu* theater should adapt to the environment of TV performance
Prospects	TV or new media *Pingshu* is better	TV or new media *Pingshu* has a vast audience and a fast transmission speed, so it has a promising future
	Theater *Pingshu* is better	Theater *Pingshu* can retain traditional *Pingshu* culture, so it has a promising future
	Both are good	Both are media for developing *Pingshu* with their own advantages: TV and new media *Pingshu* have advantages in communication, but its payment modes may result in losing audience; theater *Pingshu* has disadvantages in communication, but has advantages in retaining the audience and the culture of *Pingshu* theaters

4. Findings and Discussions

Through a comprehensive analysis of the interview data, it could be seen that in the different settings of the *Pingshu* theater and TV, the performers have different feelings, audiences, and difficulties. The performers have different views on the prospects of theater *Pingshu*, TV *Pingshu*, and new media *Pingshu*.

4.1 Beijing *Pingshu* performers feel better when performing in a *Pingshu* theater than on TV

The performers thought that theater *Pingshu* was better than TV *Pingshu* mainly in two respects, namely the atmosphere and the flexibility of performance.

4.1.1 Theater *Pingshu* is better than TV *Pingshu* in respect of the atmosphere of performance

The charm of *Pingshu* is the interaction and communication with the audience, so it is best to perform *Pingshu* in a *Pingshu* theater than on TV.

First of all, due to its nature, "*Pingshu* requires a live interaction between the performers and the audience." (Tang Ke) This kind of interaction is longed by every performer. Tang Ke said, "Performing in a *Pingshu* theater is communicating with people … The communication of the souls and minds between the ones on the stage and off the stage cannot be replaced by anything, such as the lens of TV cameras." The performers should empathize with their audiences and gain their recognition which is not only for their performances, but also for the art of *Pingshu*. The performers can feel the audience's love and respect for *Pingshu*. Tang said, "I'm faced with three lenses when I perform on TV. The feelings are so different when I perform in front of live audience and lifeless cameras." To Liang Yan, "it feels better" if the television station invited some people to the recording studio, even old ladies who never listened to *Pingshu* before. According to Liang, "it is much better than facing nobody."

Second, the audience's reaction is the source of inspiration and motivation to the performers. It is a test for the performers whether the audience can be mobilized to interact. Ma Jianping said, "The atmosphere of a *Pingshu* theater helps the performers bring out their emotions and tell the story in a more emotional way." Liang Yan said, "If you are in the face of only cameras from different angles, what's your feeling? There is no communication and no interaction. It will inspire the performers' creativity if there are audiences."

As a result, these *Pingshu* performers agreed that it should be vigorously advocated to perform *Pingshu* in a *Pingshu* theater. Tang Ke, who has experience of performing in *Pingshu* theaters and on TV, said, "Beijing *Pingshu* is a kind of stage art. Personally speaking, the best performing venue is on stage at a theater instead of at a TV or radio station." Liang Yan vividly described the daily routine of a *Pingshu* theater and its special culture:

> "In a *Pingshu* theater, you can drink tea, eat sunflower seeds and peanuts. This is part of the theater culture. At a concert, it is very inappropriate if you drink tea or eat sunflower seeds. No way. When you are watching movies in a movie theater, you'd better not eat anything crispy. Only in a *Pingshu* theater can you drink and eat, because it won't bother the performer's performance. I never forget my lines because of the noise. Instead, it helps me with my performance. I'm happy to hear it because it inspires my creativity. This is a kind of interaction. If the audience doesn't eat sunflower seeds, it indicates that they are not attracted by my performance. They fall asleep. We are happy to see the audience drinking tea, eating sunflower seeds, and discussing with others, because we consider it as a good reaction."

Liang thought that "oral arts have to be performed in small theaters". There is no distinction between high and low in art. Each art form needs suitable environment to develop. "*Pingshu* is a form of traditional Chinese art which should be given suitable environment for its development." (Liang Yan)

Compared with the boring and quiet recording atmosphere of TV, the *Pingshu* theater is warm with the audience's interaction. Performers who are used to performing in the *Pingshu* theater will feel uncomfortable when performing on TV. Their mentality changes from "performing for the audience" into "finishing this task". This will lead to a cold atmosphere and the performers' loss of passion for creativity and thus a lower sense of satisfaction.

4.1.2 TV *Pingshu* has a great limitation on the performance in terms of time and content, giving the performers little flexibility

First of all, the TV programs have strict control over the time, and TV *Pingshu* lasts no more than 26 or 27 minutes. However, the *Pingshu* theaters usually offer each performer one hour with flexible time at the beginning and ending. Thus, when recording on TV, the performers feel the time is too short to finish a complete story. Ma Jianping said, "TV directors will delete many chapters because of the time limit." Liang Yan said, "You won't get even one extra minute on TV. You need to have a good timing, which means you have to find the suspense of the story as you tell it and prepare for the ending."

In addition, compared with theater *Pingshu*, TV *Pingshu* has fewer choices when it comes to the content and improvised performance. Liang Yan said, "It's more casual in the *Pingshu* theater. You can tell stories which you can't tell on TV. For example, last time I recorded stories in *Xihan* at TV station, the massive slaughter and the burning down of Epang Palace by General Xiangyu are too violent to be recorded. Thus, I focused on the description of Hongmen banquet where witty and strategic conversations are exchanged." The performers thought TV *Pingshu* required high-quality contents suitable for audience of all ages because of its wide coverage. Thus, when performing on TV, the performers cannot be as casual and relaxed as in a *Pingshu* theater.

4.1.3 TV *Pingshu* has a high tolerance to mistakes

For TV *Pingshu*, if a performer makes a mistake during the recording, he can start all over again. He will finally present a flawless performance. Ma Jianping said, "You will never make mistakes as you perform on TV. The final performance presented to the TV audience must be perfect. However, theater *Pingshu* requires the performers to make no mistakes during the one-hour performance." The performers thought that theater *Pingshu* had a higher demand for ability than TV *Pingshu* because the audience was on site.

4.2 The quality of the audience in a *Pingshu* theater is better than those in front of a TV camera

There are two situations in TV *Pingshu*: performers speak to the cameras with or without audiences. the audiences in a recording studio are different from those in a *Pingshu* theater in that they are usually paid by the TV station to record the program. Here only the situation with audiences is discussed.

4.2.1 The audiences in a *Pingshu* theater and those in a recording studio have different degrees of passion for *Pingshu*

The majority of the audiences in a *Pingshu* theater are interested in *Pingshu*, some are even fans of *Pingshu* for decades. However, some of the audiences in a recording studio are not familiar with *Pingshu*, let alone interested in it.

Tang Ke said, "Each of them (the audiences in a TV studio) was paid 50 yuan by the TV station. They may not like *Pingshu*. The performers on stage feel differently when performing in front of 50 people who don't like *Pingshu* and 50 people who love it." Unlike the audiences who get paid in the TV station, those coming to a *Pingshu* theater buy tickets of *Pingshu* performances. Some regular audiences have come to the *Pingshu* theater for decades. They have turned their interest in *Pingshu* into a habit, which is indispensable in their lives.

These patrons who have been listening to *Pingshu* for a long time in the theater are called "*Shuzuo*", who have great passion for theater *Pingshu*. They usually listen to *Pingshu* together. They have become friends with the performers and other audiences during the long-time communication. They have their fixed seats. They chat with and refill the water for each other. They have a tacit understanding with the performers and give gifts to the performers in the festivals to show their love. "The whole theater will gradually turn into an internal social group." (Yang, 2013) As long as there is a performance, *Shuzuo* will come to the theater. Thus, the theater will reserve the seats for them. According to Liang Yan, the custom of reserving the front seats for regular audience is formed in this way:

> "What does the culture of *Pingshu* theaters include? You feel the distinctive cultural atmosphere as soon as you enter a theater. After buying the ticket, you will be led to the seat. As you can see, unlike in a movie theater where you have an assigned seat, you can choose your seat in a *Pingshu* theater, except for the first row. Why? This is culture. For instance, you arrive at 11:30 a.m., while a patron arrives at 1:30 p.m. Why should he sit in the first row but you shouldn't? Because he has been a regular customer for ten years while this is your first time. It is the culture of *Pingshu* theaters that regular customers have fixed seats. He earned himself the recognition for being our fan for ten years. You can have a fixed seat if you stay with us for that long. We ask for your pardon, but we have to give favor to our regular customers."

4.2.2 The audiences in a *Pingshu* theater and in a TV recording studio have different degrees of understanding of the content and performance skills of *Pingshu*

The audiences in a *Pingshu* theater have a deeper understanding of the content, characteristics and performance skills of *Pingshu* than those in a recording studio. Ma Jianping introduced, "The audiences in a *Pingshu* theater are usually long-time listeners. With rich experience, they know when to applause and how to interact with the performers. However, the audiences in a recording studio have less interaction with the performers because they are less familiar with the skills of *Pingshu*." With years of experience and a good knowledge of *Pingshu*, the audiences in theater are more interested and devoted to the performance and give applause spontaneously to interact with the performers.

4.2.3 The age structure of the audiences in a *Pingshu* theater is different from that of those in a recording studio

The audiences in a *Pingshu* theater are mainly youngsters and middle-aged people, while those in a recording studio are mainly old people. Liang Yan once made comparison between the former and the latter: "The audiences in the recording studio are mainly old women paid by the TV station. They are all retired and have nothing to do. Thus, it's a good deal for them to be an audience in the studio with two free meals. … As you can see, the audiences in Xuannan Pingshu Theater are mainly young people and parents with their kids. Now, the audiences are mainly people of my age, thirty to forty years old. They bring their children who are ten to twenty years old." Tang Ke also mentioned, "When you come to Xuannan Pingshu Theater, do you see more young audiences or more old audiences? I believe the number of young audiences is larger than the old. Of course, there are old audiences who have spent most of their life listening to *Pingshu*."

The performers have pointed out that the audiences in the recording studio are mainly old people, while the audiences in the *Pingshu* theater are mainly youngsters and middle-aged people. Youngsters and middle-aged people play an important role in the inheritance of *Pingshu*. The audience is very important to the development of *Pingshu*. Without the audience, *Pingshu* will no longer exist. Under some guidance, the children of these young and middle-aged audiences will come to *Pingshu* theaters, which is a process of inheritance ensuring the audience for *Pingshu* in the new era.

Many *Pingshu* performers used to be *Shuzuo*, the patrons. Among the young audiences, there are people who would like to learn *Pinghu*. They have a clear purpose when sitting there as audience, which is to become a *Pingshu* performer after learning performance skills and knowledge. They usually practice on less famous informal occasions, and get to know other *Shuzuo* and performers to exchange expertise in the theater. The enthusiastic young learners even give presents to performers for the purpose of building up a closer relationship and gain feedback on and support for their practice. (Yang, 2013)

4.3 The difficulties of performing in a *Pingshu* theater and on TV are different

The *Pingshu* performers interviewed have said that the difficulties of performing in a *Pingshu* theater and on TV are different. Generally speaking, performing in a *Pingshu* theater is more difficult, as it requires more abilities of the performers.

4.3.1 The ability to make up for mistakes during the performance

Pingshu performers are not afraid of making mistakes when recording in a TV station, because the audiences in front of TV sets are presented with a perfect performance. However, performing in a *Pingshu* theater is a different story. It requires a great ability of making up for mistakes, because you are standing in front of the audiences who can realize your mistakes immediately. Ma Jianping said, "We may have a slip of the tongue or other mistakes when performing in a *Pingshu* theater. We can hardly avoid mistakes. When performing on TV, we will present the audience with a perfect performance." Ma Jianping thought when performing on TV, the performer could correct the mistakes; whereas performing in a theater, the performer had only one chance, so he must have a quick response to the mistakes he made. Thus, performing on TV is easier than performing in a *Pingshu* theater, and the latter requires more abilities. Yang (2013) has mentioned that the audience will know the mistake as long as the performer makes it, which is called *"Zhaimao"* in jargon. Sometimes the audiences even give boos and hisses to the performer. Thus, the performer should be able to handle the pressure and face the mistakes with a good mentality. Also, he should study ways of correcting mistakes indirectly and find chances of responding in the following performance. Performers can gain experience in constant *Zhaimao* by the audience.

4.3.2 The ability to adapt to the reaction of the audience

Compared with TV *Pingshu*, performing in a theater requires performers to control the scene better. Tang Ke, according to his own experience, gave the following explanation, "The tastes of theater audience are more complex. One hundred or three hundred people sit here on the spot with different demands. They appreciate the performance from different angles, which means you are confronted with hundreds of demands. You should be good at finding their common needs, and then satisfy these needs." When performing in a *Pingshu* theater, the performer must have the abilities of synthesizing and observing and be able to change the performing style and content when an unexpected situation occurs, in order to satisfy the audiences' needs and win their recognition. Liang Yan also mentioned, "The unexpected happens in a *Pingshu* theater. For example, a child bursts into tears, or someone's cell phone drops on the floor, or someone spills the tea. All these emergencies require an instant response. This is exactly the difficulty of performing in a theater because it is a kind of live art. No other art is like this." In a *Pingshu* theater, the audiences are more complex and the environment is relatively noisy with unexpected situations. In order to cope with these emergencies and achieve a good performance, a performer must be able to communicate clearly with the audiences what he wants to express and holds their attention in a noisy environment.

4.3.3 The ability of instant performance

In *Pingshu* performance, the key to success is the performer's ability to perform well. In order to tell familiar stories in an interesting way, performers usually add their own reasonable associations. "Each performance is a process of recreating a story and reshaping the characters." (Yang, 2013) It is a great test for the skills and experience of the performers. This creativity and improvisation can hardly be shown on TV. Tang Ke said, "TV *Pingshu* doesn't require improvisation. You just keep telling the stories. The difficulty of performing in a theater lies in that you constantly improvise as you give the performance. It is a test for your skills, experience, and ability of meeting the audience's needs."

In a way, TV *Pingshu* has changed the nature of *Pingshu*; it is a kind of storytelling without comments. Its audiences, who have never had the taste of real theater *Pingshu*, will have a false impression. Tang Ke thought that "TV *Pingshu* and theater *Pingshu* have different requirements. The real *Pingshu* is in the *Pingshu* theater, not on TV, where *Pingshu* is reduced to telling a story. TV *Pingshu* misleads the audience into a wrong understanding of *Pingshu*. Now, the audience thinks TV *Pingshu* is the real *Pingshu*."

4.3.4 TV *Pingshu* is more difficult than theater *Pingshu* in terms of adaption to a new environment

The biggest difference between TV *Pingshu* and theater *Pingshu* is that the performers have to face different environment. *Pingshu* performers, who are used to performing in the theater, are familiar with the stage and the audiences who are eating sunflower seeds. They feel comfortable in this environment. However, they are faced with only lifeless cameras in a recording studio. Tang Ke, according to his experience, gave the following explanation, "You have to adapt to a tempo which is different from that of performing in the theater, otherwise you will be eliminated by the new media." *Pingshu* performers thought that TV *Pingshu* required an ability to adapt to a different environment and a new tempo.

4.4 Comparison between the prospects of theater *Pingshu* and TV *Pingshu*

Today, traditional theater *Pingshu* coexists with TV *Pingshu*. Both of them advance the development of *Pingshu*. When asked about which one is better, the participants gave different opinions.

Some thought that TV or new media *Pingshu* had a promising future from the aspect of communication. "I am afraid that TV *Pingshu* is better in terms of communication. I'm not talking about good or bad, but only about communication," said Jia Lin. He believed that TV or new media *Pingshu* was better in terms of communication. Liang Yan also said, "It is obvious that the new media is spreading at a surprising rate and greatly affects TV programs which used to have a large audience. We cannot underestimate new media which will have great development in the future." Both of them believed that only when people had a deep understanding of an intangible cultural heritage, could it develop and have a future. Thus, *Pingshu* needs to be communicated to people. "Communication" is the prerequisite for development. With a fast speed of communication and a large number of audiences, TV and new media can popularize *Pingshu* in a better way.

Tang Ke disagreed with this point: "Of course, it is the theater *Pingshu* (that has better prospects for development). TV *Pingshu* is a special phenomenon in a special media environment. It can't represent real *Pingshu*." Mr. Tang thought that theater *Pingshu* had better prospects than TV *Pingshu* and new media *Pingshu*, because theater *Pingshu* could retain both the traditional culture of *Pingshu* performance and the culture of authentic *Pingshu* theaters.

Some participants thought that theater *Pingshu* and TV or new media *Pingshu* had their own distinctive advantages from aspects of inheritance and the audience's choice. Liang Yan pointed out, "I won't deny that new media has its advantages with regard to the speed, coverage, and space. However, we are talking about inheritance rather than development." As a matter of fact, TV and new media *Pingshu* do have a promising future. However, Liang Yan, as an inheritor of *Pingshu*, is committed to see that *Pingshu* is preserved with its authentic style and tradition, before any consideration of further development is discussed. Both theater *Pingshu* and TV *Pingshu* have their own advantages. Ma Jianping said, "They all have promising futures. TV is actually a medium for *Pingshu*. A theater is a field for live *Pingshu* performance. Both TV *Pingshu* and theater *Pingshu* are *Pingshu* performance via different media. Online *Pingshu* is also a kind of *Pingshu* broadcast via the medium of the Internet. There is neither good media nor bad media. The audiences choose what they prefer. If you have time, you can patronize the theater. If time is limited, you can watch it on TV or listen to it via the Internet."

5. Summary

In general, the main differences between theater *Pingshu* and TV or new media *Pingshu* lie in the feelings and abilities of performers. Compared with performing in the recording studio, the performers prefer *Pingshu* theaters where the interaction with the audience serves as a source of inspiration for them, though it requires more abilities of the performers when they are facing the audience. Performing on TV requires the performers to adapt skillfully to the new tempo and environment in which they have no interaction with the audience to inspire their creativity. Due to the nature of *Pingshu*, the audience is indispensable. According to the interviews, the audiences in *Pingshu* theaters are mainly youngsters and middle-aged people, together with some old people who have listened to *Pingshu* for years. The audiences in recording studios are mainly old people who are hired by TV stations and have little understanding of *Pingshu*. It can be seen that the *Pingshu* theater as the original place for *Pingshu* is expected to continuously develop. TV and new media *Pingshu* will attract a large number of audiences with the advantages of fast speed and wide coverage. Theater *Pingshu* is the foundation of *Pingshu*, and TV and new media *Pingshu* take advantage of new technology. Future studies should focus on how to pass on and develop *Pingshu* through the combination of these two ways.

Finally, the limitation of this study is that there is no real field observation of TV *Pingshu*, and the understanding of its nature is based on the participants' accounts. The study only focuses on the analysis of the recording of TV *Pingshu* and does not investigate the feelings and thoughts of the audience in front of TV sets. The lack of literature on this field poses another difficulty for this research. However, this study may shed light on the research methods, and the status quo and the development of *Pingshu*.

References:

Liang, Yan. Beijing Pingshu [M]. Beijing: Beijing Arts and Photography Press, 2015.
Wang, Jingshou, Wang, Jue, & Zeng, Huijie. Review of Chinese Pingshu Art [M]. Beijing: The Economic Daily Press, 1997.
Yang, Xudong. A Study on Contemporary Beijing Pingshu Theaters [M]. Beijing: The Ethnic Publishing House, 2013.

北京评书艺术发展障碍的研究[1]

马子涛[2]　田皓宇[3]　邢泽举[4]

【摘要】　本研究通过对评书观众和演员的采访分析，发现北京评书与相声、脱口秀等同类语言艺术有很大区别。加之观众欣赏品味不同，北京评书和其他同类语言艺术之间的相互影响不会很大。所以评书的传承和发展要靠行业自身的努力。阻碍评书发展的因素包括对评书演员要求高，评书演员培养时间长，评书艺术传承难，年轻人对传统文化有偏见，表演场地不足，听书时间有限制等。当前新的传播途径对评书艺术发展虽有一些积极影响，但更多的是负面影响。评书对年轻人是有吸引力的。北京评书发展应该得到的支持包括政府扶持、观众认可、推广方面的探索与支持，以及书目的创新。

【关键词】　北京评书　障碍　影响　支持　吸引力

一、研究意义

评书为曲艺的一种，是一门有悠久历史的民间说唱艺术。表演方式为一人演说，通过"梁子，扣子，摆砌末，拔口"等艺术手段，讲述历史及现代故事（梁彦，2015）。北京评书是评书的主要分支，它形

---

1. 本篇论文辅导老师为北京外国语大学国际教育集团升学规划部教师郭倩。
2. 北京外国语大学附属中学1+3项目十年级学生。
3. 北京外国语大学附属中学1+3项目十年级学生。
4. 北京爱迪国际学校WACE项目十年级学生。

成于北京，盛行于京、津、冀、东三省等地。近年来，北京评书发展前景并不好，老一辈评书名家接连逝去，新一代说书人逐渐匮乏，书坛后继乏人。同时，书馆演出极为稀少，电视也不再播出评书节目，电子评书虽还在勉强支撑，但听众不多。北京评书的传承与发展都是亟须解决的问题(杨旭东，2013)。

2008年北京评书申遗成功，这对于评书的发展与传承有了些许帮助。本选题以北京评书为研究对象，研究其发展障碍；以宣南书馆为调查点，对其中的观众和演员进行访谈；并结合非遗保护，思考这个曾经在民众生活中占据重要地位的曲艺艺术，如何回归当下这个文化多元的社会。

二、文献综述

通过检索国内有关北京评书发展障碍的文献与相关书目，笔者发现目前并没有针对北京评书发展障碍的实证性研究。相关文献主题集中在以下三个方面。

(一) 北京评书发展历史

评书最开始是一种民间的说唱艺术，后来渐渐演变成一种类似于讲故事的语言艺术(杨旭东，2013)。它具有民族性、地域性，最接近人民的生活，也能反映一个时代的兴衰、民族的精神(梁彦，2015)。评书的表演形式简单、通俗易懂，所以很容易被人们接受。其中北京评书成形于唐宋，兴起于明清，历史十分悠久(梁彦，2015)。

(二)北京评书发展趋势

北京评书本质上在随着时间而发生改变。王华新(2012)认为,北京评书的发展已离不开新媒体的传播。新媒体为评书发展提供了更大的平台,让更多人有接触北京评书的机会。

北京评书的发展,应该时刻处于一种"居安思危"的状态。"安"在于它深厚的历史沉淀,而"危"是因为它独特的时代性。所以,目前评书所需要的是在原本的基础上进行创新(汪景寿等,1997)。

但是当前北京评书发展堪忧,面临着表演场地不足、后继乏人等问题(梁彦,2015)。现在的新娱乐与适应时代的碎片化信息大量涌入各式媒体,北京评书渐渐不被关注,淡出了电视媒体视野,并又回到了广播市场(王华新,2012)。

(三)北京评书书场研究

北京评书的书场建设,是观众"回归现场"的重要条件,也可以让评书更趋于完整。除此之外,北京评书书场还做到了传承。书场给评书演员提供了一个观摩学习、实践锻炼的平台,让演员的技艺更加炉火纯青(杨旭东,2013)。

综上所述,我们初步了解到,北京评书作为一种历史久远的艺术形式,它具有很强的地域性与时代性。本文对现代北京评书发展的障碍进行研究,与当前已有研究的角度不同,因此,本研究具有一定的创新意义和参考价值。

三、研究方法

本研究采用结构式访谈方法收集数据,并通过对数据进行编码分析,取得一些发现。

(一)数据分析

1. 采访对象

2018年7月16—28日,我们分别对三位评书演员和八位观众进行了采访,他们是:梁彦、马剑平、唐柯,以及观众1、观众2、观众3、观众4、观众5、观众6、观众7和观众8。

表1:采访对象个人信息

姓名	年龄	从业时间	擅长表演内容	特点
梁彦	37岁	12年(2007年拜连丽如为师)	《西汉》	表演颇具文采,善于讲述逸闻典故,语言优美,口齿清晰
马剑平	35岁	8年	擅长相声、评书	声音洪亮,表情丰富
唐柯	38岁	20年	擅长京韵大鼓、西河鼓书及鼓曲伴奏	口齿清晰,声情并茂
观众1	中年			书场常客
观众2	中年			书场常客
观众3	中年			书场常客
观众4	12岁			书场常客,间或表演
观众5	中年			书场常客

续表

姓名	年龄	从业时间	擅长表演内容	特点
观众6	45岁			书场常客
观众7	中年			书场常客，间或表演
观众8	中年			书场常客，间或表演

2. 数据收集

本研究采用结构式访谈形式，向宣南书馆演员与观众询问以下六个问题：

1）相比于同类语言艺术，例如脱口秀、相声等，您认为评书有何不同？

2）同类语言艺术，例如脱口秀、相声等，对评书发展是否造成了影响？

3）除了同类语言艺术，评书的发展还有什么其他障碍？请举例说明。

4）当前评书新的传播途径对评书艺术的发展造成了怎样的影响？

5）评书对年轻人是否有吸引力？为什么？

6）如果北京评书想要得到更好发展，应该得到哪方面的支持？

（二）数据分析

通过反复阅读访谈记录，我们得到以下编码。

表2：数据分析结果

研究主题	编码	定义
评书与同类语言艺术的区别	评议性和灵活性	古事而今说，佐以评论
		每一次表演都是一次故事的再创作和人物形象的再塑造
	书目特色	书目多
	内容特色	讲述历史和文化
	语言特色	文学水平高
	目的特色	传播为人处世的道理，劝人向善
	时间特色	评书的篇幅都比较长，连续性强，需要分成多次讲述，节奏比较慢；想要听完一部完整的书历时较久，需要听众有时间坚持
	观众特色	观众的理解和接受程度更高，受众范围广
同类语言艺术对评书发展造成的影响	没有影响	评书与相声和脱口秀相比有很大区别，所以不会彼此影响
	有积极影响	相声融合了评书的叙事，而在评书中也有很多相声抖包袱的手法，所以这两门艺术相互促进和融合
评书发展的其他障碍	评书演员的培养要求高，时间长	培养一名评书演员绝非易事，并非一朝一夕能完成；演员要学习的东西多且难
	传承难	传承人不足
	对传统文化的偏见	人们越来越追求新生事物，对传统文化不够重视
	场地少	现有的书馆太少，不能让更多的人去听评书
	听书人时间有限	因为时间原因，听众来不了

续表

研究主题	编码	定义
当前新的传播途径对评书艺术发展造成的影响	帮助发展	新的传播媒介帮助扩大评书的覆盖面和影响力,增加评书的受众
	阻碍发展	新媒体的发展阻碍了说书人与听众之间的互动,对时间的限制无法让演员充分发挥,演员只能忠实于故事文本
		因为新媒体的出现,人们能接触到的娱乐种类和层次更多了,人们会选择适合自己的娱乐方式,不一定会选择评书
评书对年轻人的吸引力	有吸引力	评书里有许多知识,评书用讲故事的方式让人接受枯燥的历史,并告诉听众处世的方法
北京评书应得到的支持	政府支持	政府的场地、资金支持
	行业推广和宣传	评书演员应该走出北京,去外地表演,让大家有更多机会接触评书
	观众认可	观众喜爱并支持评书
	书目创新	书目老旧,缺乏创新

四、发现与讨论

(一)评书与同类语言艺术的区别

1. 评议性和灵活性是评书的精髓

相较于脱口秀和相声,评书的评议性和灵活性非常突出。梁彦老师概括,"评书是说书人口头讲述的故事,以古事而今说,佐以评论的叙事艺术。'评'是评议,'书'是故事。夹叙夹议成为评书的基本程式"(梁彦，2015)。"评"是"书"的灵魂，没有"评"则成了"死书"，艺谚云"评书无评，如目无睛"(杨旭东，2013)。观众6也表示："评书的主要功夫不在书上而在评。你根据我说的评论内容，会被我带着产生倾向性。这个就是所谓评书的魅力。"由此可见，评书重点在于它的评，当说书人把自己的观点加入书中时，这本书才会被称为"评书"。

评书的评议涵括丰富，彰显了评书演员的知识和经验积累。评书演员唐柯老师说："评书就是这个样子，靠一张嘴。但是这一张嘴能够表达出来的问题靠的是深厚的积淀。"将"个人生活经历嵌入对历史故事的叙述当中，是书场表演的重要特征之一。艺人在书场中并不是简单的重复，每一次表演，都是一次故事的再创作和人物形象的再塑造"(杨旭东，2013)。观众2也说："评书跟小说不一样，演员要说评书，他有一次二次创作，不是照本宣科。而且每个演员都有自己的特点，根据自己掌握的知识，往里边加了很多东西。"正如梁彦(2015)说的"一遍拆洗一遍新"，评书表演非常灵活，对同一部书的每次表演都会不同。

2. 评书的书目多

相较于相声和脱口秀，评书的书目更多。梁彦(2015)归纳，自清代以来，经过历代艺人的拆洗和磨炼，评书留存下来多部经典作品。从民国至今，不少说唱西河大鼓的演员改说评书，因此又有一些西河大鼓的"大书"被改编为评书。观众2说："传统书目像《西汉》，它都是经过起码有几十年，再往前说，有上百年磨合出来的。前面老先生给写出来，慢慢多少年，评书演员一点一点磨合，慢慢大家磨合出一个比较完整的(作品)。"二十世纪三四十年代，一些文人墨客与评书艺人合作编纂了一些评书作品；新中国成立后，新编评书题材广泛，具有相当大的规模。所有这些书目加起来有百部以上，它们按照内容可分为四类：长枪袍带书、短打公案书、神怪书和新书。

3. 评书讲述历史，传承文化

相比同类语言艺术，评书的内容更侧重于历史；它讲述市井文化，分析人情世故。观众8说："评书里面的文化底蕴很多，它是讲文化、讲人情、讲内涵的。"所以北京评书不只是在讲故事、评论故事，这里面更是蕴含着从古至今积淀下来的丰富文化内涵。观众7解读道："评书让人了解历史，我们中国人的民族自豪感是通过对历史的了解来呈现的。历史需要我们后来人去传承、去发展。"由此可以看出，观众认为评书帮助人们了解历史，从而增强自我认知和自信，促进历史的传承和发展。

4. 评书格调高雅

相较于相声和脱口秀，北京评书的语言和文字表达更为高雅，体现的文学素养和文化水平更高。观众2说："评书比较高雅，从文字角度、语言角度上，它都有自己的特点。"梁彦老师指出："'赋赞儿'是评书中所使用的诗、词、赋、赞、对联等文体的总称，被评书界视为珍宝，且经过一代代说书人不断提炼改进，形成了稳定的艺术程式，使观众获得独特的艺术享受。"除"赋赞儿"外，还有用来在演出开始时吸引观众注意力、让其安静的定场诗。定场诗多引自小说、史书和诗词集，具有一定的文化底蕴（梁彦，2015）。

5. 评书高台教化

相声和脱口秀是"取悦"观众、"逗人乐的"；而评书的表演目的正如观众7所说，"咱们说书唱戏劝人方，三条大路走中央。它高台教化"。评书"谈古论今",通过讲述和评价历史故事,向观众传递为人处世的道理;它劝人向善,教人方正行事,"具有高台教化,启迪民智的作用";它说的都是"醒世良言",所以评书艺人也被尊称为"说书先生"。(梁彦,2015)评书艺术家的一项重要职责,就是教育民众。唐柯老师认为,"与同类语言艺术相比,评书有它的历史和社会责任"。"评书作品中蕴含着丰富的人生哲理和高尚的道德观念,在情节的展开中潜移默化地教育人、感化人"(王华新,2012)。

6. 评书讲述时间长

评书书目都比较长,需要分成多次讲述,节奏也比较慢,想要听完一部完整的书历时较久,需要听众有时间坚持。观众3讲道:"评书的劣势就在于要想续上是比较难的。如果你听现场,要持续不断地去跟进,对于现代人来讲,这个时间是很难把握的。"评书演员马剑平老师也说:

> "相声、脱口秀更像快餐,评书更像大餐;那么大餐要烧得慢,快餐要来得容易。现在的生活节奏比较快,所以脱口秀也好,相声也好,会比较火。那么评书可能会滞后一些,但是评书真正的发源是老百姓,他这个生活没有那么大压力,他没有那么紧张的节奏,能够真正彻底地放松下来。他有时间去听,所以评书就会发展下来,这是时代所趋。"

评书演员认为,评书是在人们生活较为轻松和缓慢的时代背景下产生的。那时人们有时间定期去书馆听书,进行娱乐和放松,所以能够跟着听完一整部书。而现在生活节奏快,人们很忙碌,很难挤出那么多时间长期地去跟一部书。这也是短小又逗乐的相声和脱口秀非常流行的原因：既搞笑、解压、让人放松，又短小精悍，没有要连续听的压力。

7. 评书听众范围广

相较于相声，各地的观众更能理解和接受评书这种曲艺形式。观众8说："相声北方人喜欢听，南方人就不喜欢。但评书是全国都有：江南就有评话评弹，到四川有四川评书，东北有东北评书，听说陕西还有陕西评话。还有秦腔，这些都是评书的分支。"相声在南方很少有人可以听懂，因此它具有地域局限性。但评书不仅可以讲述大众一般都能听懂的历史故事，而且还有很多分支分散在全国各地。所以评书更为大众所接受，适合更多人听和推广普及。

虽然评书与相声、脱口秀等同类语言艺术有所不同，但在表演技巧方面还是有相同之处的。评书表演会借鉴相声的手法，比如抖包袱——说笑话，现挂——即兴开玩笑。观众3说："从表演技巧方面来讲，现在我觉得评书和单口相声没有特别大的差别。王玥波也是说相声出身的，他很多东西都是在抖包袱。"评书观众认为，曲艺不分家，很多曲艺门类都有互相借鉴的现象（杨旭东，2013）。

（二）同类语言艺术对评书发展造成的影响

笔者采访的11人中，有8位认为同类语言艺术对评书的发展没有影响。观众8认为："虽说是同类语言艺术，但喜好他们的群体不一样，他们有不同的观众，所以不会相互影响。"同时，评书要想发展，更多的是需要自身努力。观众6概括说："关键还在于评书自身的发展。你如果自己发展得好，你的演员培养得好，你就会有好的发展。

所以我不认为有其他东西制约评书发展。"被采访者认为，虽然评书和其他曲艺一样，都属于语言艺术，但它们有不同的受众，所以不会阻碍彼此的发展。当代北京评书要从自身出发，找到传承和发展的问题所在。

有两位受访者认为，相声对评书发展有积极影响，两门艺术互相促进，借鉴了彼此的内容和表演技巧。观众3表示："现在评书里面也开始用相声抖包袱的方式去处理一些细节，相声的基本叙事功能是基于评书的架构来实现的。很多演员都是拜两门艺术的师父，这两门艺术互相融合。"相声融合了评书的叙事，而在评书中也有很多相声抖包袱的手法，即逗乐。很多评书演员也都"师从两门"："郭德纲早期也说过评书，后改说相声"（杨旭东，2013）。

(三) 评书发展的其他障碍

1. 评书演员要求高、培养时间长

培养一名评书演员绝非易事。观众3表示："评书是一个人的舞台，精不精彩，都是一个人功夫的体现。"评书是一个人的戏，"集生旦净末丑于一身"（梁彦，2015），所以一名评书演员要学的东西有很多，要下的功夫要很深；而且成为一名合格的评书演员，也并非一朝一夕就能实现。观众1说："学这东西太难，不是谁想学三天俩早上就能学出来。培养一个评书演员很难。"评书的学习不是短时间能够见成效的，这就决定了评书的传承是个长时间的过程（杨旭东，2013）。

2. 评书传承难

评书在传承方面也受到了较大阻碍，而传承包括评书演员的传承和观众的传承。传承人的不足限制了评书发展。观众7说："艺术人才欠缺。说书的人才太少，屈指可数。另外一点是观众需要培养。"马剑平老师也作出类似表述："评书的发展障碍就是人才缺失，就是能说书的人太少，能够真正上台说大书的人太少。"可以说，目前评书演员队伍面临青黄不接的尴尬局面，老一辈评书艺人已经年近古稀，而新一代年轻演员数量少，而且技艺尚不成熟（王华新，2012）。除此之外，观众7表示："社会的主导力量，应该给评书一个尊重其自身规律的发展空间，而不是做表面成绩，要做一个真正的传承。"马剑平老师认为，虽然现在评书已引起社会的重视，但因为培养一名评书演员很难，需要很长时间，所以不能操之过急；否则就会变成只做表面功夫，而很难真正出成绩。

3. 对传统文化的偏见

随着新媒体、新娱乐的产生，新文化也产生了。人们越来越追求新生事物，这导致传统文化渐渐地不被人们重视。观众6说："一说评书，大家就认为它是一个传统的东西。认为老的就不好，只有创新才是好的。"这位观众还表示："现在国民对于传统文化的认识程度相比以前是要普遍降低的，这是最大的障碍，这是一个环境问题。"在现如今这个属于创新的时代，大家都在追求"新"，传统文化的不被熟知与不被重视也成为评书文化发展道路上的一种阻碍。

4. 场地不足

场地不足导致不能让更多的人走进书场去观看评书表演。按照杨旭东（2013）的统计，"北京城区评书表演场所实际上只有四家"。观众8说："书馆太少，老先生年龄越来越大，如果后边的中青年演员现在能迎头赶上，能开更多的书馆，恢复老书馆的这种形式是最好的。"评书观众认为，书馆在规模和数量方面的局限性也阻碍了评书发展。

5. 听书的时间限制

书馆的地域固定性及说书场次和时间的限制，导致书馆覆盖范围小、辐射的观众少，这些也成为阻碍评书发展的因素。观众4表示："因为日常的一些加班，可能有的老听众来不了。"时间冲突与路程和距离限制使得许多观众不方便到现场听书或连续听书，但评书又需要不断听才能跟得上故事情节的发展进度，如果几次不听，很可能故事就接不上了，这就导致听众的流失。观众1表示："因为评书特别长，是需要耐着性子去听的东西。但是现在不论是在网络上还是在日常工作、生活中，大家都觉得快就是好。"现在人们生活节奏快，很难抽出较长时间去消遣娱乐。评书是一种收听周期很长的艺术形式，只有那些"有闲"人群才能真正享受，这就使其听众范围大大缩小，影响了评书的发展（王华新，2012）。

(四) 当前新的传播途径对评书艺术发展造成的影响

新的传播媒介对于扩大评书覆盖面、影响力和增加评书受众都很有帮助，但同时也改变了评书的时空设置。艺人和书座（老观众）普遍不认可在广播等媒介中"跑梁子"的做法，即由于广播等对于评书播出时间的限制，演员只能讲故事，不能过多地发挥和加入评论。书座认为，没有演员和观众互动的评书不算"玩意儿"，只有在书场表演的才是真正的评书。评书夹杂在众多可选择的新兴精神享受方式中，已被边缘化（杨旭东，2013）。

1. 积极影响

新媒体的传播使评书艺术覆盖面更广，能让更多人了解评书。观众3的观点是:"更多的人去了解评书,这也是最重要的。互联网是一个很好的传播方式。"评书观众认为互联网等新媒介在传播方面促进了评书艺术的推广。

2. 消极影响

传播媒介所能做到的主要是扩大评书艺术的传播范围,但它对北京评书的发展也造成了不容忽视的负面影响。首先,新媒体的表现形式屏蔽了说书人与听众之间的互动。观众3表示:"现场的演员跟观众能互动,这个效果是电视里跟广播里根本达不到的。"通过媒介传播的评书是虚拟表演,它切断了表演者和观众的联系。即使有时加入掌声和笑声,演员和观众也无法达成书场中的那种默契(杨旭东,2013)。其次,网络音视频一般播放时间很短,无法将篇幅较长的评书充分、完整和连贯地展现给听众。马剑平老师说:

"现在网络比较发达,其实我也在网上去播一些评书,比如在微博上。但是它们现在都是以短视频为主,短视频就制约了评书。很多东西没法在这短短的五分钟或十分钟之内说清楚,可能就要一个小时,要四十分钟才行。还没有把精华展现出来视频就结束了。"

评书演员认为,北京评书是一门长篇且连续性很强的艺术,网络并不适合表现北京评书的这一特点。为了适应虚拟表演对时间的严格控制,评书演员只能叙述故事文本,无法自由发挥;而听众对这些故事内容已熟知,因此失去了兴趣。"新的媒介不能挽救传统民间说唱的生命,它所带来的负面效果更为明显。"(杨旭东,2013)

除此之外，因为新媒体的出现，人们能接触到的娱乐种类和层次更多了，信息也变得更加碎片化与效率化。人们会选择适合自己的娱乐方式，而不一定会选择评书。观众8说："很多人欣赏的层面本来就不同，尤其现在是多元化社会。"评书演员也认为新媒体带来的多元文化使人们有了更多的选择，这些选择与传统娱乐艺术形成了竞争。"时尚流行的艺术形式主导着文化演出市场，成为民众娱乐休闲的主要选择，并开始重塑观众的欣赏习惯，挤压了现场表演的生存空间；制度化的工作、生活也限制了人们自由活动的时间。"（杨旭东，2013）

（五）评书对年轻人的吸引力

在11位受访者中，有9人回答评书对年轻人有吸引力。通过分析采访数据我们发现，这些受访者认为评书能够吸引年轻人的主要原因是其中蕴含着大量知识，包括历史、传统文化、处世道理等。评书又用高台教化的方式、幽默风趣的语言，结合社会经验，教给年轻人人情世故。并且听评书对于年轻人来说是一个有趣的体验。

1. 评书的知识性

评书中蕴含着许多历史与文化知识，因为其大多数书目都是传统书目。而且这些书目在几百年间由评书艺人不断演绎和磨合，囊括了各个时代的文化。观众2说："我说这个年轻人，你要喜欢历史，喜欢文学，你就要听评书，因为这里边有很多知识。"

听评书是学习知识非常好的方式。观众3回答道："主要在于大家想通过什么方式去了解这个世界和汲取知识，因为并不是所有人都排斥去了解传统文化和历史。评书是一种非常生动的形式，所以我觉得年轻人应该不会对这种事情完全排斥。"

2. 评书的思辨性

听书还可以了解人情世故和为人处世的道理，以及一些书本中学不到的、经过社会实践才能获取的生活经验。马剑平老师说："评书绝对是高台教化。把所有的历史典故结合现代人的心理状态给你分析出来，然后教你如何做人，告诉你人情世故，所以现在人很爱听评书。什么是高台教化？高台教化就是在说书先生说书时将知识传授给你，并教你向善，辨别是非。"不同年代的说书人会有不同的"评"，但相同的是，他们都通过"评"来教会观众如何做人做事，这对于初入社会的年轻人是十分有帮助的。

3. 评书的节奏感

评书这种缓慢长篇的独特表演形式会吸引年轻人。观众6说："今天的这个社会效率高、节奏快，那评书会给年轻人一个非常独特的体验，他们就会感受到其实一个小时坐在底下不说话，只接受信息而不表达是挺有意思的一个体验。"在这个快节奏的社会，评书成了为数不多的慢节奏的表演方式，对于习惯了快节奏的年轻人来说，在书馆里坐三个小时听书，是他们中很多人都没有过的体验，所以评书会吸引他们。

值得注意的是，所有被采访者都是书场观众或演员，他们在这个问题上的回答有一定的偏向性。他们对评书的了解和喜爱对身边的年轻人具有潜移默化的影响，因此这些年轻人更有可能接触评书，更了解评书，对评书更有好感，所以他们不一定能够代表所有相同年龄层次的人。此外，这11位受访者中，只有1位是年轻人，其余都是中年人。这些中年人凭自己的经验和主观判断回答这个问题，所以不一定能够真实反映年轻人的观点。

为保证收集信息的客观性和准确性，笔者横向比对了另外一组同学的采访数据，他们的研究主题是"北京中学生对北京评书的认知度调查"。在该研究中，接受采访的45名中学生中有43人（95.5%）表示评书对他们有吸引力，同时能说出评书吸引他们的一些具体特点。通过对比两项研究的采访数据，笔者能够得出评书对大多数年轻人有吸引力这一结论。

(六) 北京评书应得到的支持

笔者在采访书场观众以及评书演员时发现，说到发展北京评书需要得到的支持，被提及最多的是政府的大力支持。观众8说："我们希望国家有更大的扶持力度，现在帮助已经有了，但将来还有很长的路要走。"唐柯老师强调："资金、场地支持，包括宣传的力度应该更大，对它的整个发展空间、方方面面都应该有一些支持。"评书观众认为，政府的扶持应该是全方位的，包括宣传、为书馆提供资金和场地等。梁彦老师也提道："宣南书馆能坚持到现在，离不开政府的支持。"由于评书艺人连丽如系北京评书国家级传承人，她得到了宣武区文化部门免费提供的场地，场内的票务工作和现场服务也完全由其徒弟们承担（杨旭东，2013）。崇文、宣武、东城三个书馆，均以所在地区文化馆为主要演出场地。所以评书想要更好地传承与发展，最需要政府的扶持。

观众的认可也十分重要。观众2说："政府的扶持、观众的认可，还有说书环境，这三个都需要去培养。你看现在北京评书说书的地方很少，原来北京有大大小小上百个说书馆，现在消费的地方屈指可数。"观众的认可应该是出自对评书这门传统艺术的喜爱和对"传统书场的高度认可与呼唤"（杨旭东，2013），具体体现在对书馆的支持。在采访时我们了解到，在宣南书馆表演结束后，还会有一些观众主动留下来帮助书馆打扫卫生，他们用朴实的行动表达了对书馆的支持。

北京评书在推广方面也需要支持，即去探索新的媒介和模式，让更多人去认识评书、喜欢评书。观众3说："评书有没有一种方式是突破原有的这种大家一段一段去追的方式，把一些很经典的段子集中起来，然后去外地表演，比如开设一个专场，或类似的方式。"对比现在的一些娱乐方式，如游戏、综艺节目等，评书的参与和观看人群并不大，主要原因在于宣传和推广力度不够。在现今多媒体的大环境下，关于评书的宣传寥寥无几，这导致评书的受益人群可能只是那些懂评书和爱评书的人，不会有更多的增长。而且很多人并不是不喜欢评书，只是不知道评书。所以评书想要更多的人去了解它、喜爱它，需要在宣传方面得到有力支持。

几名观众在采访时还不约而同地提到了书目创新。观众6说："从评书的内容上讲，是不是也应该有一些新的贴近生活的评书？像六七十年代出现过一批新评书，这些新评书实际上在某种程度上起到了推动评书发展的作用"。可以说，"书目老旧，创新不足"是当代评书艺术的现状（王华新，2012），评书需要在书目或故事内容上再次创新。只有创新，评书艺术才能更好地生存和发展，才能有更多的书和故事可评。

五、总结

北京评书与同类语言艺术有很大不同。北京评书评议性的艺术特点体现在对历史故事的改编和评论上,它的表演语言和内容相比同类语言艺术有更深的文化和历史底蕴,它的表演目的是知古鉴今、劝善规过,它的书目数量也要比同类语言艺术多,它的受众分布地域也比同类语言艺术更广。由于评书的内容多是历史故事,因此篇幅很长,如果在书场表演,要分多次才能完成。现代人的生活节奏和压力阻碍了他们定期去书馆听书。所以如何让这门艺术符合现代生活节奏,让更多的人可以享受这门艺术,是值得进一步探究的问题。

由于观众的欣赏品味不同,北京评书和其他同类语言艺术之间的相互影响不会很大。评书要传承和发展,更多的应该靠行业自身的努力。

不论是从对中年人还是年轻人的采访来看,评书都是吸引年轻人的,主要是因为评书中有许多年轻人可以学到的东西,如历史知识、人情世故等。并且听评书对年轻人来说也是个独特的体验。北京评书面临着传承方面的阻碍,而想要一门传统的民间艺术继续传承与蓬勃发展,年轻人对它的熟知与热爱是必不可少的。所以,我们应该想办法让更多年轻人接触书场中的北京评书,进而热爱北京评书。

新媒体的产生和发展扩大了评书的影响力和传播范围,但同时对北京评书这门具有连续性和慢节奏特点的传统艺术产生了冲击。碎片化的趋势并不适合北京评书。而对于慢节奏的北京评书来说,在发展上我们能做到的只是多关注与多支持。当然也可以通过类似的研究,向大家介绍这门传统的艺术,让它为更多人所熟知。

北京评书要想得到更好的发展，首先应该得到政府支持，无论是在场地、资金方面，还是宣传方面，政府的支持应该是全方位的。观众认可也十分重要，因为只有观众认可，这门艺术才有发展空间。北京评书在推广方面的支持应该是去探索新的传播方式，让更多人了解北京评书并热爱它。书目创新方面也应受到重视，如果从当前社会中提取新的评书元素，那么评书会吸引更多听众，从而实现再次振兴。

参考文献：

梁彦.北京评书[M].北京：北京美术摄影出版社，2015.
汪景寿，王决，曾惠杰.中国评书艺术论[M].北京：经济日报出版社，1997.
王华新.中国评书艺术及其当代发展研究[D].河北：河北大学，2012.
杨旭东.当代北京评书书场研究[M].北京：民族出版社，2013.

A Study on the Obstacles to the Development of Beijing *Pingshu*

Shen Yiwen[1] Ma Zitao[2] Tian Haoyu[3] Xing Zeju[4]

Abstract: This study aims to investigate the obstacles to the development of Beijing *Pingshu*. Relying on data gathered through structured interviews with *Pingshu* performers and audiences in a *Pingshu* theater, this study shows that Beijing *Pingshu* is very different from other similar oral performance arts such as crosstalk and talk show. In addition, due to the different tastes of the audience, Beijing *Pingshu* and other oral performance arts will not have a great impact on each other. Therefore, the inheritance and development of Beijing *Pingshu* rely on its own efforts. Factors impeding the development of *Pingshu* include high requirements on the performers, long training time, difficulties in the inheritance, prejudice of young people towards traditional culture, lack of performance venues, and limited time for live performance. Although there are some positive impacts on the development of *Pingshu* by the new media, such as the Internet, there are more negative impacts. *Pingshu* is attractive to young people. The development of Beijing *Pingshu* relies on the government support, audience recognition, aggressive promotion, and innovation in its stories and performance.

Keywords: Beijing *Pingshu*, obstacle, influence, support, attraction

---

1. Associate professor of English, Beijing Foreign Studies University.
2. The 10th grade student of the 1+3 program of The Affiliated High School of Beijing Foreign Studies University.
3. The 10th grade student of the 1+3 program of The Affiliated High School of Beijing Foreign Studies University.
4. The 10th grade student of the WACE program of AIDI International School.

1. Significance of the Study

Pingshu is one of the popular forms of oral literature, a folk rap art, with a long history. The performance is a one-man speech, which tells historical and modern stories through artistic means. Beijing *Pingshu* is the main branch of the art form, popular in Beijing, Tianjin, Hebei, and the Three Northeast Provinces, etc. In recent years, the market of Beijing *Pingshu* is shrinking, and with the passing of the older generation of performers, there is a shortage of successors. Moreover, there are few live performances in the *Pingshu* theater, and *Pingshu* programs on TV are near extinction. Though Internet *Pingshu* is growing, it does not have a large audience. The success of Beijing *Pingshu*'s application for intangible cultural heritage in 2008 has somehow helped the development and inheritance of *Pingshu*. Still, the inheritance and development of Beijing *Pingshu* is an urgent problem that demands immediate action (Yang, 2013).

The aim of this paper is to study the obstacles to the development of Beijing *Pingshu*. A survey was conducted in Xuannan Pingshu Theater, where the audiences and performers were interviewed. By discussing the obstacles and protection of this intangible cultural heritage, we hope to shed some insight on the revival of the art and bring it back to people's lives.

2. Literature Review

After a thorough research in the cnki.net on the obstacles to the development of Beijing *Pingshu*, we found the empirical research on this topic was very few. The research on *Pingshu* mainly focuses on the following three aspects.

2.1 History of Beijing *Pingshu*

Pingshu was originally a folk rap art, but gradually evolved into a language art similar to storytelling (Yang, 2013). *Pingshu* is an art very close to the life of people. It can also reflect the rise and fall of an era, and the spirit of the nation (Liang, 2015). *Pingshu* performance is popular because it is simple and easy to understand. Beijing *Pingshu* has a very long history. It was formed in the Tang and Song dynasties and gained its popularity in the Ming and Qing dynasties (Liang, 2015).

2.2 Trends in the development of Beijing *Pingshu*

The essence of Beijing *Pingshu* is changing with time. Wang (2012) said that the development of Beijing *Pingshu* was inseparable from the dissemination of new media which provided a bigger platform for the development of *Pingshu*, and gave more people access to the art form.

Beijing *Pingshu* should "prepare for the bad times when in good time". "Good time" lies in its rich accumulation of cultural heritage, whereas "bad time" is due to the unique nature of the performance. Therefore, what is needed for its development is to innovate on the original stories (Wang et al., 1997).

However, the current development of Beijing *Pingshu* is worrying, facing such problems as inadequate performance venues and lack of successors (Liang, 2015). Nowadays, new forms of entertainment and shorter episodes are flooding into all kinds of media. Beijing *Pingshu* is gradually ignored, fading out of the vision of TV media and returning to the broadcasting market. (Wang, 2012)

2.3 Research on the Beijing *Pingshu* theater

The construction of *Pingshu* theater is important for audiences to "return to the scene". It also makes the performance more complete. In addition, *Pingshu* theaters have the function of giving young performers a platform for learning and practicing, so as to help them gain more experience (Yang, 2013). To sum up, we have learned that Beijing *Pingshu*, as an art form with a long history, has a strong regional and temporal significance. This study, focusing on the obstacles to the development of Beijing *Pingshu* in modern times, is different from the previous studies, and hence it is innovative and valuable.

3. Research Methods

The data were collected by the authors through structured interviews, and the findings were obtained through coding and analysis of data.

3.1 Data analysis

3.1.1 Participants

From July 16 to 28, 2018, we interviewed three *Pingshu* performers and eight audiences (See Table 1) respectively.

Table 1: Biographical information of the participants

Name	Age	Career time	Expertise	Characteristics
Liang Yan	37	12 years (a student of Master Lian Liru since 2007)	*Pingshu* scholar and performer	Literary performance, beautiful language, and clear delivery
Ma Jianping	35	8 years	Crosstalk and *Pingshu*	Loud voice and rich expressions
Tang Ke	38	20 years	*Jingyun Dagu* and *Xihe Gushu*	Clear tongue and clear voice
A1	Middle age			Regular customer
A2	Middle age			Regular customer
A3	Middle age			Regular customer
A4	12			Regular customer, performing occasionally
A5	Middle age			Regular customer
A6	45			Regular customer
A7	Middle age			Regular customer, performing occasionally

continued

Name	Age	Career time	Expertise	Characteristics
A8	Middle age			Regular customer, performing occasionally

3.1.2 Data collection

The data were collected by the authors through structured interviews. Six questions were asked:

1) Compared with similar language arts, such as talk show, crosstalk and so on, how do you think *Pingshu* is different?

2) Do other oral performance arts, such as talk show and crosstalk, have any impact on the development of *Pingshu*?

3) Apart from other similar language arts, what other obstacles are there to the development of *Pingshu*? Please give examples.

4) What is the impact of the new media, such as the Internet, on the development of *Pingshu*?

5) Is *Pingshu* attractive to young people? Why?

6) What kind of support should it get for further development of Beijing *Pingshu*?

3.2 Data analysis

By reading the data over and over again, we get the following codes.

Table 2: Data analysis results

Theme	Code	Definition
The difference between *Pingshu* and similar language arts	Commentary and creativity	Ancient stories, contemporary comments
		Each performance is to recreate a story and rebuild an image
	Number	Large number of stories
	Content features	About history and culture

continued

Theme	Code	Definition
The difference between *Pingshu* and similar language arts	Language features	High literary level
	Educational features	Spread the truth of life and persuade people to be good
	Time features	*Pingshu* is lengthy, and the continuity is important; it needs to be divided into many parts, and the pace is slow; it is time-consuming for the audiences if they want to listen to a complete *Pingshu* story
	Audience features	The audience has a higher level of understanding and acceptance, and *Pingshu* has a wide range of audience
The influence of similar language arts on the development of *Pingshu*	No impact	*Pingshu* is very different from crosstalk and talk show, so it will not be affected
	Positive effect	The two art forms, *Pingshu* and crosstalk, promote and learn from each other
Other obstacles to the development of *Pingshu*	Demanding and long training process	It is by no means easy to train performers, and they have to learn much and it is time-consuming
	Inheritance is difficult	There is a shortage of successors
	Prejudice against traditional culture	People like to pursue new things and pay less attention to traditional culture
	Limited venue	The existing *Pingshu* theaters are too few for more people to enjoy
	Time constraint	The audience could not come because of time constraint
The impact of the new media on the development of *Pingshu*	Helpful	The new media help to expand the coverage and influence of *Pingshu*, and increase the number of the audiences
	Hindrance	The development of new media hinders the interaction between the performers and the audiences. The limitation of time prevents the performer from giving full play of his or her ability; the performer only remains faithful to the stories
		Because of the emergence of new media, people can come into contact with more types and levels of entertainment, and will choose the most suitable one

continued

Theme	Code	Definition
The appeal of *Pingshu* to young people	Attractive	There is a lot of knowledge in *Pingshu*, which makes boring history acceptable through stories; *Pingshu* tells young people how to do things
Support for Beijing *Pingshu*	Government support	Venues and financial support from the government
	Promotion and publicity	*Pingshu* performers should go out of Beijing and perform in other places so as to give more people access to *Pingshu*
	Audience approval	The audiences love and support it
	Story innovation	The stories are old and lack innovation

4. Findings and Discussions

4.1 The differences between *Pingshu* and other oral performance arts

4.1.1 Commentary and creativity are the essence of *Pingshu*

Compared with talk show and crosstalk, the commentary and creativity of *Pingshu* are prominent. Liang (2015) pointed out that "*Pingshu* is the story told orally by the performers. It is an old story with a modern perspective. Its narrative with commentary style is the basic formula of *Pingshu*. 'Ping' in Chinese means commentary; 'shu' means stories which are often well-known history stories." Commentary is the soul of *Pingshu*. (Yang, 2013) A 6 said, "The main power of *Pingshu* is not in the story but in the comment. Audience can take sides when they agree with the comments. This is the charm of *Pingshu*." *Pingshu* is just an ordinary story-telling until performers add their comments and opinions in it. Thus, the key point of *Pingshu* is its comments.

Though stories can be the same, commentary can vary greatly since different *Pingshu* performers have different point of views. They tell stories creatively, incorporating their social understanding and personal experience. "One person with his mouth – this is the way *Pingshu* is," Tang ke said. "But what he expresses through the mouth is his rich accumulation of understanding of people and society." "Personal life experiences embedded in the narrative of the historical story is one of the important features of *Pingshu* performance. Each performance is not a simple repetition, but a story and character recreation." (Yang, 2013) A 2 said, "*Pingshu* is different from novels. When performing *Pingshu*, the performer goes through a process of recreation, instead of simply telling the stories from the novel. Every performer has his own characteristics, and adds a lot of stuff to it, based on his own understanding and features." The performance of *Pingshu* is very creative, and *Pingshu* is varied from performance to performance, even with the same story.

4.1.2 The large number of *Pingshu* stories

Compared with crosstalk and talk show, there are more *Pingshu* story pieces. Liang (2015) concluded that since the Qing dynasty, a number of classic works had been preserved through generations of performance and recreation. From the founding of Republic of China to the present, many performers of other oral performance arts, such as *Xihe Dagu*, have changed to be *Pingshu* performers, so some of the "long and heavy story pieces" of *Xihe Dagu* have been adapted to *Pingshu*. A 2 said, "The traditional stories like *The Western Han Dynasty* have up to one hundred years of history. At the beginning, an experienced *Pingshu* performer wrote it out, and after many years of performing and recreating by many performers, slowly it evolves into a more complete master work." In the 1930s and 1940s, some writers and artists worked together to compile new works. Since the founding of the People's Republic of China, the number of new stories has been on the rise. The total number of *Pingshu* works has reached more than a hundred. They are classified into four categories according to the content: war, law, ghost, and new stories.

4.1.3 *Pingshu* is about history and culture

Compared with other oral performance arts, *Pingshu* focuses more on history, telling the culture of the common people and analyzing the society. A 8 said, "There are many cultural implications in *Pingshu*. It is about culture, human feelings, and self-cultivation." So *Pingshu* does not only tell stories and comment stories, but it also contains rich cultural connotations passed on from the ancient times. "*Pingshu* gives people an understanding of history," A 7 said. "*Pingshu* helps people understand history, and the national pride is presented through our understanding of our own history. History needs us to inherit and develop." *Pingshu* helps people understand their own history, thus enhancing their self-awareness and confidence, and promoting the inheritance and development of history.

4.1.4 *Pingshu* is elegant in style

The language expression of Beijing *Pingshu* is more elegant, and the literary and cultural level is higher. "It is elegant. It has its own characteristics from both the features of vocabulary and language as a whole," said A 2. Liang (2015) pointed out that "'*Fuzan*' is the general term for the poetry, lyrics and couplets used in *Pingshu*. '*Fuzan*' is regarded as treasures which, after continuous improvement through generations of performers, bring artistic enjoyment to the audience." In addition to this, prelude poems are used to attract the attention of the audience, and to make them quiet when a performance starts. Many of the prelude poems, extracted from novels, historical books, and poems, are of high literary value (Liang, 2015).

4.1.5 *Pingshu* is educational

Crosstalk and talk show are "entertaining". But the purpose of *Pingshu*, succinctly summarized by A 7, is that "*Pingshu*, talking about the past and the present, is used to convey to the audience the ethical way to do things. It advises people to be good and righteous." *Pingshu* is educational and enlightening. One of the important duties of performers is to educate the public. Therefore, the performers are called by the audiences "*Pingshu* teachers". (Liang, 2015) Tang Ke believed that "compared with other oral performance arts, *Pingshu* has its historical and social responsibilities". "*Pingshu* contains rich philosophy of life and high moral values, and imperceptibly educates and revives people through the development of the plot." (Wang, 2012)

4.1.6 *Pingshu* takes a long time to deliver

Stories of *Pingshu* are usually very long, and they are performed in series in *Pingshu* theaters, where the pace is slow. The audiences, if they want to listen to a complete story, need to listen to the live performance once or twice a week for at least half a year, sometimes even three years. A 3 said, "the disadvantage of *Pingshu* is that it is difficult to follow, particularly when you listen to the live performance and want to continue. It is very difficult for people nowadays to have such a fixed time for a prolonged period." Ma Jianping, the performer, also said, "Crosstalk and talk show are more like fast food. But *Pingshu* is more like a big meal. The meal needs a long time to cook and the fast food comes easily. Now the pace of life is faster, so talk show and crosstalk are well received and popular. Well, *Pingshu* lags behind, because *Pingshu* originated from the common people's life in the old days when they didn't have so much pressure, with no fast pace. They could really relax completely. Only when people have time to listen to *Pingshu*, can *Pingshu* have the base for development. This is the trend of the era."

Performers believed that *Pingshu* would develop only when people's life was more relaxing and slows down. If people have time to go to the theater regularly for fun and relaxation, they can finish a whole story by enjoying live performance. Now the fast pace and busy life make it difficult for people to squeeze out so much time to listen to *Pingshu* for a long time. This is why short and funny crosstalk and talk show are so popular. They are both relaxing and short, and there is no pressure if one does not want to listen to them continuously.

4.1.7 *Pingshu* is inclusive

Compared with crosstalk, audiences from different parts of China can understand and accept *Pingshu*. A 8 said, "The people in the north like to listen to crosstalk, but not the people in the south. But *Pingshu* is available all over China, for example, in the south of the Yangtze River, Sichuan province, and northeastern provinces. And in Shaanxi province, *Pingshu* has another name '*Shaanxi Pinghua*'." Crosstalk is rare in the south, so it is limited to areas. *Pingshu* not only tells historical stories that the general public can understand, but also has many branches scattered throughout the country. Therefore, *Pingshu* is more widely accepted and suitable for wider promotion.

Although *Pingshu* is different from other oral performance arts such as crosstalk and talk show, there are still similarities in the performance skills, and *Pingshu* will draw on the techniques of them, such as telling jokes or improvising a joke on the context. "In terms of performing skills, I don't think there is a big difference between *Pingshu* and the one-man crosstalk," A 3 said. "The *Pingshu* performer, Wang Yuebo was trained as a crosstalk performer, and now he uses lots of crosstalk techniques in *Pingshu* performance." It is generally agreed that it is hard to distinguish one oral performance art from another; and the arts all have learned from each other (Yang, 2013).

4.2 The impact of other oral performance arts on the development of *Pingshu*

Of the eleven people interviewed, eight believed that other oral performance arts have no impact on the development of *Pingshu*. A 8 argued that "although it is similar in terms of form and language, different oral performance arts have different audiences and tastes, and they will not affect each other." A 6 concluded, "The key lies in the development of *Pingshu* itself with excellent performers and excellent market. I don't think it's something else that restricts the development of *Pingshu*." It is generally believed that Beijing *Pingshu* should start from its own strength and address the problems that hinder the inheritance and development.

Two interviewees said that crosstalk had a positive impact on the development of *Pingshu*, because the two art forms complemented each other, drawing on each other's content and performance skills. A 3 said, "Now *Pingshu* begins to use crosstalk techniques, such as 'telling jokes unexpectedly' to deal with some details; the narrative ability of crosstalk is based on *Pingshu*'s structure. It is obvious to notice the merging of the two art forms." In *Pingshu*, there are also a lot of comic jokes which are funny. Many of the performers "follow two masters"; one is from crosstalk and the other from *Pingshu*. "Guo Degang learned *Pingshu* in the early days, and then converted to crosstalk." (Yang, 2013)

4.3 Other factors impeding the development of *Pingshu*

4.3.1 The requirements to the performers are high and the training time is long

It is no easy task to train a *Pingshu* performer. "*Pingshu* is a one-man performance. The wonder relies on that one person, and his talent," said A 3. "A single *Pingshu* performer acts as all the characters in the play." (Liang, 2015) It takes much time before one becomes a qualified performer. It demands tremendous observation, imitation, practice and effort from the learners. The learning process takes years, yet nobody can predict in the early stage if the person really has the potential and perseverance to grow into a successful performer eventually. "It's very hard to learn and one cannot be successful without years of efforts," said A 1. This determines that *Pingshu* inheritance is a long and hard process (Yang, 2013).

4.3.2 It is difficult to pass on *Pingshu*

The inheritance of *Pingshu* faces great obstacles, such as the shrinking number of both performers and audiences. The shortage of inheritors limits the development of *Pingshu*. There are only a few people who can give *Pingshu* performance. The other problem is the lack of enthusiasm of audiences.

"There is a shortage of artistic talents," said A 7. Ma Jianping also said, "The obstacle to the development of *Pingshu* is the lack of talents. At present, there are only a few who can give performance and even less who can give a whole series of long historical stories." "Nowadays, the older generations are too old to go on the stage and the younger generation are too young and too few in number. And the younger generation does not have mature skills." (Wang, 2012) In addition, A 7 said, "The mainstream of the society should give *Pingshu* a space that respects its own laws of development, demanding a real inheritance rather than some superficial achievements." Ma Jianping pointed out that even though *Pingshu* had aroused the attention of the society, it was very difficult to get a positive result in the near future because it was a very long process of training performers and cultivating the interest of the audience. The development of *Pingshu* has its own rules; to break it only results in superficial achievement but it is not sustainable.

4.3.3 Prejudice against traditional culture

With the emergence of new media and entertainment, a new culture has also emerged. People are increasingly pursuing new things, leading to the gradual neglect of traditional culture. "The word *Pingshu* is associated with oldness and tradition which have negative connotation. People regard highly of new and innovative things, and look down on the old and tradition," said A 6. "This is a major obstacle that the value of tradition is decreasing in the mind of general public. This is the social context." In this era of innovation, we are all pursuing "newness", and the lack of knowledge and attention to traditional culture has become an obstacle to the development of *Pingshu*.

4.3.4 There is a shortage of venues

The lack of space has prevented people from going into *Pingshu* theater to watch *Pingshu* performance. According to Yang (2013), "There are in fact only four places in Beijing to watch live *Pingshu* performance." A 8 said, "There are too few theaters, and the performers are getting older and older. But if the young and middle-aged ones can now catch up and more *Pingshu* theaters are open, the situation can be much better." The limitations in size and quantity of *Pingshu* theaters have hindered the development of *Pingshu*.

4.3.5 Time constraints for listening to *Pingshu*

Another obstacle to the development of *Pingshu* is the geographical location of the *Pingshu* theater, as well as the limitations on the number and time of performance, which have resulted in a small coverage of audience. "Some regular listeners may not be able to come because of their business obligations," said A4. Time conflict, traffic and distance all make it very inconvenient for many audiences to come to the theater for live *Pingshu* performance. But because *Pingshu* is a series of stories which are all closely related, one must listen continuously to keep up with the development of the story. If one fails to listen to it several times, it is likely that he will get lost of the plot. This leads to the loss of the audience. "Because *Pingshu* is very long, we need to have patience to listen to it, but now, whether on the Internet or in our daily life, we all feel it is good to be quick," said A1. Nowadays, people live in fast pace, and it is hard to spare much time for entertainment. *Pingshu* demands a very long devotion of time and energy from the audiences. Therefore, the prerequisite greatly narrows the market of audience and hence hinders *Pingshu*'s own development. (Wang, 2012)

4.4 The impact of new media of communication on the development of *Pingshu*

4.4.1 Helpful

The new media helps expand the coverage and influence of *Pingshu*, and increases the audience for *Pingshu*. "It's important for more people to know it," said A3. "The Internet is a good way to promote it." The audiences believed that new media, such as the Internet, have helped the promotion of the art.

4.4.2 Hindrance

The new media also has negative impact on the development of Beijing *Pingshu*. Firstly, the new media has blocked the interaction between performers and audiences. Experienced audiences think that *Pingshu* is not authentic without proper interactions between performers and audiences. They believe that only in *Pingshu* theater that *Pingshu* is performed in its most natural and authentic way. "This interaction between performers and audiences in *Pingshu* theater can't be achieved on TV or on the radio," A 3 said. It cuts the performers off from the audience. This is not a real performance but a virtual one even with applauses and laughter added. *Pingshu* has been marginalized because of numerous new and alternative ways of enjoyment. (Yang, 2013) Secondly, Internet audio and video pieces are generally very short in time. It cannot provide a full and comprehensive play of a lengthy *Pingshu* piece. Ma Jianping said,

> "Now the Internet is fully developed. In fact, I also post some of my *Pingshu* performance on the Internet, for example on Weibo, but they are mostly short videos, which I believe restrict the performance. A lot of things can't be explained in this short 5 or 10 minutes. It must take an hour or 40 minutes. The video is over before it reaches the peak."

The performers believed that Beijing *Pingshu* was a long and sequential art, and the Internet was not suitable for the performance. In order to adapt to the strict control of time in virtual performances, the performers can only tell the story but cannot give the comment freely. The audiences, who are already familiar with the story line, lose interest in it. "The new media cannot save the lives of traditional oral performance arts, and its negative effects are more obvious." (Yang, 2013)

In addition, because of the emergence of new media, people can access more types of entertainment. Information is more fragmented and people are more time-conscious. In this sense, *Pingshu* has lost its advantage. "A lot of people have different preferences, especially in a pluralistic society," said A 8. New media has brought about more choices which are in competition with traditional entertainment arts. "Modern and popular art forms dominate the entertainment market and become the choice of people, and begin to reshape the leisure hobbies of the general people and squeeze the living space of the live performance of traditional oral performance arts. Institutionalized life style also limits the free time of people." (Yang, 2013)

4.5 The appeal of *Pingshu* to young people

Of the eleven people interviewed, nine replied that *Pingshu* was attractive to young people. Through data analysis, we found that *Pingshu*'s main attraction to young people was that it was loaded with knowledge of history, traditional culture, and ideological systems. The commentary through humorous language teaches young people the operation of the society and the relationships based on rich social experience. Beyond that, listening to *Pingshu* is an interesting experience for young people.

4.5.1 The intellectual nature of *Pingshu*

Pingshu reveals much historical and cultural knowledge to young people, because most stories told in *Pingshu* are from traditional works. Moreover, after hundreds of years of interpretation by the performers, these stories have been scrutinized through the lens of culture of each era, which young people can learn. A 2 said, "If a young man likes history and literature, he should listen to *Pingshu*, because there is much he can learn from it."

Listening to *Pingshu* is a very good way to learn. A 3 replied, "The main element is how you want to understand the world. If one wants a comprehensive understanding of traditional culture and history, *Pingshu* is a vivid form. So I don't think young people should say they are totally excluded from this kind of art form."

4.5.2 The dialectic feature of *Pingshu*

Pingshu helps to understand the world and obtain life experiences through social practices, instead of from books. Ma Jianping said, "*Pingshu* is definitely educative. By analyzing historical figures from the mentality of modern people, *Pingshu* tells you how to be a decent man, and how the world operates. What is education? Education is not only to teach you knowledge, but also to show you right and wrong." Performers of different ages have different comments, but they all teach the audience how to behave. This is very helpful for young people who just enter the society.

4.5.3 The pace of *Pingshu*

Another attraction is that the slow and long performance of *Pingshu* is a unique experience for young people. A 6 said, "Today's society is efficient, fast-paced. But *Pingshu* will give young people a very unique experience. One will feel strange but interesting that they can actually sit down and listen for an hour, simply receiving information." "In this fast-paced society," he said, "*Pingshu* has become one of the few slow acting styles for young people who are used to the fast tempo." *Pingshu* must be a special experience. It is a rare experience for many young people to sit for three hours in the *Pingshu* theater and listen to *Pingshu*. So *Pingshu* attracts young people.

It is worth noting that all the interviewees are either professional performers or enthusiastic audiences. It is possible that their answers to this question are biased. Their knowledge and love of *Pingshu* have a subtle influence on the young people around them. Therefore, those young people are more likely to be exposed to *Pingshu*, to know about *Pingshu*, and to have a favorable impression on *Pingshu*. In this sense, the young people may not be representative. Second, only one out of the eleven interviewees is a young man; others are middle-aged. Their subjective judgments do not necessarily reflect the views of young people.

In order to double check the objectivity and accuracy of the finding, the authors made a cross-reference to the data of another young researcher group who have studied on Beijing middle school students' recognition of *Pingshu*. Their data shows that 95.5% of the middle school students interviewed said *Pingshu* is attractive to them, and that they are able to identify some of the outstanding features that make *Pingshu* attractive. Hence, our finding that *Pingshu* is attractive to young people is reliable.

4.6 Support for Beijing *Pingshu*

The data demonstrate that the strong support from the government is most frequently mentioned for the development of Beijing *Pingshu*. A 8 suggested that our government should provide more support than what we have now, for the development of *Pingshu* has a long way to go. "We want a more comprehensive support from the government," Tang Ke said. "We need more space, more funding, and more extensive promotion." Liang Yan said, "The Xuannan Pingshu Theater cannot survive without the support of government." The rent of the theater is paid by the cultural department of Xuanwu District, and the ticketing work and on-site services in the theater are carried out entirely by the students of Lian Liru, the national inheritor of Beijing *Pingshu* (Yang, 2013). The three theaters in Chongwen, Xuanwu and Dongcheng districts use their regional cultural centers as their main venues for performances. It is obvious that the development of *Pingshu* has a close link to the support of the government.

Audience recognition is also very important. A 2 said, "The government's support, the audience's approval, the management of theaters and training of young performers are critical factors. Compared with hundreds of *Pingshu* theaters in the old days, there are only a few places for live *Pingshu* performance in Beijing now." The audience's recognition should be based on the love of this traditional art, and it is also "a call for the return of traditional *Pingshu* theaters" (Yang, 2013). *Pingshu* lovers show their affection to the art by their substantial support to the theater. In the interview, we learned that after each performance, some audiences took the initiative to help cleaning up in Xuannan Pingshu Theater. They have expressed their support for the theater with simple actions.

Beijing *Pingshu* also needs support in its promotion, and it needs to explore new media and models, so that more people will know *Pingshu* and like *Pingshu*. A 3 said, "We can try a new model of performing *Pingshu* by gathering all classic pieces of different stories to make a tour around the country." Compared with the current forms of entertainment, such as games and variety shows, the distribution of audience of *Pingshu* is not wide. The main reason is publicity and promotion. In this multimedia era, there is very little publicity about *Pingshu*, which may lead to the limited number of people who know about *Pingshu*. A lot of people, who lack experience of listening, may fall in love with it once they encounter the charm of *Pingshu*. So a strong support in publicity for *Pingshu* is necessary for more people to understand it and love it.

Data show that many audiences mention the innovation of *Pingshu* through creating more stories. "In terms of the content of *Pingshu*, should there be some new stories that are close to life, like those in the 1960s and 1970s?" A 6 said. "Those new *Pingshu* stories have in fact played a role in promoting the development of *Pingshu*." "Old stories without innovation" is the current state of contemporary *Pingshu* (Wang, 2012). The audiences believed that *Pingshu* had made an innovation in the 1960s and 1970s to revitalize the art. Only by innovation can the art of *Pingshu* survive and develop, and more books and stories can be told and commented.

5. Summary

Beijing *Pingshu* is very different from other oral performance arts. Its main features are reflected in the adaptation and commentary of historical stories. Its language is more liberal and its content is richer in cultural and historical knowledge. The purpose of the performance is educative, and to advise audiences on moral well-being. It also has more series of stories than other oral arts, with its audiences more widely distributed. Because the content of *Pingshu* is mostly historical stories, *Pingshu* is usually very long. It will take many times to finish in a theater. The fast pace and pressure of people nowadays prevent them from going to the theater to listen to live performance regularly. So how to adapt this art to the rhythm of modern life so that more people can enjoy it is the next step worth exploring.

As the audiences have different tastes, there are little mutual influence between Beijing *Pingshu* and other similar oral performance arts. So the inheritance and development of *Pingshu* more depend on the efforts of the practitioners.

Based on our research, we have found that Beijing *Pingshu* is attractive to young people. There are so many things that they can learn from *Pingshu*, the history, the culture, and the society. It is also a unique experience for them to listen to *Pingshu*. Beijing *Pingshu* is faced with inheritance obstacles, and young people's familiarity and love for an ancient folk art is essential if it is to continue to inherit and flourish. Therefore, we should find ways to let more young people come into contact with Beijing *Pingshu*, and then love it.

The development of new media has expanded the influence and dissemination of *Pingshu*, but at the same time it hurts this traditional art that demands interaction between performers and audiences. What we can do with Beijing *Pingshu* is to support it and promote it.

For the better development of Beijing *Pingshu*, support of the government is crucial, whether it is the money, the venue, or the publicity. The audience recognition is also very important, because this art gains room for development with wider market. Beijing *Pingshu* should explore new ways of communication, so that more people can understand and love it. Attention should also be paid to story innovation; and writing new *Pingshu* stories is another crucial way for Beijing *Pingshu* to revitalize now.

References:

Liang, Yan. Beijing Pingshu [M]. Beijing: Beijing Arts and Photography Press, 2015.

Wang, Huaxin. Research on Chinese Pingshu Art and Its Contemporary Development [D]. Hebei: Hebei University, 2012.

Wang, Jingshou, Wang, Jue, & Zeng, Huijie. Review of Chinese Pingshu Art [M]. Beijing: The Economic Daily Press, 1997.

Yang, Xudong. A Study on Contemporary Beijing Pingshu Theaters [M]. Beijing: The Ethnic Publishing House, 2013.

北京中学生对北京评书的认知度调查[1]

那日苏　贾婷毓　王御龍[2]

【摘要】 我们通过对北京中学生进行结构式访谈，并分析访谈数据，发现他们对北京评书的认知有三个特点：北京中学生对于北京评书有广泛的浅层了解但缺乏深度了解；北京评书对北京中学生的吸引力主要来自北京评书本身的特色以及说书人的魅力；北京中学生听北京评书的渠道多样，但主要集中在手机和广播两种渠道。我们还发现，虽然现在北京评书对北京中学生有一定的吸引力，但是北京评书要想进一步发展，还是需要政府的措施、多媒体的传播，以及评书本身的创新。

【关键词】 北京评书　北京中学生　了解度　评书的吸引力　听书渠道　支持评书传播

一、研究背景与研究目标

　　北京评书是有历史底蕴的传统文化的一个代表，但随着时代的变迁，它在社会上的地位和受欢迎的程度却越来越低。我们认为，对传统文化的保护和发扬，必须从青年人做起，必须让青年人了解它、喜爱它。只有这样，这个传统文化的表现形式才有可能发扬光大。基于这一想法，我们对北京中学生群体进行调查研究，希望借此发现北京的

---

1. 本调研报告科研指导教师为北京外国语大学专用英语学院副教授沈忆文。
2. 本调研报告的三位作者均为北京外国语大学附属中学1+3项目十年级学生。

青年人对北京评书的认识和了解程度,探究他们的听书兴趣以及听书渠道,以期依据这些数据对北京评书的改进和创新提出建议。希望北京评书在保留其传统艺术特色的前提下,能够提高大家对它的认知度并让更多人喜爱这项传统文化,北京评书从而能够长远地保留、传承下去。

二、文献综述

笔者用"对北京评书的认识""评书的听众""青年人对评书的了解"等作为关键词,在中国知网上进行检索,没有发现任何相关的内容。由此,我们认为本研究具有一定的开拓性意义。

三、研究方法与研究步骤

(一) 数据收集

1. 采访对象

  总受访人数:70人

  男性:23人

  女性:47人

  年龄:14—17岁之间

  学校:1)北京普通高中(以北京外国语大学附属中学为主)

     2)私立国际学校(以北京外国语大学国际高中为主)

2. 数据收集

本研究采用结构式访谈的模式,通过电话或者面对面访谈,询问了中学生以下问题:

您是否听过评书？

听过：

1）您在哪里听书？

2）您多久听一次书？

3）您了解哪些名家？

4）评书为什么吸引您？

5）您还记得您第一次听评书的经历吗？

6）北京评书已经成为中国国家级非物质文化遗产，是中华文化的传承，那么您对它的发展有没有什么建议呢？

没听过：

1）您对评书有什么了解？（请用几个词概括一下）

2）您为什么不听评书？

3）北京评书已经成为中国国家级非物质文化遗产，是中华文化的传承，那么您对它的发展有没有什么建议呢？

（二）数据分析

我们通过反复阅读、分析数据，最终获得以下编码。

表1：数据分析结果

主题	编码
了解度	广泛的浅层了解但缺乏深度了解
吸引力	评书的特色和收听的便利性
收听渠道	多样性与集中性
推广建议	多方联合与多种渠道

四、研究分析与讨论

通过对数据的归纳和总结,我们有四个主要发现:1)北京中学生对北京评书有广泛的浅层了解但缺乏深度了解;2)北京评书对北京中学生的吸引力来自评书本身和评书表演艺术家,而非来自收听的便利性;3)收听北京评书的渠道很多,但中学生集中选择手机和广播;4)评书的推广需要各方人士通力合作,并且需要各种渠道联合行动。下面我们将从北京中学生对评书的了解度、评书的吸引力、收听渠道以及对评书推广的建议四个方面分别进行分析和讨论。

(一) 对北京评书的了解度

通过采访,我们发现对北京评书有浅层了解的北京中学生人数较多,但是有深度了解的中学生的人数却很少。多数北京中学生听过北京评书,且对北京评书的基本特色有一定了解;但坚持每天听书的人不多,而且大多数中学生对评书表演艺术家知之甚少,对评书艺术特色的阐述也只停留在表面,并没有真正理解评书艺术的精髓。

1. 广泛的浅层了解

表2:听过北京评书的北京中学生人数占比(总人数N=70)

编号	是否听过书	人数(n)	百分比(n/N)
1	听过	44	62.9%
2	没听过	26	37.1%

表3：北京中学生听北京评书的频率（总人数N=44）

编号	频率	人数(n)	百分比(n/N)
1	每天	11	25.0%
2	每周	4	9.1%
3	每月	4	9.1%
4	每年	4	9.1%
5	不确定	18	40.9%
6	只听过一次	3	6.8%

由表2和表3可知，62.9%的同学听过北京评书，且其中有93.2%听过不止一次。也就是说，绝大多数北京中学生由于各种原因与评书有过接触。有些同学选择继续听下去，有些同学听过几次后就放弃了。

表4：北京中学生对北京评书特色的了解（总人数N=45）

编号	特色	人数(n)	百分比(n/N)
1	故事性	16	35.6%
2	趣味性	14	31.1%
3	评议性	11	24.4%
4	表演艺术性	11	24.4%
5	教育性	3	6.7%

注：部分学生提到的北京评书特色多于一个。

由表4可知，多数北京中学生对北京评书有基本的认识和了解。在听过评书的学生中，大家的认识集中在故事性、趣味性、评议性、表演艺术等几个方面；而对于没有听过评书的学生，他们对评书特色的了解程度也不逊色于听过评书的同学，他们可以准确说出北京评书的一些特色，如北京评书是"一种幽默或者有吸引力的语言表达的形式，把故事讲给听众""了解故事的人利用自己的文化知识，对书籍内容加以讲述和评论"等，这些特色和听书的同学提到的特色大同小异。

2. 缺乏深度了解

由表3可知，每天坚持听书的同学只有11人，占比25.0%；每周都听书的同学占比9.1%。迄今为止，只听过一次评书的同学有3人，占比为6.8%。其余同学则是偶尔听，例如每月听几次，或者时间不确定。从数据可以看出，多数学生听书的频率不高或时间不确定。如一位学生所说："时间不确定，只要碰到就会听一会儿。"由此可知，多数学生与评书的接触不多，不可能对北京评书产生深层次的了解。

由表4可知，不论是听过还是没有听过评书的学生，他们对评书特色的了解只在皮毛，没有深入到这门艺术的精髓。

评书是说书人口头讲述故事，以古事而今说，佐以评论的叙事艺术。关于评书的基本程式，"评书"二字已经揭晓了答案："评"是评议，"书"是故事。评，是评书之精髓，根据书中故事情节的发展，或引经据典，或有感而发，评人、评事、评情、评理、评历史曲直、评人物功过，醒世警俗，画龙点睛；书，是评书之要素，故事起承转合，跌宕曲折，人物命运因之变化。因此，夹叙夹议成为评书的基本程式。然而，评书之所以不同于故事，还在于评书要说理，说理要说事，说事要说人，说人要说心。评书要说理，是要有主题，扬善抑

恶,褒是贬非。(梁彦,2015)

北京中学生对北京评书的认识多停留在讲故事层面。一部分同学认为他们是因为故事的吸引力和评书的趣味性而听评书,一部分同学提到评书的"评"字在这门艺术中举足轻重的作用。而恰恰"评"这个字才是这门艺术的精髓,是区别于其他口头文学的重要特性。此外,很少有学生意识到评书"扬善抑恶,褒是贬非"这样的高台教化作用,只有少数学生提到评书的教育性(6.7%)。由此可知,由于中学生与评书的接触时间不够,而且没有用心体会评书的深层意义,简单地把评书等同于讲故事,因此我们认为他们对评书的了解还停留在表面。

表5:北京中学生对评书表演艺术家的了解(总人数N=44)

编号	提到名家的个数	人数(n)	百分比(n/N)
1	不了解	18	40.9%
2	一个	13	29.5%
3	两个	9	20.5%
4	三个及以上	4	9.1%

由表5可知,近30%的中学生可以说出两个或两个以上知名评书表演艺术家的名字,如连阔如、袁阔成。有近30%的同学能提到一个艺术家的名字。40.9%的同学表示"这个我不了解"。

尤其值得关注的是,中学生对青年评书演员了解不多,只有3名学生提到青年演员,在所有听过北京评书的学生当中占比为6.8%。但据梁彦(2015)指出,大批青年评书演员正在成长,并且已经取得一些成就。王玥波、李菁、贾林、祝兆良、张怡、张硕等是其中的佼佼者。由此可知，大部分同学对北京评书只有浅层了解，需要更多地接触评书后才会产生深层了解。

(二) 吸引力：评书的特色和收听的便利性

关于北京评书对于北京中学生的吸引力，我们共采访了45位学生，其中有2人对北京评书完全没有兴趣，约占受访学生总数的4%；其他43名同学都认为北京评书对他们是有吸引力的。通过对这43名学生的访谈数据做编码，共整理出92条编码条目。我们发现，北京评书对于中学生的吸引力主要来自五个方面：评书本身的特色、说书人的吸引力、学生个人的收获、收听的便利性和放松方式。

表6：北京评书主要吸引力（条目总数N=92）

编号	吸引力	条目频数 (n)	百分比 (n/N)
1	评书本身	63	68.5%
2	说书人	13	14.1%
3	个人收获	10	10.9%
4	收听便利性	5	5.4%
5	放松方式	1	1.1%

由表6可知，北京评书本身的艺术特色对中学生的吸引力最大，条目频数占条目总数的68.5%；其次是说书人的吸引力和学生从听书中得到的收获；收听的便利性、放松方式等其他方面对学生的吸引力并不大。由此可见，吸引中学生听评书的关键在于评书艺术本身，以及他们对评书表演艺术家的由衷钦佩。

1. 北京评书本身的特色

北京评书本身特色的吸引力又可以分为故事情节、听书有趣、评议性等多个方面。

表7：北京评书本身特色的吸引力（条目总数N=63）

编号	特色吸引力类别	条目频数（n）	百分比（n/N）
1	故事情节	16	25.4%
2	听书有趣	14	22.2%
3	评议性	11	17.5%
4	生动形象	10	15.9%
5	容易理解	7	11.1%
6	传统文化	3	4.8%
7	大众化	1	1.6%
8	不同于其他口头表演艺术	1	1.6%

注：表中百分比相加大于100%是由保留一位小数的四舍五入所致。

由表7可见，对于评书本身的特色，并没有某一种特色是中学生集中喜欢的。故事情节是吸引中学生听书最为重要的特色，占评书本身特色吸引力条目总数的25.4%。有16名学生在访谈中提到评书中的历史故事非常精彩：有同学认为"评书的故事情节挺吸引我的"；有同学觉得"它引人入胜的故事特别吸引我"；有同学强调"（评书）讲的故事非常富有戏剧性"；还有同学提道，"我觉得评书吸引我应该是因为它讲的一些历史故事很生动"。

同时我们也看到，评议性占评书本身特色吸引力条目总数的17.5%，可见有部分同学在听书的时候，不仅关注了故事本身，也被说书人对故事的评论所吸引。如有同学提到"评书表演艺术家的独到见解";也有同学说,"说书人把他自己的一些感情色彩代入进去"。还有同学说:"说书人他们自己独特的价值观也特别吸引我。"更有同学说:"(说书人)将书中那些难以理解的内容,例如说教类的道理讲了出来。"甚至有同学的说法更加明确:"我觉得评书能批判,它能反映出社会上的美丑、真假和善恶,能反映人性或者社会上的一些问题。"我们认为,中学生正处在开始了解世界、认识世界的阶段,评书中的评论对他们尤其重要,因为他们需要正确的价值观和世界观的指引。说书人对人性和社会问题的分析,对社会上的美丑、真假、善恶的评论,对历史功过的褒贬,都起着高台教化的作用,是中学生非常需要且欢迎的。

评书生动形象的表达也是很多同学认为其具有吸引力的因素。有同学说:"评书吸引我主要在于说书比较生动。"也有同学说:"感觉说书人的表演十分生动形象,能够让我有兴趣听进去故事。"有同学认为:"评书可以把书中的人物心理描绘得更形象。"也有同学认为评书的代入感比较强,"比较有画面感""让人有一种身临其境的感觉"。所以评书语言和表演的生动性都是吸引中学生的因素。

有同学认为评书之所以吸引人,"是因为它是中华传统文化"。但只有3名同学提到评书艺术是中华传统文化的代表,条目频数仅占评书本身特色吸引力条目总数的4.8%。这说明学生对评书的历史渊源和文化承载还认识不足。

2.说书人的特点

说书人的特点又可以分为表演艺术、风格多样、知识渊博三个方面。

表8：说书人的特点（条目总数N=13）

编号	说书人特点	条目频数(n)	百分比(n/N)
1	表演艺术	11	84.6%
2	风格多样	1	7.7%
3	知识渊博	1	7.7%

由表8可知，对于说书人的特点，中学生最能感受到的就是表演艺术。其中有同学说："他的那个语气……挺吸引我的。"也有同学说："他说的就比较有韵律感。"还有同学认为"说书人在说书的时候非常有感情"，而且"一些音调的起承转合会让人从心里注意"。从这些话中可以看出，评书是一门口头表演艺术，学生通过说书人的感情投入、音调变化、声音韵律感等来体会评书艺术的魅力。

3.个人收获

对于个人收获，我们把数据总结成文学/历史知识、增长见识这两个方面。

表9：北京中学生听评书的个人收获（条目总数N=10）

编号	收获类型	条目频数(n)	百分比(n/N)
1	文学/历史知识	7	70.0%
2	增长见识	3	30.0%

有中学生在访谈中提道："因为评书是一种口头上的文学表现形式，它能帮助我们更好地去理解一些难懂的篇目。比如四大名著，看纸质的书会觉得比较枯燥，没有意思，但是如果听评书的话就会有趣许多。"也有同学说："评书不仅可以增加我的历史常识，也可以让我

学习到历史故事中的一些谋略，还有一些教训之类的，因为读史使人明智。"还有同学认为："评书对名著加以评论，同时让人增长见识，感觉挺受益。"在受访的45名中学生中，只有10名同学提到个人收获是评书吸引他们的原因。但我们认为，随着听评书时间的增加，越来越多的同学会感受到评书给他们的学习和见识带来的裨益。

4. 收听的便利性和放松方式

由表6可知，有5名同学提到收听的便利性，占采访总人数的5.4%；只有1名同学提到听评书是一个很好的放松方式。这说明随着技术的进步，收听的便利性已经不能吸引多数中学生参与听评书这项活动；而且当下休闲放松的方式有很多，听评书不是中学生的首选。因此这两项在评书的吸引力方面占比很小。

（三）收听渠道：多样性与集中性

通过对访谈数据的分析，我们发现目前中学生听北京评书的渠道有很多种，如广播、电视、光盘、手机等等；使用手机和广播听书的人数最多，超过一半。而第一次接触评书的渠道对于日后听书渠道的选择没有很大的影响。

1. 渠道的多样性

表10：北京中学生的听书渠道（总人数N=44）

编号	渠道	人数(n)	百分比(n/N)
1	手机	23	52.3%
2	广播	10	22.7%
3	学校活动	5	11.4%

续表

编号	渠道	人数(n)	百分比(n/N)
4	书馆	4	9.1%
5	电视	1	2.3%
6	光盘	1	2.3%

注：表中百分比相加大于100%是由保留一位小数的四舍五入所致。

由表10可知，中学生的听书渠道多样化，访谈中提到的有6个。有同学提到"在自家汽车或者出租车的收音机里听书"，也有人认为听书"就是用光盘跟手机APP"，还有4名同学提到去"东城的一个文化书馆"听书。

从数据中我们也发现，随着时代的变迁，人们听书的渠道越来越多。有一位受访学生说："小时候是拿收音机听书，然后是用电视机看直播，然后是每天上下学，听我父亲汽车上的广播播放的一些评书节目。"

2.手机和广播的集中性

表10显示，52.3%的同学使用手机听书，22.7%的同学使用广播听书。使用手机和广播听书的人数占所有受访者的75.0%。由此可以看出，虽然可选择的渠道有很多，但多数中学生集中选择了手机和广播这两个渠道。

表11：每天听书的北京中学生使用的听书渠道（总人数N=9）

编号	渠道	人数(n)	百分比(n/N)
1	手机	7	77.8%
2	广播	1	11.1%
3	学校活动	1	11.1%

由表11可以看出，在每天听书的中学生中，77.8%使用手机听书。综合表10和表11可以看出，大多数同学选择手机听书，而且每天听书的同学更是倾向于选择手机听书。我们认为，手机为主流听书渠道的原因是中学生的课业相对繁重，很少有大块且固定的时间用来听北京评书，但手机中的软件可以随时随地播放评书，并且可以随听随停，这对于时间紧迫、但几乎人手一台手机的中学生来说无疑是极其方便的。每天听书的同学绝大多数使用手机作为听书渠道，可以充分印证这一点。而广播成为第二大听书渠道，主要归功于在汽车上听到的广播电台节目；大部分选择广播作为渠道的学生都提到了汽车上的广播。而去书馆听书作为传统的听书方式，在数据中所占比例只有9.1%，这主要是因为中学生忙碌、快节奏的生活和学习使他们无法享受去现场听书的乐趣。

表12：北京中学生第一次听书的渠道（总人数N=21）

渠道	人数(n)	百分比(n/N)
学校活动	6	28.6%
广播	5	23.8%
手机	4	19.0%
书馆	4	19.0%
电视	1	4.8%
光盘	1	4.8%

由表12可知，28.6%的学生第一次接触北京评书是通过学校活动，并且有19.0%的学生是在书馆第一次接触到北京评书的。但由表10可知，手机是中学生听评书的主要渠道。由此可见，第一次听书

的渠道对后续听书的渠道没有影响。无论通过何种渠道接触到评书，只要中学生对这门艺术产生了兴趣，他们就会选择最简便的方式继续听下去。书馆听书对中学生来说不是最佳选择，手机和广播听书是最方便、最合适的选择。

(四)评书推广的建议：多方联合、多种渠道

1.北京中学生不听北京评书的原因

数据显示，中学生不听评书的原因主要有三个：没有兴趣、没有时间、没有环境。

表13：北京中学生不听北京评书的原因（总人数N=38）

编号	原因	人数(n)	百分比(n/N)
1	没有兴趣	16	42.1%
2	没有时间	12	31.6%
3	没有环境	10	26.3%

由表13可见，中学生不听评书的原因比较单一，主要是因为没有兴趣、没有时间和没有环境。有同学提道："对评书讲述的那些内容不是很感兴趣。"也有同学提道："没有太多闲暇时间去了解评书。"还有一部分同学认为："对于现在的时代来说，'评书'这一词汇很少出现在生活里。"针对这些原因，中学生也给出了发展北京评书的建议。

2.多方联合、多种渠道

中学生对发展北京评书的建议主要包括两方面：推广责任人与推广渠道。

表14：北京中学生对评书推广责任人的建议

责任人	建议	代表性措施	代表性表述
评书艺术家	创新	增加原创篇目	原创的篇目比较少，大多都是传统的改编
	传播	增加传播力度和广度	多方面、多时间段或以多种形式进行传播
政府	保护措施	增加年轻从业人员数量	年轻的从业人员较少
	宣传措施	海外推广，将评书推广到全世界	政府应该大力推广与宣传北京评书；应该让评书发展范围更广，可以给国外的一些群体也带去精彩的中华文化
学校	培养学生对评书的兴趣	邀请评书艺人多举办一些讲座，加深学生对评书的了解	应该在校园推广评书文化，这样可以让年轻人对它感兴趣，评书就会有更好的发展

通过对数据的分析，我们把评书推广责任人分为三类——评书艺术家、政府和学校，并分别找出对应的建议和措施。

中学生对评书艺术家提出的建议包括创新与传播两个方面。针对创新，中学生的建议是增加原创篇目。例如一位同学说："（评书）原创的篇目比较少，大多都是传统的一些改编。"这表明中学生希望评书不仅能够继承传统，还能够创作出符合新时代的作品，加强中学生对现实世界的理解、分析和批判能力。针对传播，中学生提出的建议是增加传播力度和广度。一位同学说："（评书应该）多方面、多时间段或以多种形式进行传播。"这说明中学生希望评书能够通过更加丰富的渠道进行传播。综上所述，中学生希望评书艺术家能够跟随潮流，进行书目的原创，并找到更加丰富的传播渠道。

我们把中学生对政府提出的建议细分为两个方面：保护措施与宣传措施。一位同学提道："政府应该有一些政策去保护（评书），比较年轻的从业人员也比较少。"评书只有通过增加年轻从业人员的数量才能得到传承，政府可以通过给予从业人员政策或补贴来对评书艺术进行保护。宣传措施指的是对评书的宣传与推广，中学生建议通过多种渠道宣传北京评书。有同学说："政府应该大力推广与宣传北京评书。"大家对政府提出的推广建议甚至包括向海外进行推广，例如一位同学说："应该让评书发展范围更广，可以给国外的一些群体也带去精彩的中华文化。"总之，对于中学生来说，政府主要在对评书的保护与传播方面发挥作用。

对于学校，中学生建议将评书引入校园。正如一位同学给出的建议："我觉得应该在校园推广评书文化，这可以让年轻人对它感兴趣，评书就会有更好的发展。"有些同学提到了更为具体的措施，例如通过评书艺人走进校园举办讲座来提高大家对评书的认知度。

综上所述，中学生建议评书推广责任人进行创新，培养中学生的喜好，以及寻找更加丰富的传播方式。我们认为评书推广责任人之间可以互相交流、互惠互助。评书艺术家可以参与政府的传播与保护活动，以提高政府的传播信赖度；政府对评书艺术家的传播给予支持，以增强评书艺术家传播评书的信心和力度；学校也可以邀请评书艺术家进入校园推广评书，以培养学生对评书的喜爱，甚至从学生中挑选出合适的艺术传承人进行培养。

表15：北京中学生对评书推广渠道的建议

推广渠道	代表性措施	代表性表述
线上渠道	借助网络渠道宣传；利用新媒体宣传，如电视	现代传承人的坚持和努力可以借助网络渠道进行宣传；可以利用新媒体进行宣传，如电视评书
线下渠道	报纸广告、宣传册	可以在超市一类的地方发广告进行宣传

由表15可知，中学生对北京评书推广渠道的建议主要分为线上渠道与线下渠道两方面。中学生建议多通过网络和新媒体进行线上推广，例如有同学说道："我觉得评书可以选择通过网络和新媒体进一步传播。"而对于线下渠道，如一位同学所说："可以在超市一类的地方发广告进行宣传。"中学生关于评书推广渠道的建议基本涵盖了他们日常生活所涉及的领域。

五、总结

通过数据分析，我们有四个方面的发现。第一，很多北京中学生对北京评书有基本的了解，但仅有少数中学生对它有深度了解。这主要表现在坚持每天听书的学生不多，学生对评书表演艺术家的了解也很少，且对评书艺术特色的阐述只停留在表面。第二，北京评书对于北京中学生的吸引力主要来自评书本身的故事性、趣味性，以及说书人的艺术功底，用手机收听评书的便利性并不是评书的主要优势。第三，北京中学生听北京评书的渠道有很多种，使用手机和广播听书的人数最多，这和中学生的生活状况有密切关系。第四，大部分北京中学生建议评书应该进行内容创新和渠道创新，而且评书艺术家、政府和学校应该联合起来，利用多种渠道共同促进北京评书的传承和发扬。

本研究从学生的视角，采用实证研究的方法，比较全面地分析了北京中学生对于北京评书的认识和发展建议。本研究的不足之处主要有以下两点。首先是数据问题。虽然接受采访的同学总共有70位，但由于同学们缺乏访谈经验，有很多同学答非所问，我们不知如何总结编码。对于这些数据，我们归类为无效数据，这导致最后可供我们使用的有效数据并不多，由此我们的结论也缺少数据支持。而且本研究的数据来源主要是学生的主观认知，没有从其他角度交叉印证中学生的主观印象。其次是文献问题。我们在中国知网上以"对北京评书的认识""评书的听众""青年人对评书的了解"等为关键词，搜索关于大众对北京评书的了解与喜爱方面的论文，得到的搜索结果为零。这导致我们的研究没有先例可循，也没有文献指导，因此我们在数据分析和主题提炼方面遇到很多困难，这也是研究过程中遇到的最大困难。

由此可见，本研究还有较大的改进空间和继续探究的必要性。但本研究的研究过程和结果，以及提出的问题和解决问题的方向，都具有一定的借鉴意义。

参考文献：

梁彦.北京评书[M].北京：北京美术摄影出版社，2015.

Beijing Middle School Students' Cognition of Beijing *Pingshu*

Shen Yiwen[1] Na Risu Jia Tingyu Wang Yulong[2]

Abstract: Through structured interviews with Beijing middle school students, we have three findings on their cognition of Beijing *Pingshu*. There is an extensive recognition on the superficial level but deficient in profound understanding. *Pingshu*'s attraction for the students originates from the characteristics of Beijing *Pingshu* itself and the charms of the performers. There are multi-channels for the students to listen to *Pingshu*, but the two main ones are mobile phones and radio broadcast. To promote the development of *Pingshu*, the suggestions from the middle school students are to form the collaboration of different stakeholders and utilize multiple promotion channels.

Keywords: Beijing *Pingshu*, Beijing middle school students, cognition of *Pingshu*, attraction of *Pingshu*, channels for listening to *Pingshu*, *Pingshu* promotion

1. Research Background and Objective

Beijing *Pingshu* is one of the representatives of cultural heritage which has rich cultural connotation; but with the changing of times, its popularity and adorability are both decreasing. We believe that the protection and promotion of Beijing *Pingshu* has to be started with teenagers, who are encouraged to spend time understanding and appreciating this art. Only in this way can this cultural heritage develop and be more popular. Based on this idea, we interviewed Beijing middle school students, hoping to find out their cognition of this art and suggestions to its development. We hope

---

1. Associate professor of English, Beijing Foreign Studies University.
2. The other authors of this paper are the 11th grade students of The Affiliated High School of Beijing Foreign Studies University.

that while the core of *Pingshu* is preserved, methods can be found to increase people's understanding and make more people know how to admire this kind of cultural heritage, so that *Pingshu* can last longer in the society.

2. Literature Review

After a thorough search on cnki.net using the keywords "cognition of Beijing *Pingshu*" "Beijing *Pingshu*'s audience" "Teenagers' understanding of Beijing *Pingshu*", etc., nothing has been retrieved. So we believe that our research is of a pioneering value.

3. Research Methods and Procedures

3.1 Data collection

3.1.1 Participants

Number of participants: 70

Number of males: 23

Number of females: 47

Age: 14 - 17 years old

Students' background:

1) Beijing public middle school students (mainly from The Affiliated High School of Beijing Foreign Studies University)

2) International middle school students (mainly from the International Curriculum Centre of Beijing Foreign Studies University)

3.1.2 Interview questions

This research used structured interviews with mobile phone or face-to-face mode. We asked the following questions.

Have you ever listened to Beijing *Pingshu*?

Yes:

1) Where do you listen to Beijing *Pingshu*?
2) How often do you listen to Beijing *Pingshu*?
3) What stories have you listened to?
4) Why does Beijing *Pingshu* attract you?
5) Do you remember the first time you listened to Beijing *Pingshu*?
6) What advice do you have for the development of Beijing *Pingshu*?

No:

1) What do you know about Beijing *Pingshu*? (Please use specific words to describe.)
2) Why don't you listen to Beijing *Pingshu*?
3) What advice do you have for the development of Beijing *Pingshu*?

3.2 Data analysis

After analysis, we obtained the following results.

Table 1: Data analysis results

Theme	Code
Level of cognition	Extensive in superficial recognition but deficient in profound understanding
Attraction of *Pingshu*	Characteristics of Beijing *Pingshu* and convenience of listening
Channels of listening	Diversification and centralization
Suggestions on promotion	Collaboration of different stakeholders and the use of multiple channels

4. Research Findings

Through discussing and analyzing the data, we have obtained some enlightening findings on Beijing middle school students' knowledge of Beijing *Pingshu*. We will summarize the findings into four aspects: the level of recognition, the attraction of *Pingshu*, the channels of listening, and suggestions on promotion.

4.1 Level of recognition: extensive in superficial recognition but deficient in profound understanding

Our data show that a large number of middle school students have a superficial understanding of Beijing *Pingshu*, but the number of those who have a profound understanding is small. Most middle school students have listened to Beijing *Pingshu* or watched the performance, and have some understanding of its basic characteristics. However, the number of students listening to Beijing *Pingshu* regularly is small, and they know little about *Pingshu* artists. Moreover, their explanation of *Pingshu*'s characteristics is also superficial due to their lack of knowledge of the culture essence of *Pingshu*.

4.1.1 Extensive superficial recognition

Table 2: The proportion of middle school students who have listened to Beijing *Pingshu* (N=70)

Number	Have listened before?	Number of students (n)	Percentage (n/N)
1	Yes	44	62.9%
2	No	26	37.1%

Table 3: The frequency of listening to Beijing *Pingshu* (N=44)

Number	Frequency	Number of students (n)	Percentage (n/N)
1	Every day	11	25.0%
2	Once a week	4	9.1%
3	Once a month	4	9.1%
4	Once a year	4	9.1%
5	Not sure	18	40.9%
6	Only once	3	6.8%

According to Tables 2 and 3, 62.9% of the students have listened to Beijing *Pingshu*. And most of them (93.2%) have listened to it more than once. It is obvious that most of the students have listened to Beijing *Pingshu*, but some choose to continue this practice whereas others, after a few times, have chosen to give up.

Table 4: Students' understanding of the characteristics of Beijing *Pingshu* (N=45)

Number	Characteristic	Number of students (n)	Percentage (n/N)
1	Storylines	16	35.6%
2	Fun	14	31.1%
3	Commentaries	11	24.4%
4	Art	11	24.4%
5	Educational	3	6.7%

Note: Some students mentioned more than one characteristic of Beijing *Pingshu*.

Table 4 shows that most middle school students have basic knowledge and understanding of Beijing *Pingshu*. Among those who have listened to it before, they choose to name the characteristics of the art as "attractive storylines" "funny" "have commentaries" and "performing art". Even those who have never listened to Beijing *Pingshu* know some typical characteristics. For example, someone who has never listened to *Pingshu* before mentioned, "Beijing *Pingshu* is a kind of oral performing art that is humorous and attractive." Another student said, "The essence of Beijing *Pingshu* is that someone who knows a story very well, retells it by using his own words, and adding some of his own opinions and comments." From the data, we can see that no matter whether the students have listened to it, they share the similar recognition of Beijing *Pingshu*.

4.1.2 Deficient in profound understanding

It can be seen from Table 3 that only 11 students listen to Beijing *Pingshu* every day, accounting for 25.0%, and 9.1% of the students listen to *Pingshu* once a week. So far, the number of students who have only listened to Beijing *Pingshu* once is 3, taking up 6.8%. The remaining students listen to it occasionally, or with no fixed time. We can see that most middle school students do not listen to Beijing *Pingshu* frequently and regularly. One of the interviewees said, "I'm not sure when I will listen. If I accidentally bump into it, I will listen for a while." It can be seen that most middle school students do not have much contact with Beijing *Pingshu*, and they lack profound understanding of the art.

Beijing *Pingshu* is the art of storytelling, which tells stories of the past to educate people of the present through accompanied commentaries. As for the basic components of *Pingshu*, the word itself, which means commenting and storytelling, has already revealed the answer. "Commenting" is about reviews, and "storytelling" is about stories. Commenting is the essence of the art form. Based on the development of plots in the stories, the performers either quote the classic works or give their personal comments. The comments can be on anything, such as the characters, the events, the situations, the moral standards, or the characters' merits and demerits, with the purposes of enlightening and sustaining moral standards. Stories are the key element. As the plot develops, the fate of the characters is revealed along with the performer's comments on it. Thus, the integration of narration and commentary is the distinctive feature of *Pingshu*, which differentiates it from pure storytelling. *Pingshu* talks not only about stories, but also ethical principles, in the context of human nature and social culture. In *Pingshu*, there must be a theme, which usually is about exalting the good and suppressing the evil. (Liang, 2015)

However, contradictory to the essential characteristics of Beijing *Pingshu* mentioned above, Beijing middle school students' understanding of *Pingshu*, based on Table 4, is mostly limited to storytelling. Some of them believed that they listened to *Pingshu* because of the stories and fun. Some of them mentioned "commentaries", the distinctive characteristic of *Pingshu* that separates it from other forms of oral literature. Only a few of the students mentioned *Pingshu*'s educational characteristic (6.7%), a feature that is often talked about by the performers as "exalting the good and suppressing the evil". It can be seen that most middle school students simply consider Beijing *Pingshu* as storytelling, but fail to get to the core of the art. Therefore, we believe that middle school students' understanding of Beijing *Pingshu* remains on the surface, due to their lack of contact with it.

Table 5: Middle school students' knowledge about Beijing *Pingshu* performers (N=44)

Number	Number of performers mentioned	Number of students (n)	Percentage (n/N)
1	None	18	40.9%
2	One	13	29.5%
3	Two	9	20.5%
4	Three or more	4	9.1%

Table 5 shows that only about 30% of the middle school students can name two or more Beijing *Pingshu* performers, such as Yuan Kuocheng and Lian Kuoru. About another 30% can name one performer. For example, one student said, "I only knew a few famous ones, such as Mr. Tian Lianyuan." And the rest 40.9% said, "I know none of them."

It is worth noting that the middle school students we interviewed knew very little about young performers, with only three of them mentioning the names of young performers like Wang Yuebo. But according to Liang (2015), many young Beijing *Pingshu* performers have achieved some degree of success. Among them, Wang Yuebo, Li Jing, Jia Lin, Zhu Zhaoliang, Zhang Yi, Zhang Shuo and others are the outstanding ones. We can see that most students only have a shallow understanding of Beijing *Pingshu*, and they need more contact with *Pingshu* before they can have a deeper understanding.

4.2 Attraction: characteristics of Beijing *Pingshu* and convenience of listening

We interviewed 45 middle school students about the attraction of Beijing *Pingshu*. Two were completely lacking in interest, accounting for about 4% of the total. The remaining 43 students thought Beijing *Pingshu* was attractive to them. We collected 92 pieces of codes from the 43 students interviewed.

We have found out that the attraction of Beijing *Pingshu* mainly comes from five aspects: the characteristics of the art itself, the charms of the performers, the personal gains of the students, the convenience of listening, and the way of relaxation.

Table 6: Five aspects of attraction of Beijing *Pingshu* (N=92)

Number	Attraction	Number of codes (n)	Percentage (n/N)
1	Beijing *Pingshu* itself	63	68.5%
2	Performers	13	14.1%
3	Personal gains	10	10.9%
4	Convenience	5	5.4%
5	Relaxation	1	1.1%

From Table 6, we can see that the artistic characteristics of Beijing *Pingshu* are the greatest attraction for middle school students, accounting for 68.5%. Next are the charms of the performers and the students' personal gains from listening. But the convenience of listening is not very attractive. Thus, it can be seen that the key elements in attracting middle school students are their appreciation for the art and their admiration for the performers.

4.2.1 Characteristics of Beijing *Pingshu* itself

The characteristics of Beijing *Pingshu* itself can be divided into eight aspects, including storylines, fun of the performance, commentaries and so on.

Table 7: Different characteristics of Beijing *Pingshu* itself (N=63)

Number	Characteristic of Beijing *Pingshu*	Number of codes (n)	Percentage (n/N)
1	Storylines	16	25.4%
2	Fun of the performance	14	22.2%
3	Commentaries	11	17.5%
4	Vivid expression	10	15.9%
5	Easy to comprehend	7	11.1%

continued

Number	Characteristic of Beijing *Pingshu*	Number of codes (n)	Percentage (n/N)
6	Traditional culture	3	4.8%
7	Popular among common folks	1	1.6%
8	Different from other oral arts	1	1.6%

Note: The sum of the percentage exceeds 100% because of the rounding off.

As we can see from Table 7, there isn't one single characteristic that is enjoyed by most middle school students. The storylines and the fun of the performance are the two major characteristics that attract them to listen to Beijing *Pingshu*, accounting for 47.6% altogether. Sixteen students mentioned in the interviews that the historical stories of Beijing *Pingshu* were very exciting. One student said, "The storylines of *Pingshu* attract me the most." One said, "The stories told are very dramatic." And another one said, "I think *Pingshu* appeals to me because some of the historical stories it tells are very vivid."

We also see that the characteristic of commentaries takes up 17.5% of the total with 11 students mentioning this point. It can be seen that some students, while listening to the story, are also attracted by the performer's comments on it. One of the students said, "The performers have their unique opinions." Some also said, "The performers bring in their own emotional feelings, which adds color to the performance." Another one said, "The performer's own moral values attract me." Some said, "*Pingshu* makes what is difficult to understand in the classics, such as traditional values and principles, easy to understand." Some student put it more clearly, "I think *Pingshu* can help us distinguish the beautiful and the ugly, the good and the evil of the society. It can reveal human nature or social problems." We take it that middle school students are just beginning to understand the world. Such comments are particularly important to them because they need to be guided by positive values and world views. The performers' analysis of human nature and social problems; their comments on the beautiful and the ugly, the truth and the falsehood, the good and the evil in society; and their praises and criticisms of the merits and demerits of historical figures and events, all play a role in enlightening the students, which is necessary and welcoming.

The vivid expression of *Pingshu* is also a factor that many students find attractive. One student said, "The main thing that attracts me is its vividness." One said, "The performance is very vivid and interesting." Some student thought that "*Pingshu* depicts vividly the psychological state of the characters in the story". One student believed that listeners could be easily immersed in the stories through the art of *Pingshu*; "*Pingshu* can create a sense of liveliness and let you feel you're personally on the scene". Therefore, *Pingshu*'s vivid language and expression count as another reason of its attraction.

Although it is generally believed that Beijing *Pingshu* is part of the traditional Chinese culture, only three students mentioned this point, accounting for 4.8%. This indicates that middle school students have insufficient understanding of the historical origin and cultural bearing of the art.

4.2.2 Charms of the performers

Three characteristics of *Pingshu* performers are highlighted by the students: art of performance, richness in knowledge, and diversity in styles.

Table 8: Characteristics of the performers (N=13)

Number	Characteristic	Number of codes (n)	Percentage (n/N)
1	Art of performance	11	84.6%
2	Richness in knowledge	1	7.7%
3	Diversity in styles	1	7.7%

From Table 8, it can be seen that art of performance is the key characteristic of *Pingshu* performers that attracts middle school students. One student said, "His tone ... is fascinating to me." Another commented, "He speaks in a rhythmic way." Yet another: "The performers are rich in emotion when they speak." From these words, it can be seen that *Pingshu* is a performing art. Students experience the charms of this art through the emotional engagement of the performers, the change of the tones, and the sense of musical rhythm of the voices.

4.2.3 Personal gains of the students

For personal gains of the students, the data can be summarized into two aspects: literature/historical knowledge, and enriched experience.

Table 9: Personal gains of middle school students listening to *Pingshu* (N=10)

Number	Gain	Number of codes (n)	Percentage (n/N)
1	Literature/historical knowledge	7	70.0%
2	Enriched experience	3	30.0%

The biggest gain is literature/historical knowledge. "Because *Pingshu* is an oral form of literary expression, it can help us better understand some difficult texts," one student said in the interview. "For example, if you read the Four Great Classic Novels of China, the reading process can be boring; but if you listen to their stories in *Pingshu*, it will be more interesting." Besides that, three students mentioned enriched experience in the interviews. One student said, "*Pingshu* not only increases my historical knowledge, but also enables me to have some experiences and learn life lessons from history, because history makes men wise." Another said, "It feels good to be able to comment on famous books and enrich your knowledge at the same time." However, for the 45 middle school students we interviewed, only 10 of them mentioned that personal gains were the reasons for their listening to *Pingshu*. We believe that if they spend more time listening to *Pingshu*, much more can be gained from it.

4.2.4 Convenience of listening and way of relaxation

As it can be seen from Table 6, only 5 students mentioned the convenience of listening as the attraction of *Pingshu*, accounting for 5.4% of the total. Only one student mentioned that listening to *Pingshu* was a good way to relax. This indicates that with the development of technology, the advantage of the convenience of listening can no longer attract middle school students. In addition, middle school students have many ways to relax and listening to *Pingshu* is surely not the first choice for them. So these two aspects make up a very small percentage of *Pingshu*'s appeal.

4.3 Channels: diversification and centralization

The data show that there are many channels for middle school students to listen to Beijing *Pingshu*, such as radio, TV, CDs, mobile phones, etc.; and the number of students who use mobile phones and radio is the largest. However, the channel through which students have their first contact with *Pingshu* has no significant influence on the continuation of the practice in the future.

4.3.1 Diversity of channels

Table 10: Middle school students' access channels to *Pingshu* (N=44)

Number	Channel	Number of students (n)	Percentage (n/N)
1	Mobile phones	23	52.3%
2	Radio	10	22.7%
3	School activities	5	11.4%
4	*Pingshu* theaters	4	9.1%
5	TV	1	2.3%
6	DVDs	1	2.3%

Note: The sum of the percentage exceeds 100% because of the rounding off.

Table 10 shows that middle school students' listening channels are diversified, as there are as many as six channels mentioned in the interviews. One student mentioned that he "listen(s) to *Pingshu* on the radio in the car or taxi". Another mentioned listening to *Pingshu* "through CDs and mobile phone apps". Four students mentioned that they had been to a *Pingshu* theater in Dongcheng District to watch live *Pingshu* performance.

From the data, we also find that with the change of the times, the diversity of listening channels is increasing. One student said, "When I was a kid, I used to listen to *Pingshu* on the radio. Then I watched live TV broadcast. Then on my way to school every day in my dad's car, I can listen to *Pingshu* on the car radio."

4.3.2 Centralization of choices

Table 10 shows that 52.3% of the students listen to *Pingshu* through mobile phones and 22.7% on the radio. The total number of these two groups reaches 75.0% of all respondents. Therefore, we can see that although there are many choices of channels, most middle school students choose mobile phones and radio as their main channels to listen to *Pingshu*.

Table 11: Channels used by students who listen to *Pingshu* every day (N=9)

Number	Channel	Number of students (n)	Percentage (n/N)
1	Mobile phones	7	77.8%
2	Radio	1	11.1%
3	School activities	1	11.1%

According to Table 11, of the students who listen to *Pingshu* every day, 77.8% of them use mobile phones.

From Tables 10 and 11, it can be seen that most students choose to listen to *Pingshu* on their mobile phones which is also the most preferred choice of those who listen on a daily basis. We think the reason is that the school workload of middle school students is heavy, and there is not any long and fixed time period left for them to listen to Beijing *Pingshu*. The good news is that a smart phone can be played anywhere and anytime, and it can be stopped or continued as you wish. This is extremely convenient for students who are in short supply of time, but in abundant access of mobile phones. No wonder mobile phones become the main channel of listening. We think that the reason for radio to become the second major channel is the popularity of cars. Most students who choose radio as the channel listen to *Pingshu* through car radio.

But *Pingshu* theaters, the most traditional place to listen to *Pingshu*, account for only 9.1%. The fast-paced life of middle school students deprives them of enjoying live *Pingshu* performances in *Pingshu* theaters. Their busy schedule simply has no room for such a luxury of time.

Table 12: Channels of listening to *Pingshu* for the first time (N=21)

Number	Channel	Number of students (n)	Percentage (n/N)
1	School activities	6	28.6%
2	Radio	5	23.8%
3	Mobile phones	4	19.0%
4	*Pingshu* theaters	4	19.0%
5	TV	1	4.8%
6	CDs	1	4.8%

From Table 12, it can be seen that 28.6% of the middle school students got their first contact with Beijing *Pingshu* at school, and 19.0% of them got their first contact in *Pingshu* theaters. But from Table 10, we can see that the main channel for middle school students to listen to *Pingshu* is mobile phones. This shows that the channel middle school students first used to listen to Beijing *Pingshu* has no impact on whether or not this practice is continued in the future. As long as the students have gotten interested in this kind of oral art, they will automatically choose the easiest way to listen. *Pingshu* theaters are not the best choice among middle school students; for them, mobile phones and radio are the most convenient and appropriate channels.

4.4 Suggestions on Beijing *Pingshu*'s promotion: collaboration of different stakeholders and the use of multiple channels

4.4.1 Reasons of not listening to Beijing *Pingshu*

According to the data, there are three main reasons of middle school students not listening to Beijing *Pingshu*: lack of interest, lack of time, and lack of atmosphere.

Table 13: Three main reasons of middle school students not listening to Beijing *Pingshu* (N=38)

Number	Reason	Number of students (n)	Percentage (n/N)
1	Lack of interest	16	42.1%
2	Lack of time	12	31.6%
3	Lack of atmosphere	10	26.3%

From Table 13, it can be seen that the reasons of not listening to Beijing *Pingshu* are rather focused, namely lack of interest, time, and atmosphere. Some student mentioned that they had no interest in the type of stories told in *Pingshu*. Some student said, "There is no leisure time to listen to it." Another said, "Nowadays, the word *Pingshu* rarely appears in our daily life." Targeting these reasons, the students gave suggestions on the development of Beijing *Pingshu*.

4.4.2 Collaboration of different stakeholders and the use of multiple channels

The suggestions on the development of Beijing *Pingshu* are mainly from two aspects: the collaboration of different stakeholders and the use of multiple channels.

Table 14: Suggestions to the stakeholders of *Pingshu*

Stakeholder	Suggestion	Measure	Elaboration
Performers	Innovation	Create authentic *Pingshu* pieces	There are few authentic pieces while most are adaptations of the classics
	Promotion	Increase the momentum and scope of promotion	Promote through different media, during different time periods, and in different ways
Government	Protection measures	Train young performers	Set up policies to protect the art, as there are not enough young performers
	Publicity measures	Vigorously promote and publicize Beijing *Pingshu* overseas	The government should vigorously promote and publicize Beijing *Pingshu*; let *Pingshu* develop in a wider scope, and bring splendid Chinese culture to the groups overseas
Schools	Raise the interest of students	Invite *Pingshu* performers to schools to perform live and give lectures on the art	We should promote Beijing *Pingshu* on campus; if teenagers can get interested in it, Beijing *Pingshu* will have a better future

From Table 14, we can see that suggestions to the performers, government and schools are given by the students interviewed.

The suggestions given to the performers are divided into two parts: innovation and promotion. The students felt that there is a lack of contemporary pieces based on today's society. For example, one student said, "There are few authentic pieces while most are adaptations of the classics." So they suggested that the performers use their creativity for new pieces. Another piece of suggestion is to increase the momentum and scope of promotion. One student answered, "(*Pingshu* should be) promoted through different media, during different time periods, and in different ways." This shows that middle school students want to promote *Pingshu* through more diversified channels. To sum up, middle school students hope that the performers can follow the trend of modern society in order to find a better way to promote and develop the art form.

The proposals for the government can also be divided into two parts: protection measures and publicity measures. For protection measures, one student suggested, "The government should also set up some policies to protect (*Pingshu*), as there are not enough young performers." Beijing *Pingshu* is inherited by an increasing number of young performers, and the government needs to protect the art by granting them favourable policies or subsidies. Publicity measures refer to publicity and promotion of *Pingshu*. The students interviewed suggested that the government publicize Beijing *Pingshu* through different ways. One of them said, "The government should vigorously promote and publicize Beijing *Pingshu*." Also, the government can conduct overseas promotion campaigns for *Pingshu*. One student said, "Let *Pingshu* develop in a wider scope, and bring splendid Chinese culture to the groups overseas."

As for schools, the students suggested that schools invite Beijing *Pingshu* performers to campus and organize lectures to cultivate students' interest in *Pingshu*. For example, one student said, "I think we should promote Beijing *Pingshu* on campus; if teenagers can get interested in it, Beijing *Pingshu* will have a better future."

In summary, middle school students suggested that the performers promote the art through creativity, the schools through cultivation of the students' interest, and the government through finding more diversified means of promotion. In addition, different groups of stakeholders can complement each other in the promotion process. The performers can collaborate with the government on specific measures to increase the channels of promotion; the schools can work with the performers by inviting them to campus to cultivate students' love for *Pingshu*; and the government can provide subsidies to schools for the invitation of *Pingshu* performers.

Table 15: Suggestions related to promotion channels

Media	Measure	Elaboration
Online channels	Use the Internet to promote; use new media, such as TV	Nowadays, the performers can use the Internet, TV and other media to promote and perform Beijing *Pingshu*
Offline channels	Newspaper advertisements and pamphlets	Go to places like supermarkets to hand out pamphlets

From Table 15, we can see that two main promotion channels are mentioned by the students interviewed: online and offline. For online channels, the students suggested more promotion through the Internet and new media. For example, one student said, "I think *Pingshu* can be promoted by using the Internet and new media." For offline channels, the students suggested newspaper advertisements and handing out pamphlets in supermarkets. Just like one student said, "Advertisement pamphlets can be handed out in some supermarkets." These measures all focus on ordinary people's daily life.

5. Conclusion

Focusing on a group of Beijing middle school students, this research analyzes their cognition of and suggestions on Beijing *Pingshu*. The findings are as follows. Firstly, for Beijing *Pingshu*, most students only have a superficial recognition, but lack profound understanding. This finding is supported by the fact that not many students listen to *Pingshu* every day, and they only know very little of *Pingshu* performers, and the cognition of the main characteristics stays on the surface. Secondly, most middle school students are attracted to Beijing *Pingshu* by its intrinsic characteristics, not by convenience of listening. Thirdly, the channels through which middle school students listen to *Pingshu* are diversified, but the number of students who use radio and mobile phones is the largest. This is closely related to the students' way of life. Fourthly, most students suggest that the collaboration of different stakeholders and the use of multiple channels are the ways to promote *Pingshu*.

The research, which is conducted from the students' perspective with qualitative method, analyzes comprehensively the cognition of and the development suggestions for Beijing *Pingshu* from Beijing middle school students. However, the weakness of this research is obvious. The first is the problem with data. Although we have interviewed a total of 70 students, due to the lack of interviewing experience, many students' answers to the questions are either too vague to make sense of or simply incomplete. So we have to classify these data as invalid data. As a result, there are not many valid data and our conclusions are not supported by a large amount of data. Secondly, the students' cognition of Beijing *Pingshu* is subjective and changeable. Without other sources of information for cross-references, it is hard to prove that the findings are reliable. The third issue is the problem with the references. We searched the website cnki.net using the keywords "cognition of Beijing *Pingshu*" "Beijing *Pingshu*'s audience" "Teenagers' understanding of Beijing *Pingshu*", etc., but ended up with nothing. This imposes difficulties in data analysis and coding, which is the biggest obstacle we have encountered in the research.

Even though there is much for improvement in further research, the research procedures and findings, as well as the suggestions on Beijing *Pingshu*'s promotion, are valuable to the preservation of this precious cultural heritage.

References:

Liang, Yan. Beijing Pingshu [M]. Beijing: Beijing Arts and Photography Press, 2015.